AGENTS OF ATLAS

PANDEMONIUM

Greg Pak
WRITER

Nico Leon
WITH **Pop Mhan** (#2, #4)
ARTISTS

Federico Blee (#1-2) & **Rachelle Rosenberg** (#3-5)
COLOR ARTISTS

"BEHIND THE VEIL"

Jeff Parker
WRITER

Carlo Pagulayan
PENCILER

Jason Paz
INKER

Dono Sánchez-Almara
COLOR ARTIST

VC's Joe Sabino
LETTERER

Junggeun Yoon
COVER ART

Lindsey Cohick & **Tom Groneman**
ASSISTANT EDITORS

Mark Paniccia
EDITOR

COLLECTION EDITO
ASSISTANT MANAG
ASSISTANT EDITO
EDITOR, SPECIAL PR
VP PRODUCTION & SPEC
BOOK DESIG
SVP PRINT, SALES & M
EDITOR IN CHIEF **C.B. CEBULSKI**

D1265358

AGENTS OF ATLAS: PANDEMONIUM. Contains material originally published in magazine form as AGENTS OF ATLAS (2019) #1-5. First printing 2019. ISBN 978-1-302-92011-1. Published by MARVEL WORLDWIDE, INC., a subsidiary of MARVEL ENTERTAINMENT, LLC. OFFICE OF PUBLICATION: 1290 Avenue of the Americas, New York, NY 10104. **Printed in Canada.** KEVIN FEIGE, Chief Creative Officer; DAN BUCKLEY, President, Marvel Entertainment; JOHN NEE, Publisher; JOE QUESADA, EVP & Creative Director; TOM BREVOORT, SVP of Publishing; DAVID BOGART, Associate Publisher & SVP of Talent Affairs; Publishing & Partnership; DAVID GABRIEL, VP of Print & Digital Publishing; JEFF YOUNGQUIST, VP of Production & Special Projects; DAN CARR, Executive Director of Publishing Technology; ALEX MORALES, Director of Publishing Operations; DAN EDINGTON, Managing Editor; SUSAN CRESPI, Production Manager; STAN LEE, Chairman Emeritus. For information regarding advertising in Marvel Comics or on Marvel.com, please contact Vit DeBellis, Custom Solutions & Integrated Advertising Manager, at vdebellis@marvel.com. For Marvel subscription inquiries, please call 888-511-5480. **Manufactured between 12/13/2019 and 1/14/2020 by SOLISCO PRINTERS, SCOTT, QC, CANADA.**

10 9 8 7 6 5 4 3 2 1

ONE

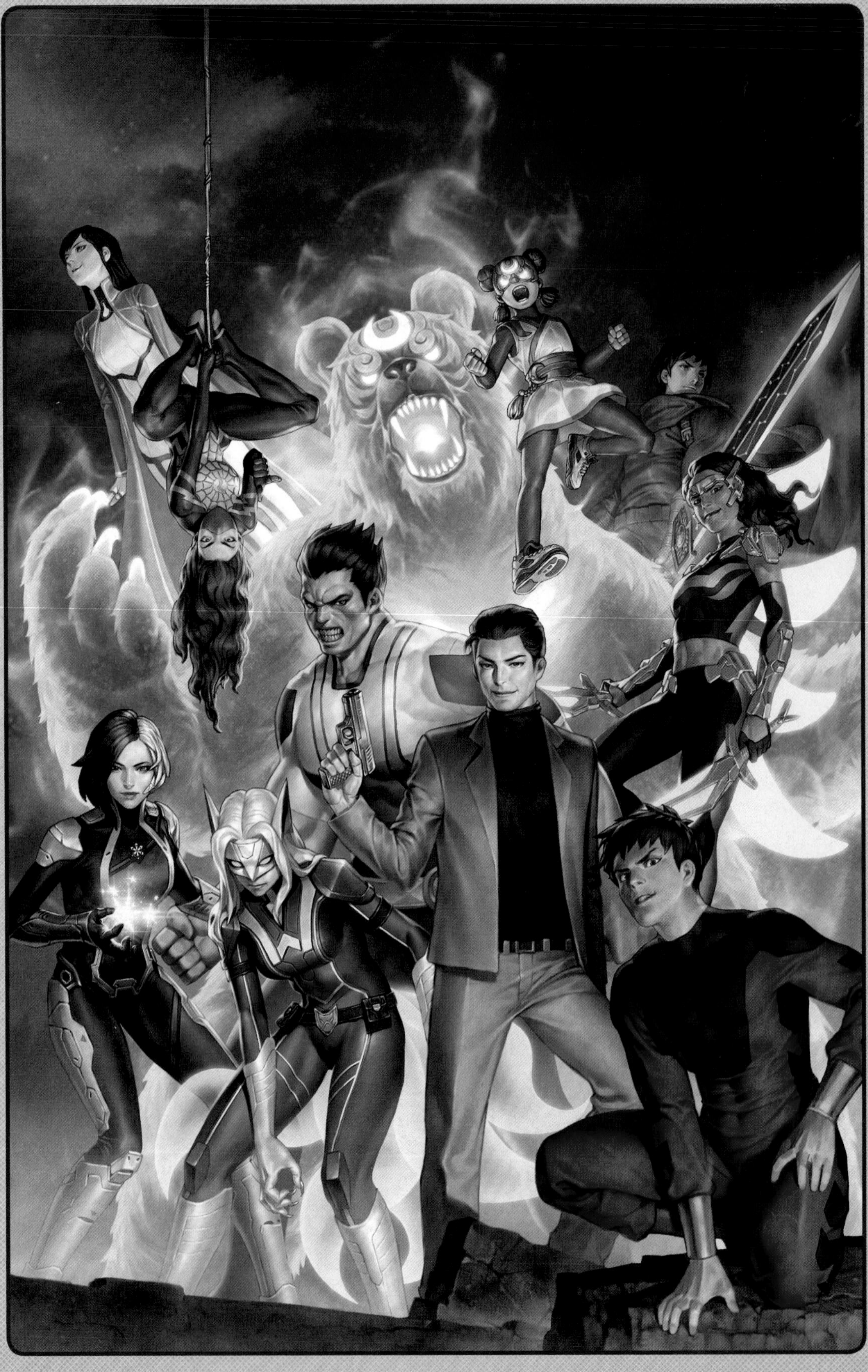

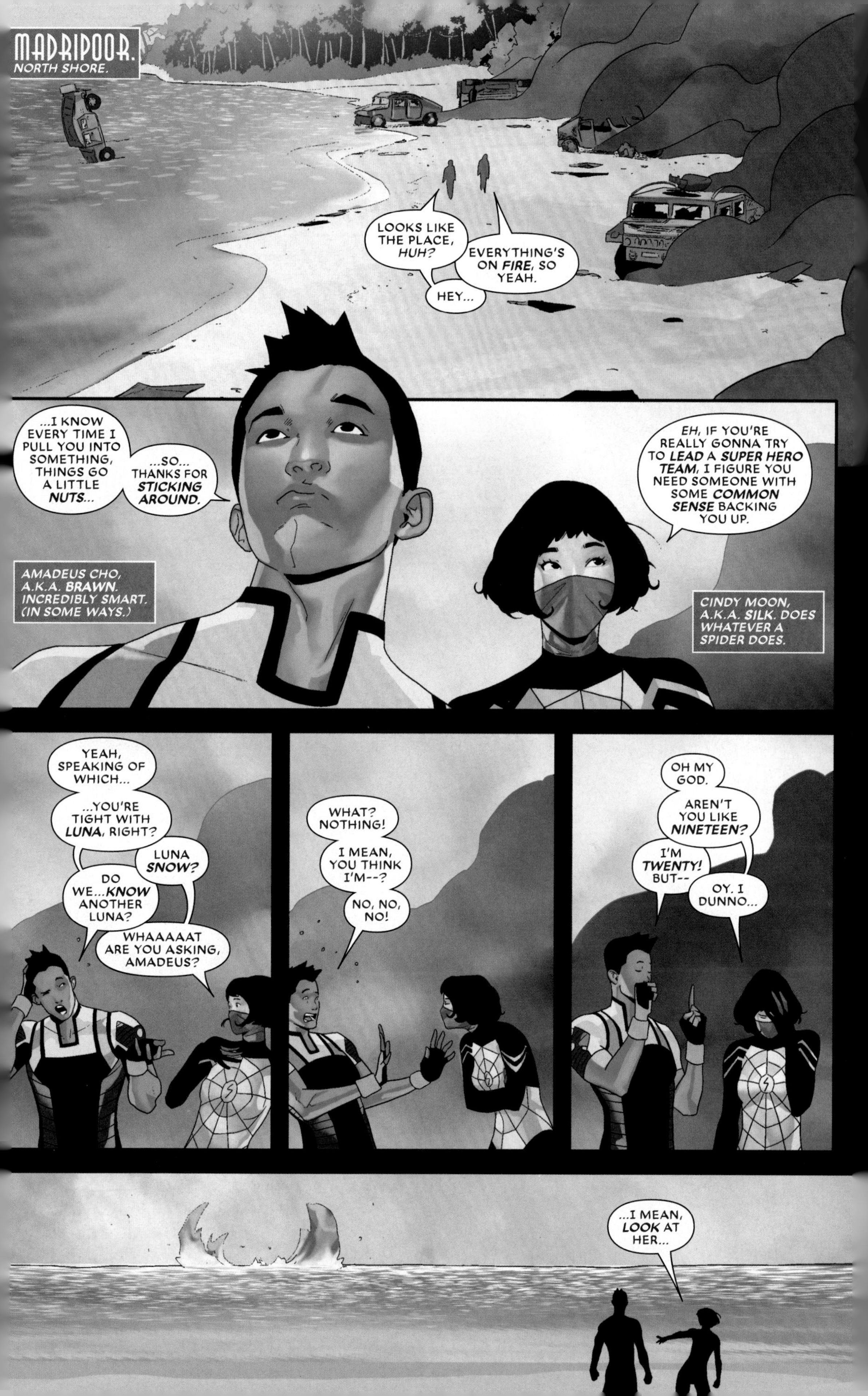
MADRIPOOR.
NORTH SHORE.
LOOKS LIKE THE PLACE, HUH?
EVERYTHING'S ON FIRE, SO YEAH.
HEY...
...I KNOW EVERY TIME I PULL YOU INTO SOMETHING, THINGS GO A LITTLE NUTS...
...SO... THANKS FOR STICKING AROUND.
EH, IF YOU'RE REALLY GONNA TRY TO LEAD A SUPER HERO TEAM, I FIGURE YOU NEED SOMEONE WITH SOME COMMON SENSE BACKING YOU UP.
AMADEUS CHO, A.K.A. BRAWN. INCREDIBLY SMART. (IN SOME WAYS.)
CINDY MOON, A.K.A. SILK. DOES WHATEVER A SPIDER DOES.
YEAH, SPEAKING OF WHICH...
...YOU'RE TIGHT WITH LUNA, RIGHT?
LUNA SNOW?
DO WE...KNOW ANOTHER LUNA?
WHAAAAAT ARE YOU ASKING, AMADEUS?
WHAT? NOTHING!
I MEAN, YOU THINK I'M--?
NO, NO, NO!
OH MY GOD.
AREN'T YOU LIKE NINETEEN?
I'M TWENTY! BUT--
OY. I DUNNO...
...I MEAN, LOOK AT HER...

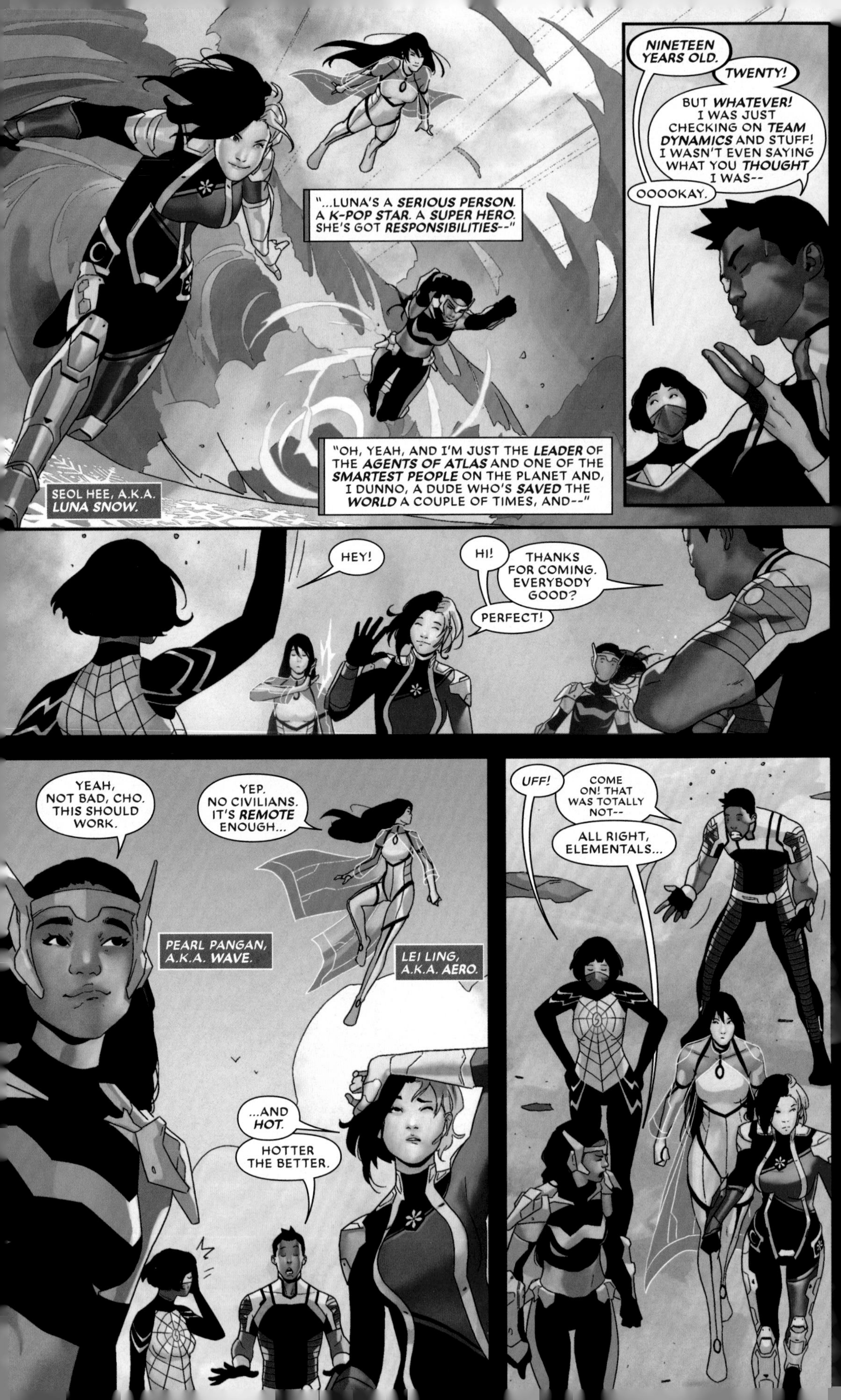
"...LUNA'S A SERIOUS PERSON. A K-POP STAR. A SUPER HERO. SHE'S GOT RESPONSIBILITIES--"
SEOL HEE, A.K.A. LUNA SNOW.
"OH, YEAH, AND I'M JUST THE LEADER OF THE AGENTS OF ATLAS AND ONE OF THE SMARTEST PEOPLE ON THE PLANET AND, I DUNNO, A DUDE WHO'S SAVED THE WORLD A COUPLE OF TIMES, AND--"
NINETEEN YEARS OLD.
TWENTY!
BUT WHATEVER! I WAS JUST CHECKING ON TEAM DYNAMICS AND STUFF! I WASN'T EVEN SAYING WHAT YOU THOUGHT I WAS--
OOOOKAY.
HEY!
HI!
THANKS FOR COMING. EVERYBODY GOOD?
PERFECT!
YEAH, NOT BAD, CHO. THIS SHOULD WORK.
YEP. NO CIVILIANS. IT'S REMOTE ENOUGH...
PEARL PANGAN, A.K.A. WAVE.
LEI LING, A.K.A. AERO.
...AND HOT.
HOTTER THE BETTER.
UFF!
COME ON! THAT WAS TOTALLY NOT--
ALL RIGHT, ELEMENTALS...

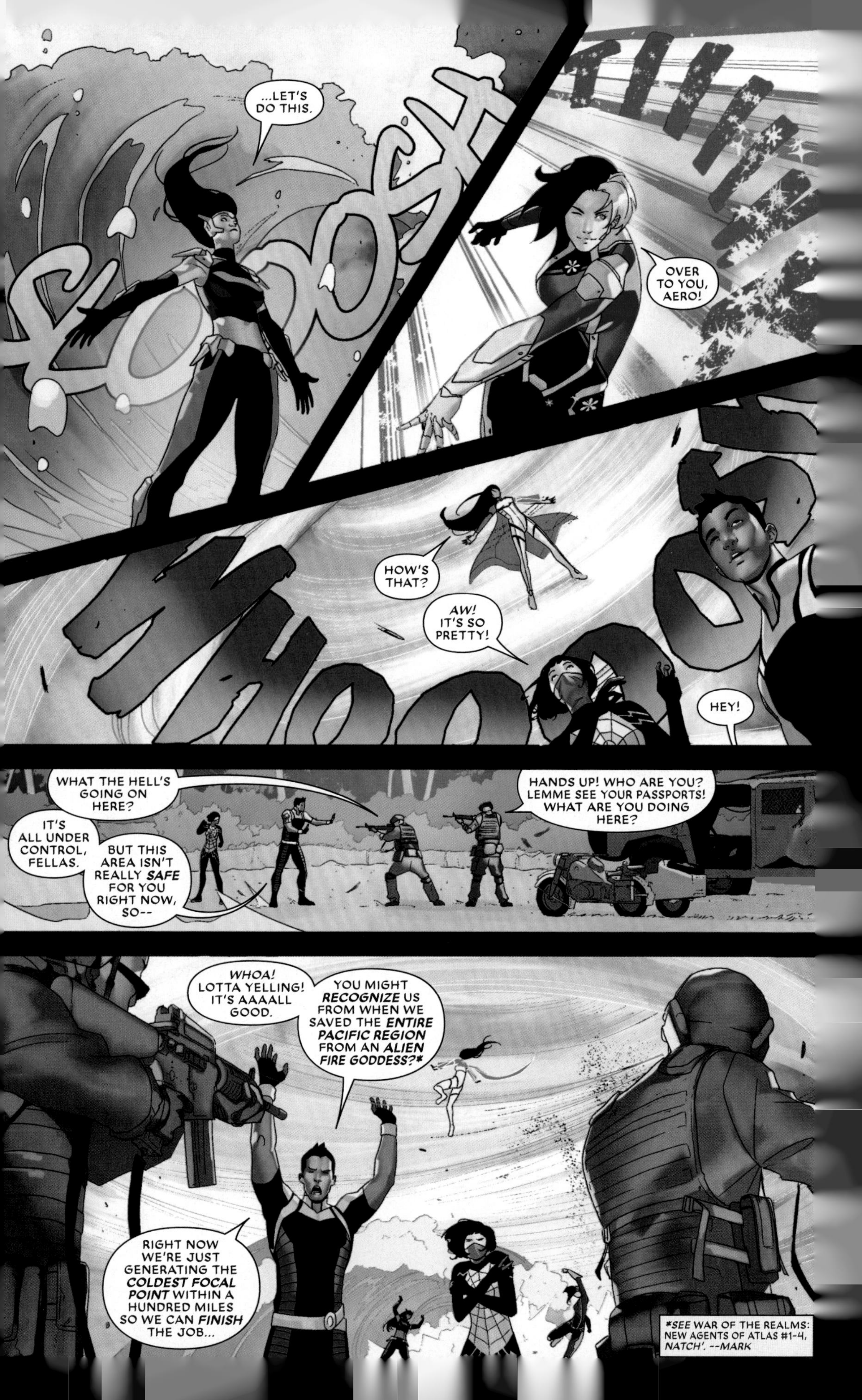
...LET'S DO THIS.
SHOOSH
OVER TO YOU, AERO!
HOW'S THAT?
AW! IT'S SO PRETTY!
HEY!
WHAT THE HELL'S GOING ON HERE?
HANDS UP! WHO ARE YOU? LEMME SEE YOUR PASSPORTS! WHAT ARE YOU DOING HERE?
IT'S ALL UNDER CONTROL, FELLAS.
BUT THIS AREA ISN'T REALLY SAFE FOR YOU RIGHT NOW, SO--
WHOA! LOTTA YELLING! IT'S AAAALL GOOD.
YOU MIGHT RECOGNIZE US FROM WHEN WE SAVED THE ENTIRE PACIFIC REGION FROM AN ALIEN FIRE GODDESS?*
RIGHT NOW WE'RE JUST GENERATING THE COLDEST FOCAL POINT WITHIN A HUNDRED MILES SO WE CAN FINISH THE JOB...
*SEE WAR OF THE REALMS: NEW AGENTS OF ATLAS #1-4, NATCH'. --MARK

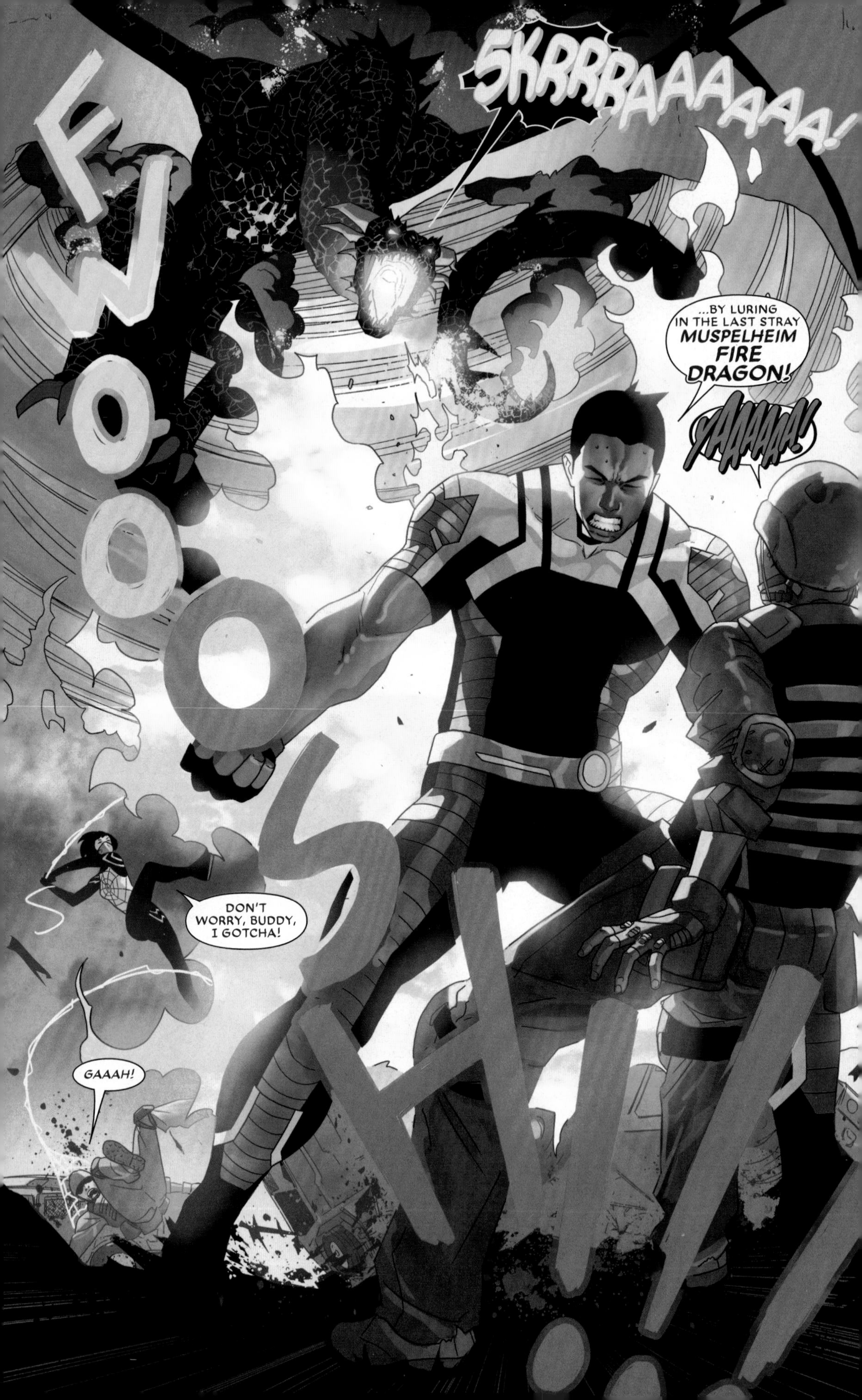

5KRRRAAAAAAA!
FWOOOOSSH!!
...BY LURING IN THE LAST STRAY MUSPELHEIM FIRE DRAGON!
YAAAAAA!
DON'T WORRY, BUDDY, I GOTCHA!
GAAAH!

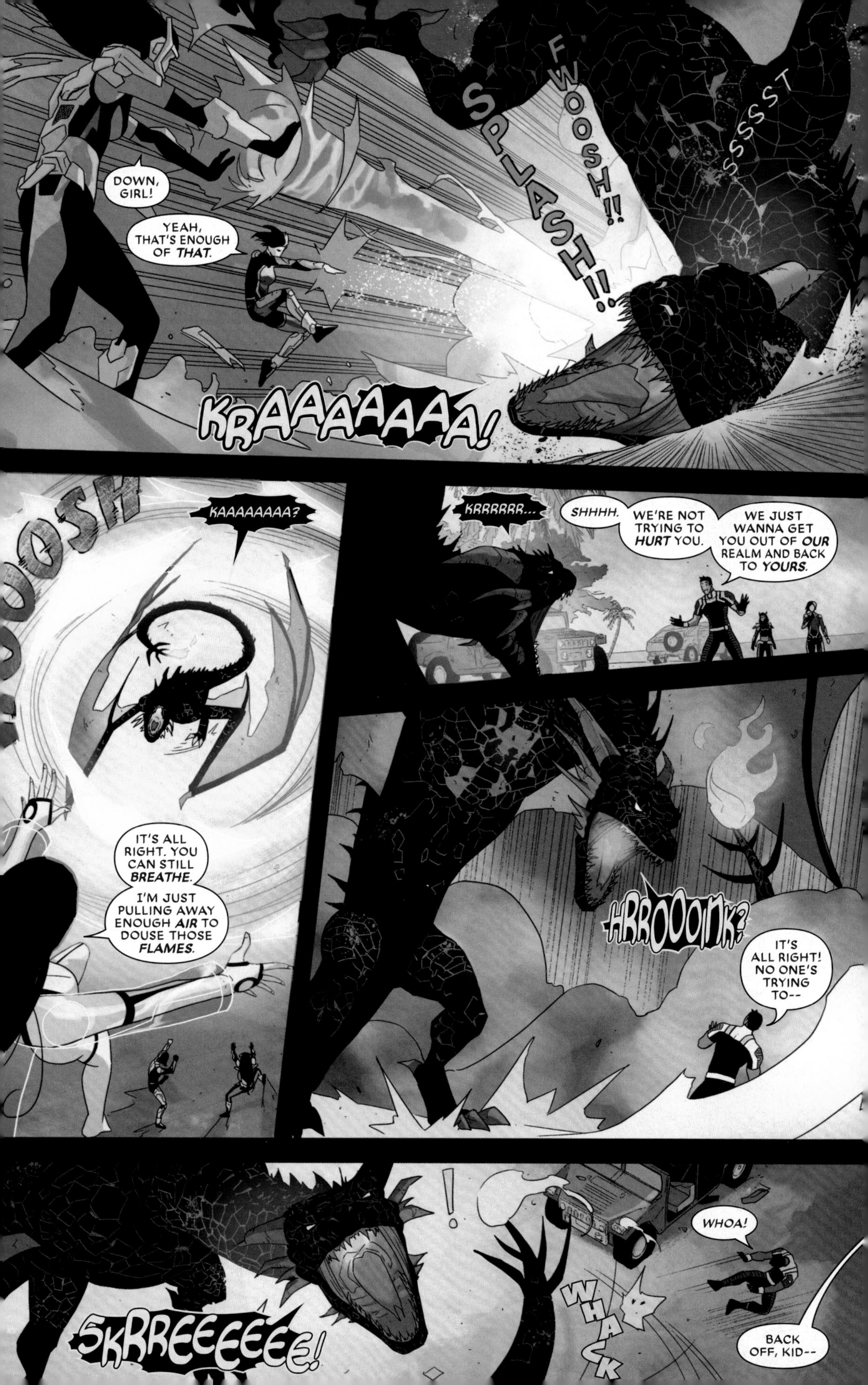
DOWN, GIRL!
YEAH, THAT'S ENOUGH OF THAT.
SPLASH!!
FWOOSH!!
SSSSST
KRAAAAAAAA!
WOOSH
KAAAAAAAA?
IT'S ALL RIGHT. YOU CAN STILL BREATHE.
I'M JUST PULLING AWAY ENOUGH AIR TO DOUSE THOSE FLAMES.
KRRRRRR...
SHHHH.
WE'RE NOT TRYING TO HURT YOU.
WE JUST WANNA GET YOU OUT OF OUR REALM AND BACK TO YOURS.
HRROOOINK?
IT'S ALL RIGHT! NO ONE'S TRYING TO--
SKRREEEEEEE!
!
WHACK
WHOA!
BACK OFF, KID--

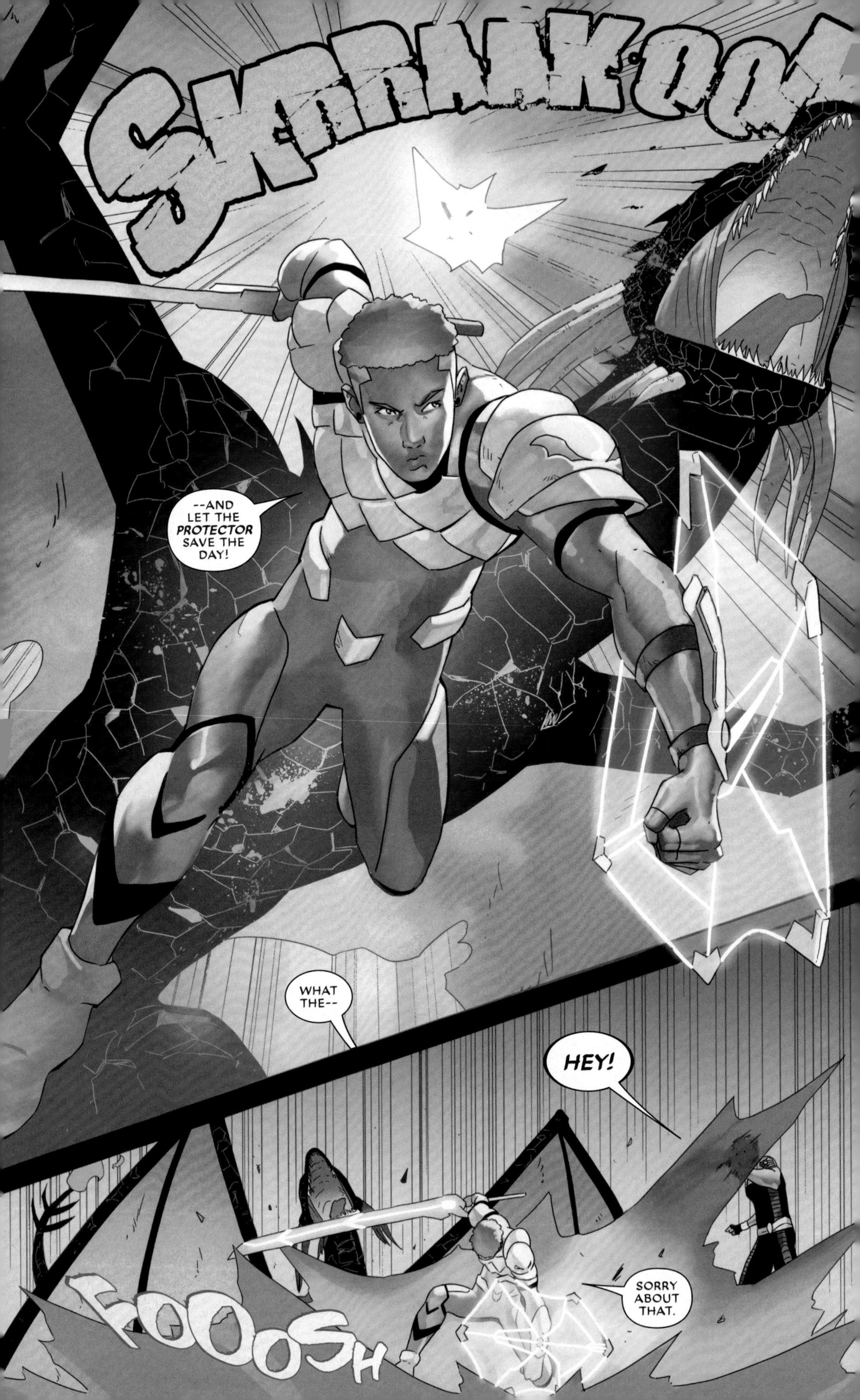
SKRRAKOOM
--AND LET THE PROTECTOR SAVE THE DAY!
WHAT THE--
HEY!
SORRY ABOUT THAT.
FOOOOSH

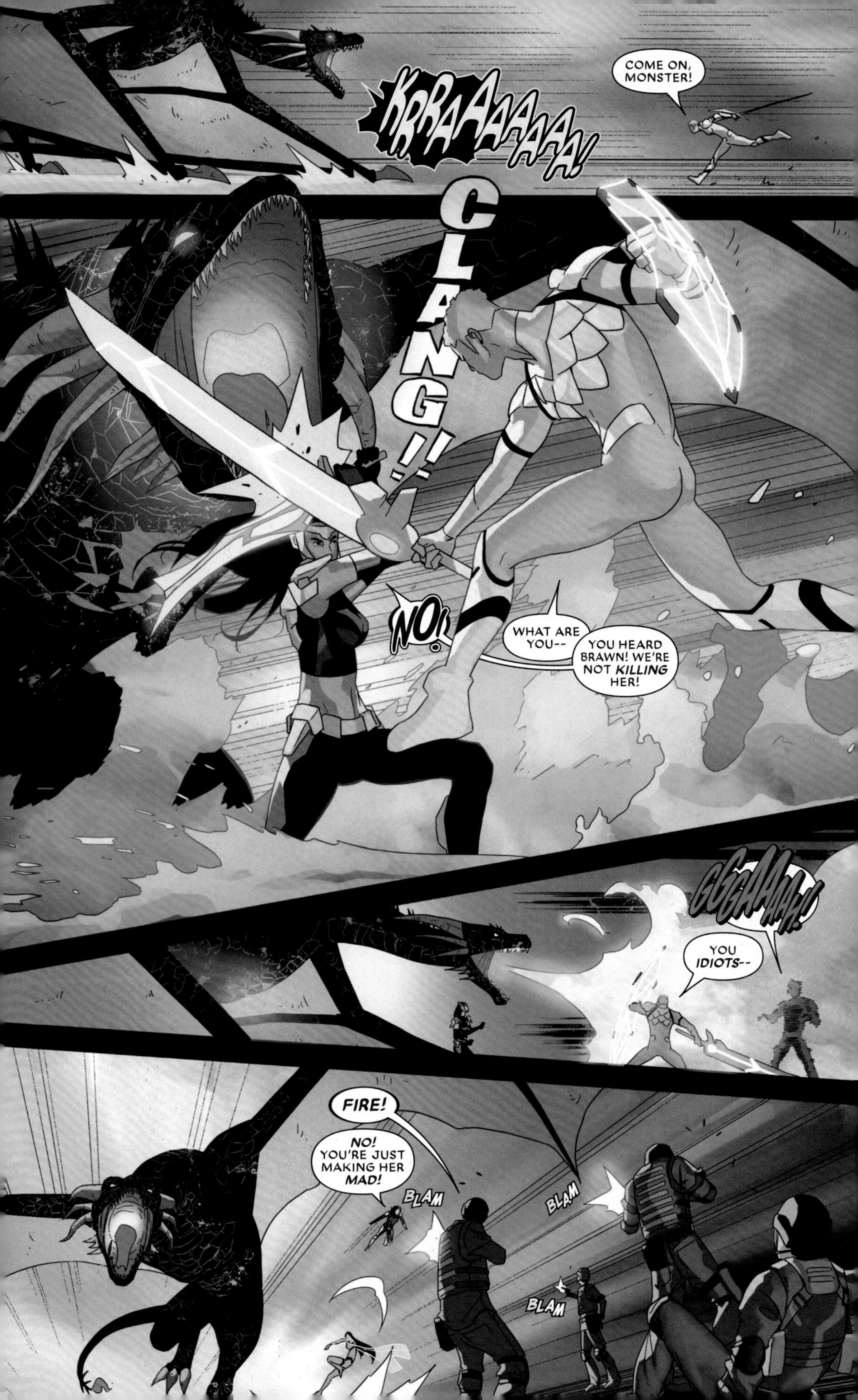
KRRAAAAAAAA!
COME ON, MONSTER!
CLANG!!
NO!
WHAT ARE YOU--
YOU HEARD BRAWN! WE'RE NOT KILLING HER!
GGGAAAAH!
YOU IDIOTS--
FIRE!
NO! YOU'RE JUST MAKING HER MAD!
BLAM
BLAM
BLAM

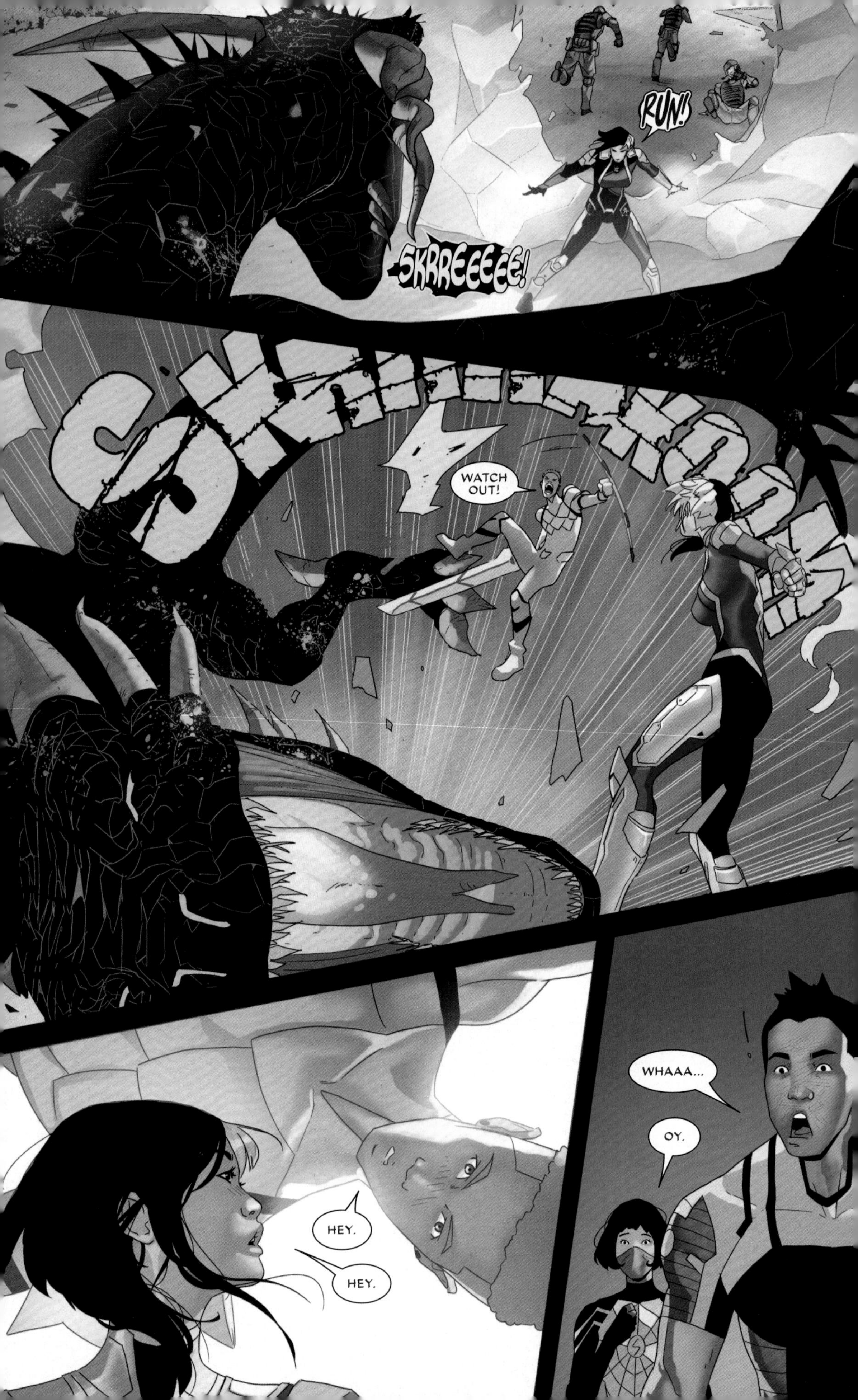
RUN!
SKRREEEEE!
WATCH OUT!
HEY.
HEY.
WHAAA...
OY.

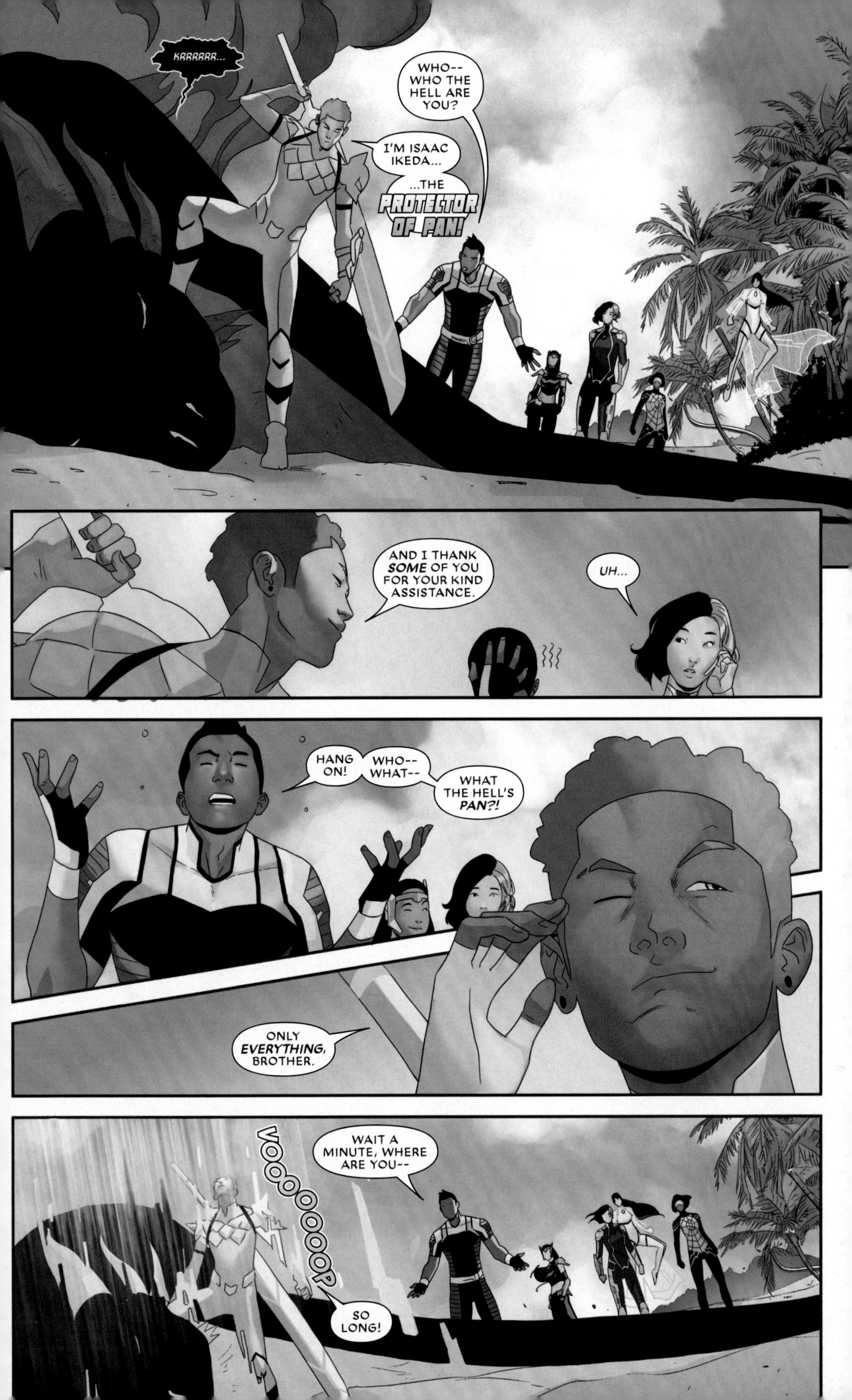
KRRRRRR...
WHO-- WHO THE HELL ARE YOU?
I'M ISAAC IKEDA...
...THE PROTECTOR OF PAN!
AND I THANK SOME OF YOU FOR YOUR KIND ASSISTANCE.
UH...
HANG ON!
WHO-- WHAT--
WHAT THE HELL'S PAN?!
ONLY EVERYTHING, BROTHER.
WAIT A MINUTE, WHERE ARE YOU--
VOOOOOOOP
SO LONG!

YEARS AGO, AN INCREDIBLE TEAM OF FBI AGENTS DISCOVERED THAT THEIR LEADER, JIMMY WOO, WAS THE HEIR TO AN ANCIENT UNDERGROUND EMPIRE KNOWN AS THE ATLAS FOUNDATION. TOGETHER WITH THE IMMORTAL DRAGON, MR. LAO, AS HIS ADVISOR, AND THE ORIGINAL AGENTS OF ATLAS — GORILLA-MAN, VENUS, NAMORA, THE URANIAN AND M-11 — JIMMY ASSUMED CONTROL OF THE WORLDWIDE SYNDICATE TO USE ITS INFLUENCE FOR GOOD.

BUT DURING THE WAR OF THE REALMS, JIMMY RECRUITED A NEW TEAM OF YOUNG HEROES LED BY AMADEUS CHO TO DEFEAT SINDR, THE QUEEN OF MUSPELHEIM AND ALLY TO MALEKITH, AND SAVED THE PACIFIC FROM DESTRUCTION!

NOW, AMADEUS AND JIMMY SEEK A PATH FORWARD FOR THE NEW TEAM AND THE ATLAS FOUNDATION IN THE WAKE OF A WORLD CHANGED BY THE FIRES OF WAR! TOGETHER, THEY ARE THE NEW...

AGENTS OF ATLAS

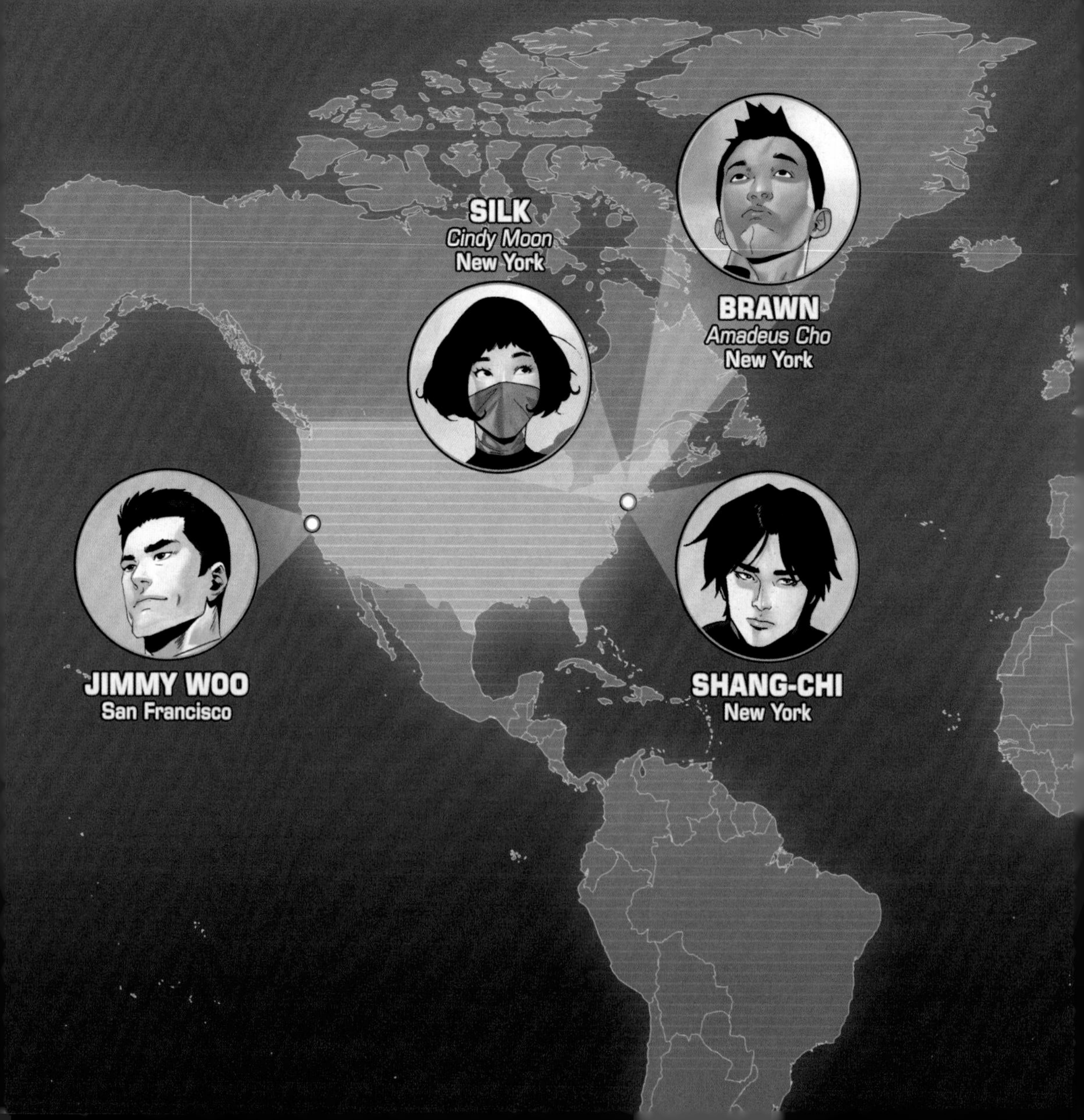

SILK
Cindy Moon
New York
BRAWN
Amadeus Cho
New York
JIMMY WOO
San Francisco
SHANG-CHI
New York

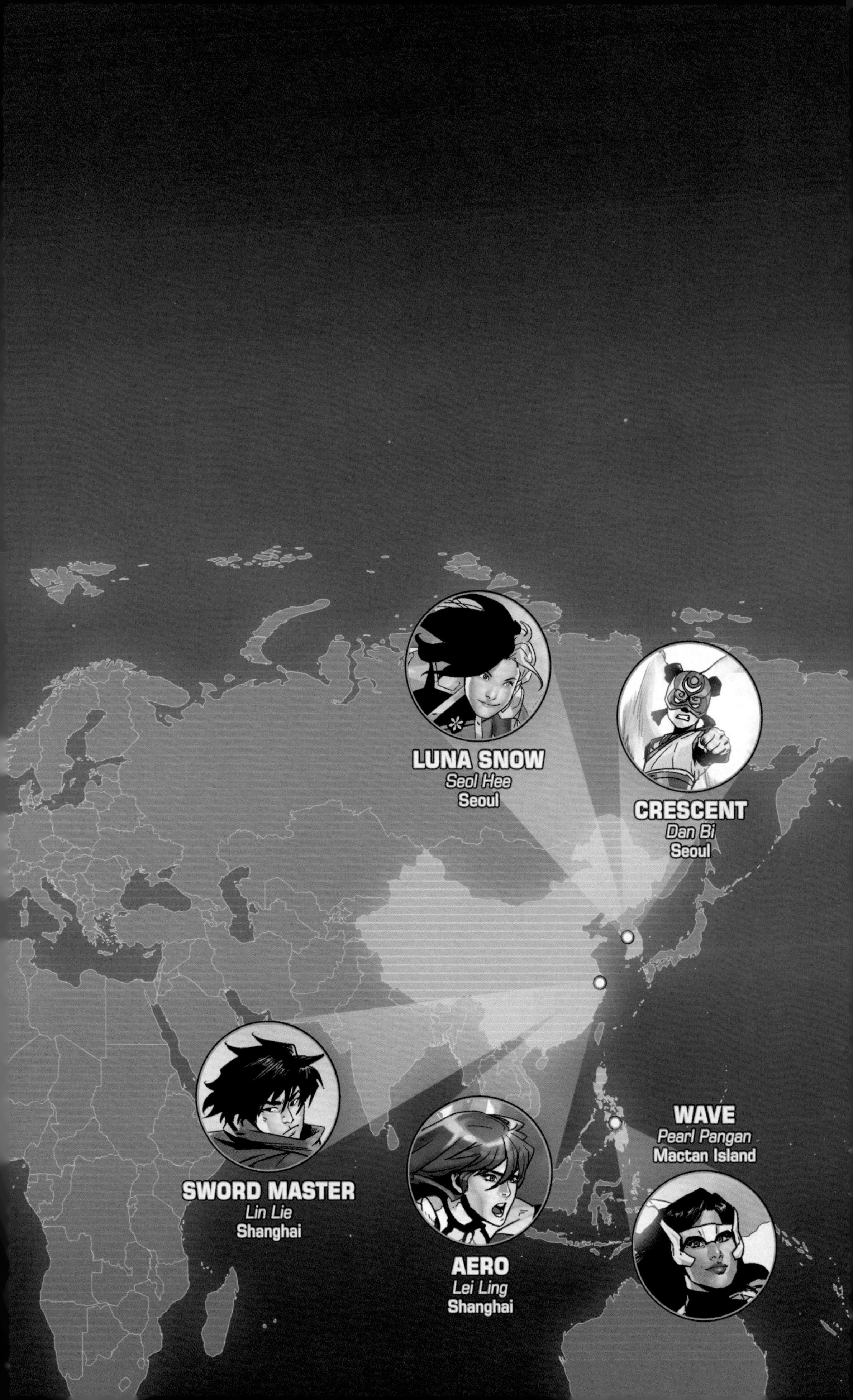
LUNA SNOW
Seol Hee
Seoul
CRESCENT
Dan Bi
Seoul
WAVE
Pearl Pangan
Mactan Island
SWORD MASTER
Lin Lie
Shanghai
AERO
Lei Ling
Shanghai

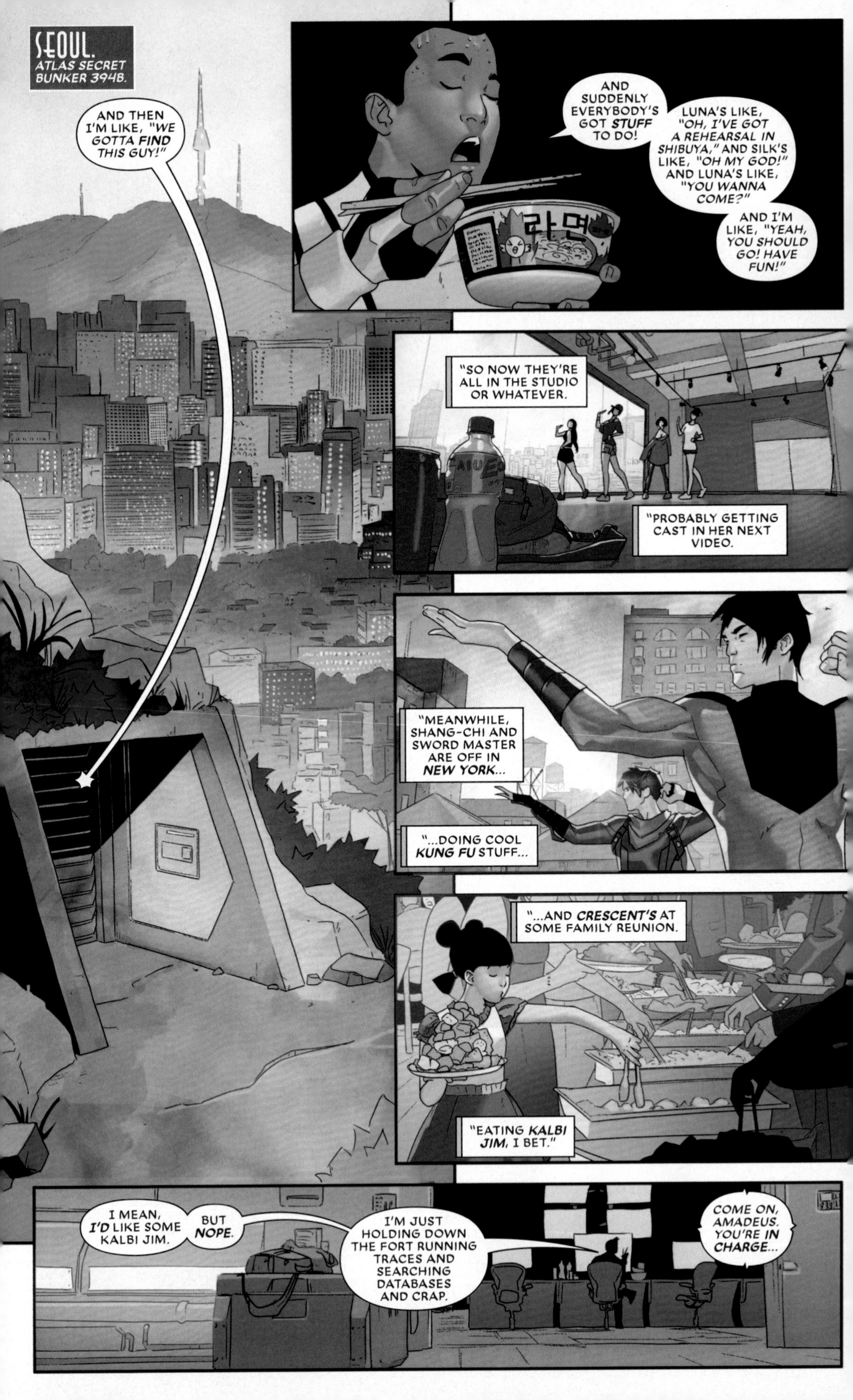
SEOUL.
ATLAS SECRET BUNKER 394B.
AND THEN I'M LIKE, "WE GOTTA FIND THIS GUY!"
AND SUDDENLY EVERYBODY'S GOT STUFF TO DO!
LUNA'S LIKE, "OH, I'VE GOT A REHEARSAL IN SHIBUYA," AND SILK'S LIKE, "OH MY GOD!" AND LUNA'S LIKE, "YOU WANNA COME?"
AND I'M LIKE, "YEAH, YOU SHOULD GO! HAVE FUN!"
라면
"SO NOW THEY'RE ALL IN THE STUDIO OR WHATEVER.
"PROBABLY GETTING CAST IN HER NEXT VIDEO.
"MEANWHILE, SHANG-CHI AND SWORD MASTER ARE OFF IN NEW YORK...
"...DOING COOL KUNG FU STUFF...
"...AND CRESCENT'S AT SOME FAMILY REUNION.
"EATING KALBI JIM, I BET."
I MEAN, I'D LIKE SOME KALBI JIM.
BUT NOPE.
I'M JUST HOLDING DOWN THE FORT RUNNING TRACES AND SEARCHING DATABASES AND CRAP.
COME ON, AMADEUS. YOU'RE IN CHARGE...

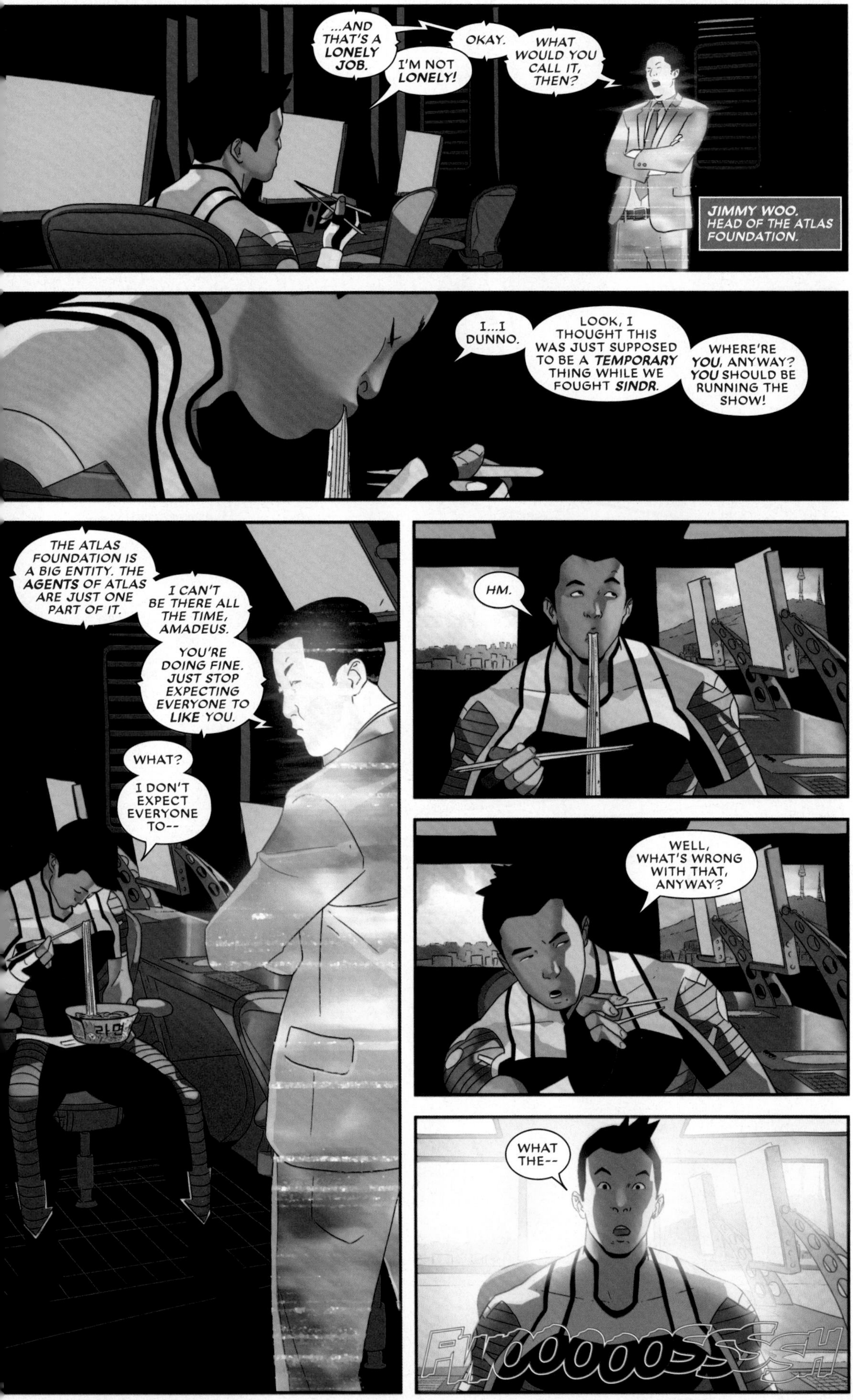
...AND THAT'S A LONELY JOB.
OKAY.
I'M NOT LONELY!
WHAT WOULD YOU CALL IT, THEN?
JIMMY WOO. HEAD OF THE ATLAS FOUNDATION.
I...I DUNNO.
LOOK, I THOUGHT THIS WAS JUST SUPPOSED TO BE A TEMPORARY THING WHILE WE FOUGHT SINDR.
WHERE'RE YOU, ANYWAY? YOU SHOULD BE RUNNING THE SHOW!
THE ATLAS FOUNDATION IS A BIG ENTITY. THE AGENTS OF ATLAS ARE JUST ONE PART OF IT.
I CAN'T BE THERE ALL THE TIME, AMADEUS.
YOU'RE DOING FINE. JUST STOP EXPECTING EVERYONE TO LIKE YOU.
WHAT?
I DON'T EXPECT EVERYONE TO--
라면
HM.
WELL, WHAT'S WRONG WITH THAT, ANYWAY?
WHAT THE--
FWOOOOOSSSH

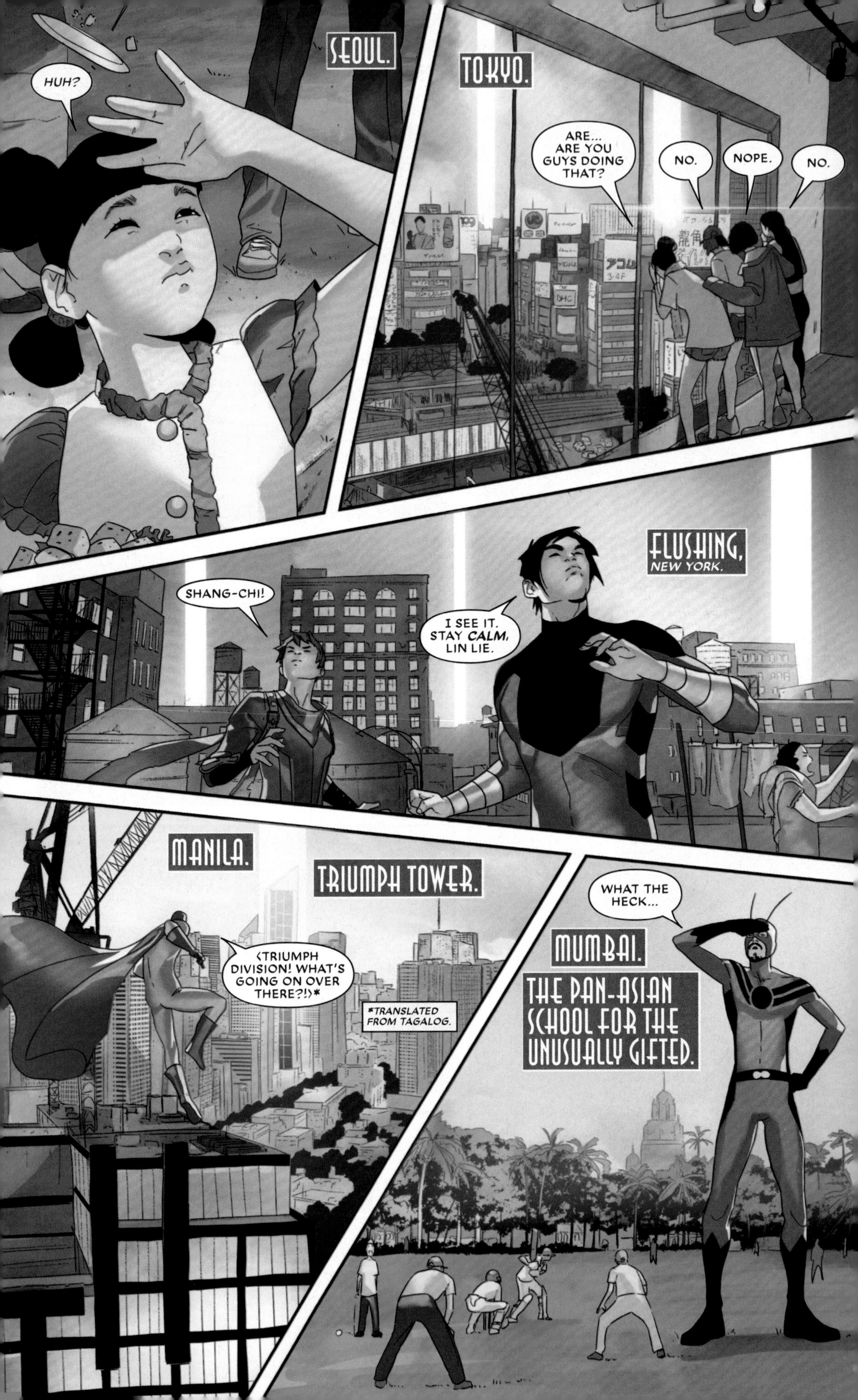
SEOUL.
HUH?
TOKYO.
ARE... ARE YOU GUYS DOING THAT?
NO.
NOPE.
NO.
FLUSHING, NEW YORK.
SHANG-CHI!
I SEE IT. STAY CALM, LIN LIE.
MANILA.
TRIUMPH TOWER.
‹TRIUMPH DIVISION! WHAT'S GOING ON OVER THERE?!›*
*TRANSLATED FROM TAGALOG.
MUMBAI.
THE PAN-ASIAN SCHOOL FOR THE UNUSUALLY GIFTED.
WHAT THE HECK...

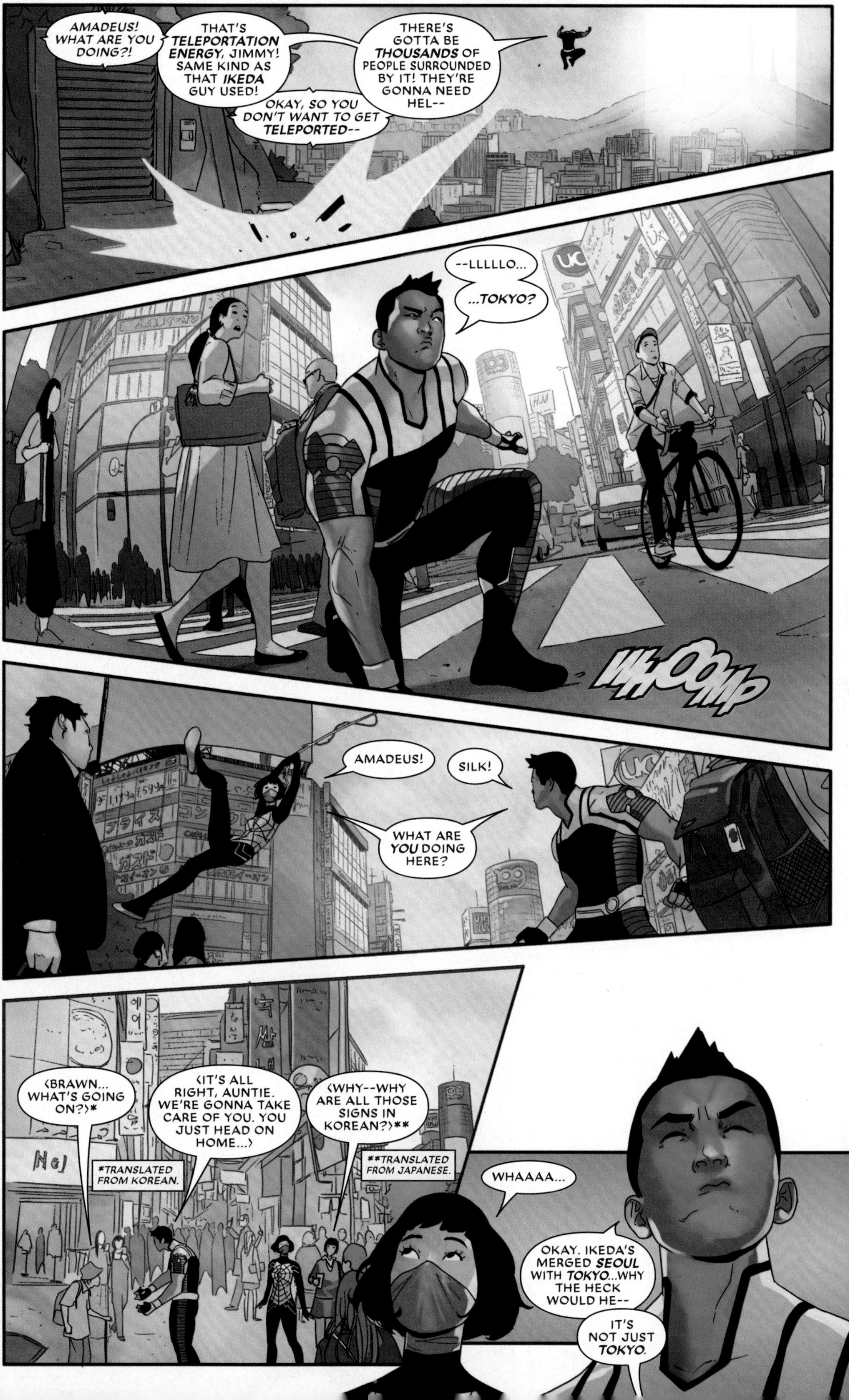
AMADEUS! WHAT ARE YOU DOING?!
THAT'S TELEPORTATION ENERGY, JIMMY! SAME KIND AS THAT IKEDA GUY USED!
OKAY, SO YOU DON'T WANT TO GET TELEPORTED--
THERE'S GOTTA BE THOUSANDS OF PEOPLE SURROUNDED BY IT! THEY'RE GONNA NEED HEL--
--LLLLLO...
...TOKYO?
WHOOMP
AMADEUS!
SILK!
WHAT ARE YOU DOING HERE?
‹BRAWN... WHAT'S GOING ON?›*
*TRANSLATED FROM KOREAN.
‹IT'S ALL RIGHT, AUNTIE. WE'RE GONNA TAKE CARE OF YOU. YOU JUST HEAD ON HOME...›
‹WHY--WHY ARE ALL THOSE SIGNS IN KOREAN?›**
**TRANSLATED FROM JAPANESE.
WHAAAA...
OKAY. IKEDA'S MERGED SEOUL WITH TOKYO...WHY THE HECK WOULD HE--
IT'S NOT JUST TOKYO.

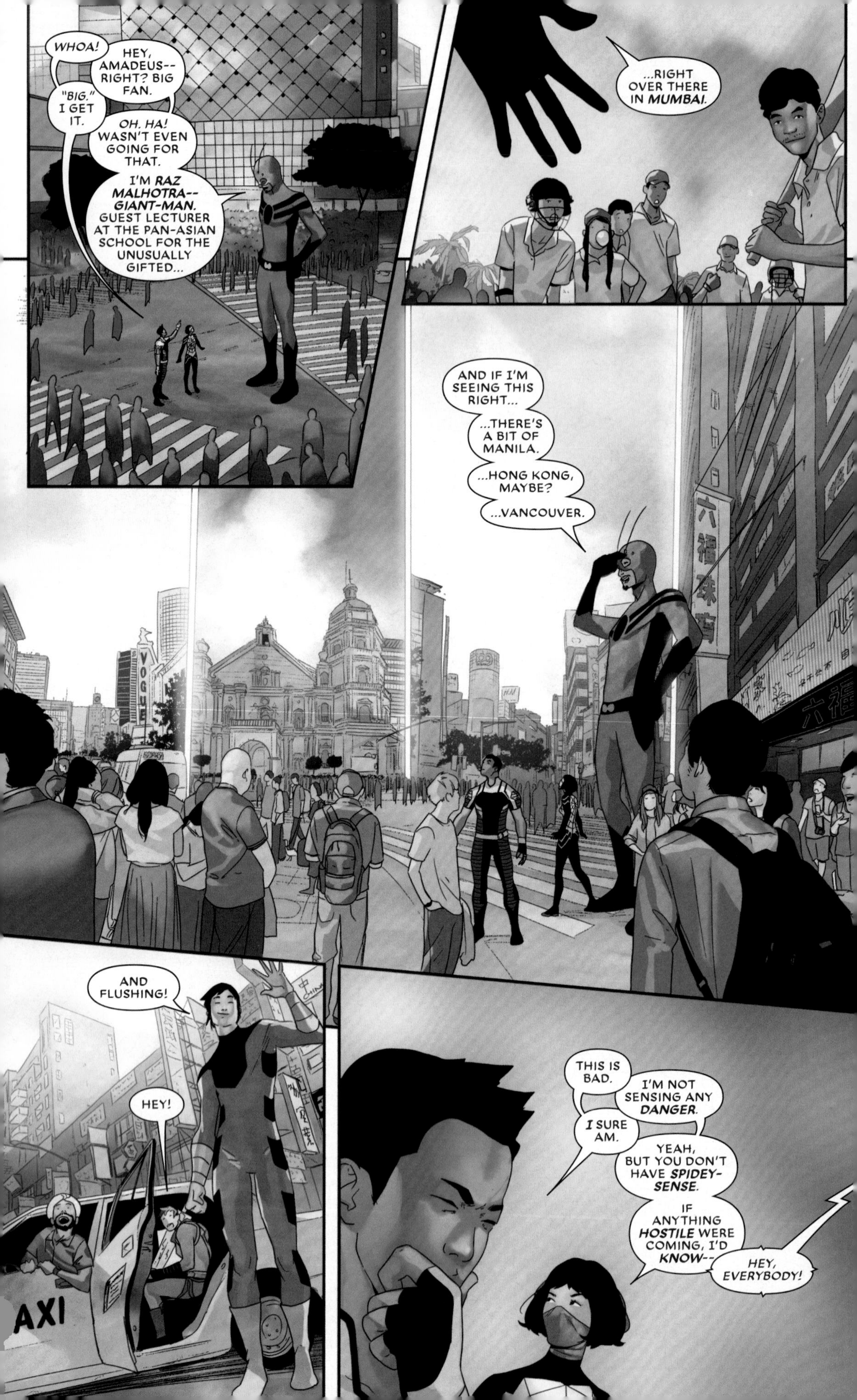
WHOA!
HEY, AMADEUS-- RIGHT? BIG FAN.
"BIG." I GET IT.
OH. HA! WASN'T EVEN GOING FOR THAT.
I'M RAZ MALHOTRA-- GIANT-MAN. GUEST LECTURER AT THE PAN-ASIAN SCHOOL FOR THE UNUSUALLY GIFTED...
...RIGHT OVER THERE IN MUMBAI.
AND IF I'M SEEING THIS RIGHT...
...THERE'S A BIT OF MANILA.
...HONG KONG, MAYBE?
...VANCOUVER.
AND FLUSHING!
HEY!
AXI
THIS IS BAD.
I'M NOT SENSING ANY DANGER.
I SURE AM.
YEAH, BUT YOU DON'T HAVE SPIDEY-SENSE.
IF ANYTHING HOSTILE WERE COMING, I'D KNOW--
HEY, EVERYBODY!

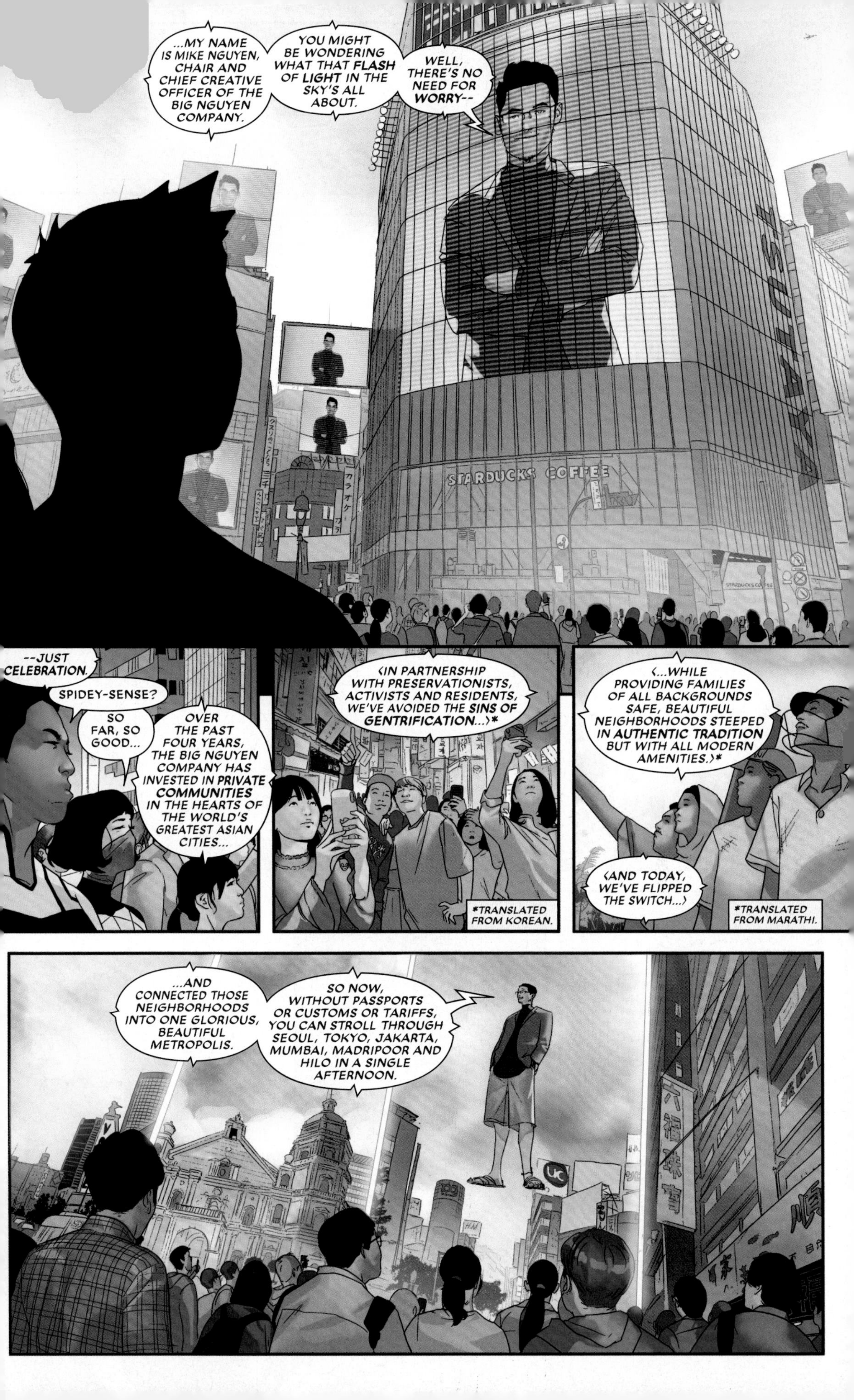
...MY NAME IS MIKE NGUYEN, CHAIR AND CHIEF CREATIVE OFFICER OF THE BIG NGUYEN COMPANY.
YOU MIGHT BE WONDERING WHAT THAT FLASH OF LIGHT IN THE SKY'S ALL ABOUT.
WELL, THERE'S NO NEED FOR WORRY--
STARDUCKS COFFEE
--JUST CELEBRATION.
SPIDEY-SENSE?
SO FAR, SO GOOD...
OVER THE PAST FOUR YEARS, THE BIG NGUYEN COMPANY HAS INVESTED IN PRIVATE COMMUNITIES IN THE HEARTS OF THE WORLD'S GREATEST ASIAN CITIES...
‹IN PARTNERSHIP WITH PRESERVATIONISTS, ACTIVISTS AND RESIDENTS, WE'VE AVOIDED THE SINS OF GENTRIFICATION...›*
*TRANSLATED FROM KOREAN.
‹...WHILE PROVIDING FAMILIES OF ALL BACKGROUNDS SAFE, BEAUTIFUL NEIGHBORHOODS STEEPED IN AUTHENTIC TRADITION BUT WITH ALL MODERN AMENITIES.›*
‹AND TODAY, WE'VE FLIPPED THE SWITCH...›
*TRANSLATED FROM MARATHI.
...AND CONNECTED THOSE NEIGHBORHOODS INTO ONE GLORIOUS, BEAUTIFUL METROPOLIS.
SO NOW, WITHOUT PASSPORTS OR CUSTOMS OR TARIFFS, YOU CAN STROLL THROUGH SEOUL, TOKYO, JAKARTA, MUMBAI, MADRIPOOR AND HILO IN A SINGLE AFTERNOON.

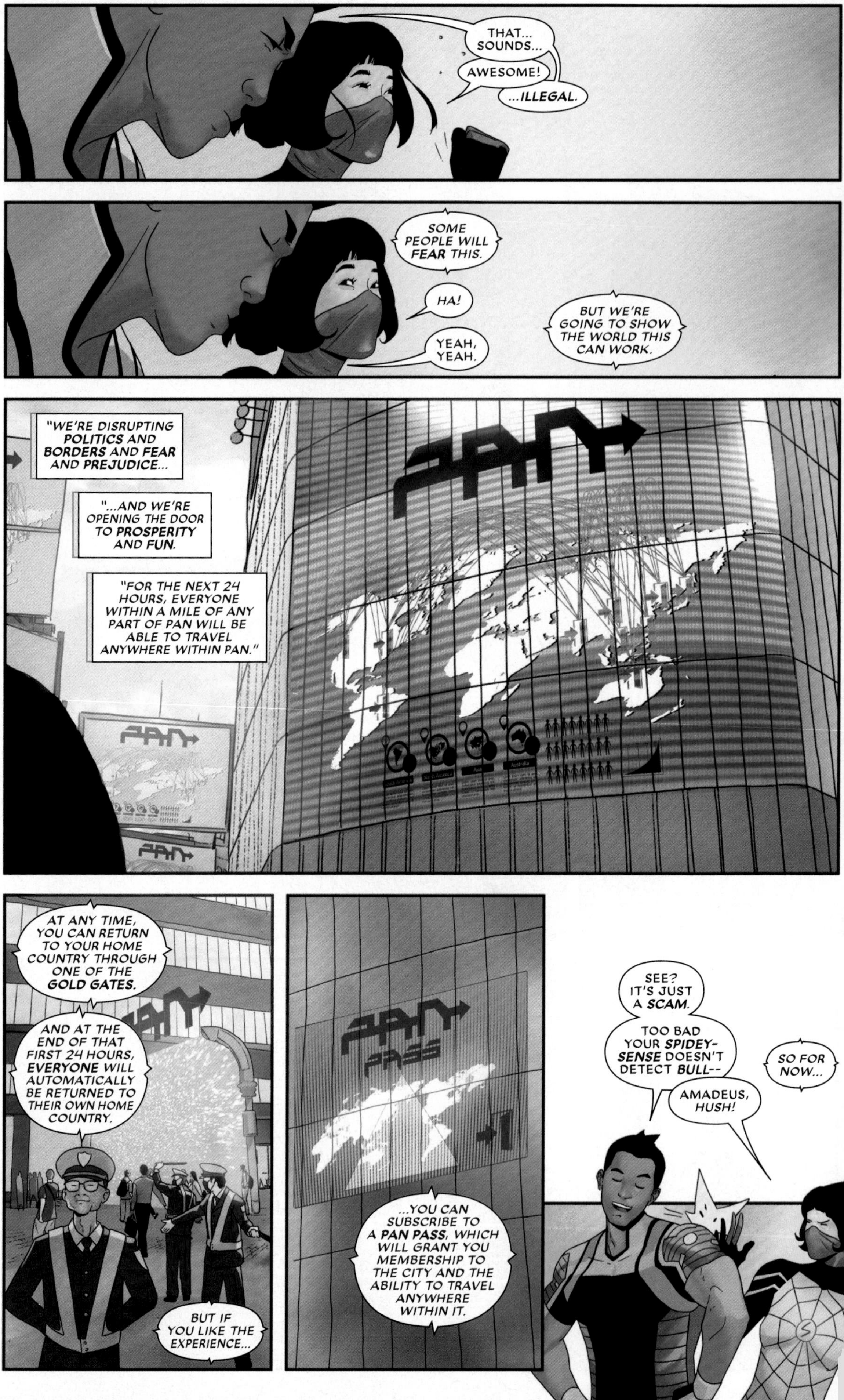
THAT... SOUNDS...
AWESOME!
...ILLEGAL.
SOME PEOPLE WILL FEAR THIS.
HA!
YEAH, YEAH.
BUT WE'RE GOING TO SHOW THE WORLD THIS CAN WORK.
"WE'RE DISRUPTING POLITICS AND BORDERS AND FEAR AND PREJUDICE...
"...AND WE'RE OPENING THE DOOR TO PROSPERITY AND FUN.
"FOR THE NEXT 24 HOURS, EVERYONE WITHIN A MILE OF ANY PART OF PAN WILL BE ABLE TO TRAVEL ANYWHERE WITHIN PAN."
AT ANY TIME, YOU CAN RETURN TO YOUR HOME COUNTRY THROUGH ONE OF THE GOLD GATES.
AND AT THE END OF THAT FIRST 24 HOURS, EVERYONE WILL AUTOMATICALLY BE RETURNED TO THEIR OWN HOME COUNTRY.
BUT IF YOU LIKE THE EXPERIENCE...
...YOU CAN SUBSCRIBE TO A PAN PASS, WHICH WILL GRANT YOU MEMBERSHIP TO THE CITY AND THE ABILITY TO TRAVEL ANYWHERE WITHIN IT.
SEE? IT'S JUST A SCAM.
TOO BAD YOUR SPIDEY-SENSE DOESN'T DETECT BULL--
AMADEUS, HUSH!
SO FOR NOW...

...GO AHEAD. TAKE THAT FIRST STEP...

...AND SEE THE WORLD!

ALL RIGHT, GET READY.

FOR WHAT?

PEOPLE ARE GONNA GO *NUTS.*

YOU CAN'T JUST THROW *THOUSANDS* OF PEOPLE FROM *DIFFERENT WORLDS* TOGETHER AND EXPECT...

⟨THIS--THIS IS *INCREDIBLE!*⟩*

⟨WE'RE GONNA BE LATE FOR LUNCH...⟩

⟨WHO *CARES?* LOOK, HAVEN'T YOU ALWAYS WANTED TO VISIT TOKYO?⟩

*TRANSLATED FROM MANDARIN.

UH... KONNICHIWA?

HA! ANN... YUNG...

ANNYEONGHASEYO!

HA HA!

HA HA!

HUH. SPIDEY-SENSE?

ALL GOOD. YOU CAN TOTALLY RELA--

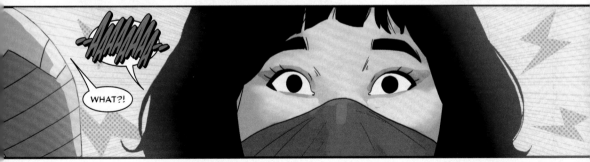

AAAAAAH!

WHAT?!

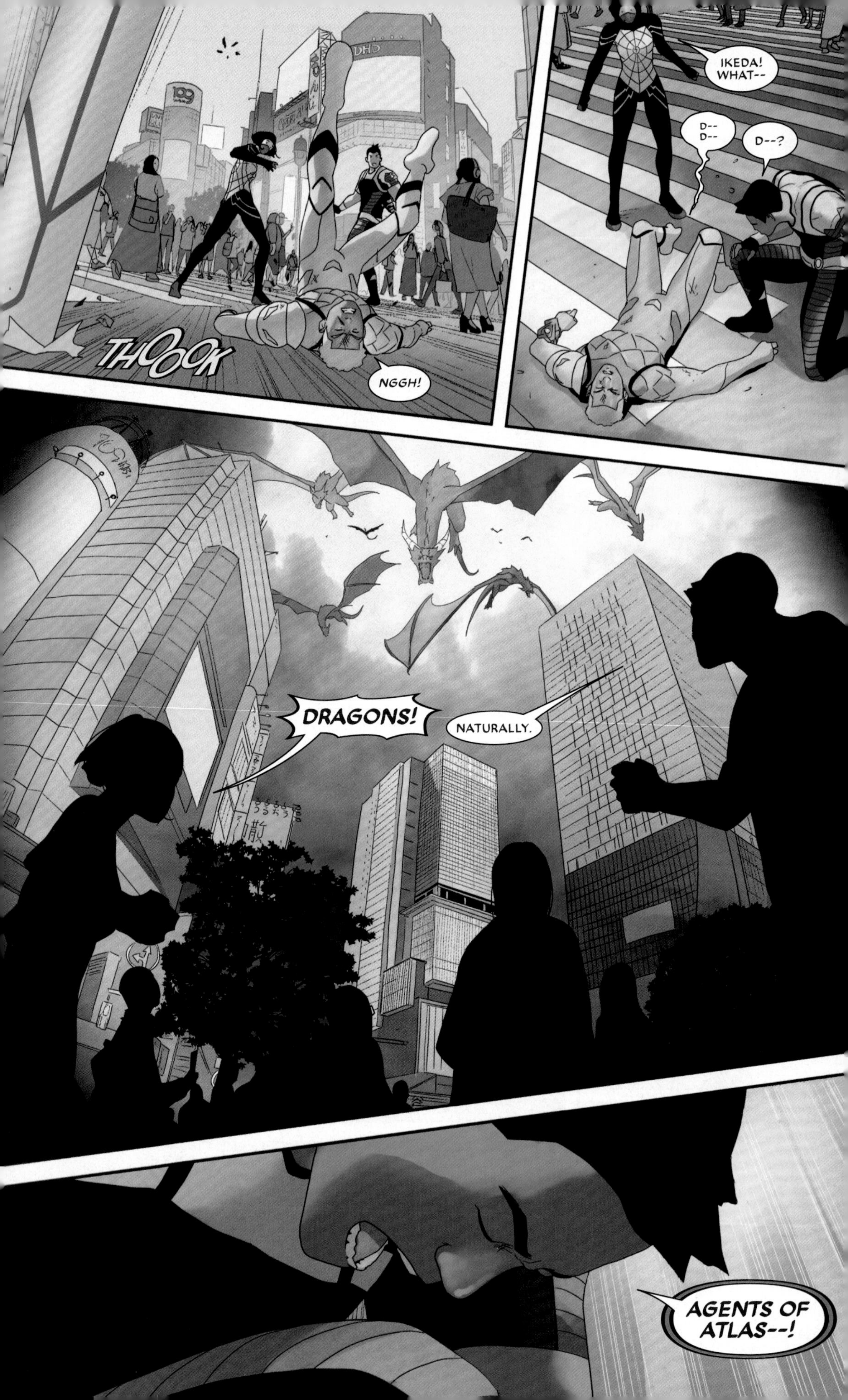
THOOOK
NGGH!
IKEDA! WHAT--
D-- D--
D--?
DRAGONS!
NATURALLY.
AGENTS OF ATLAS--!

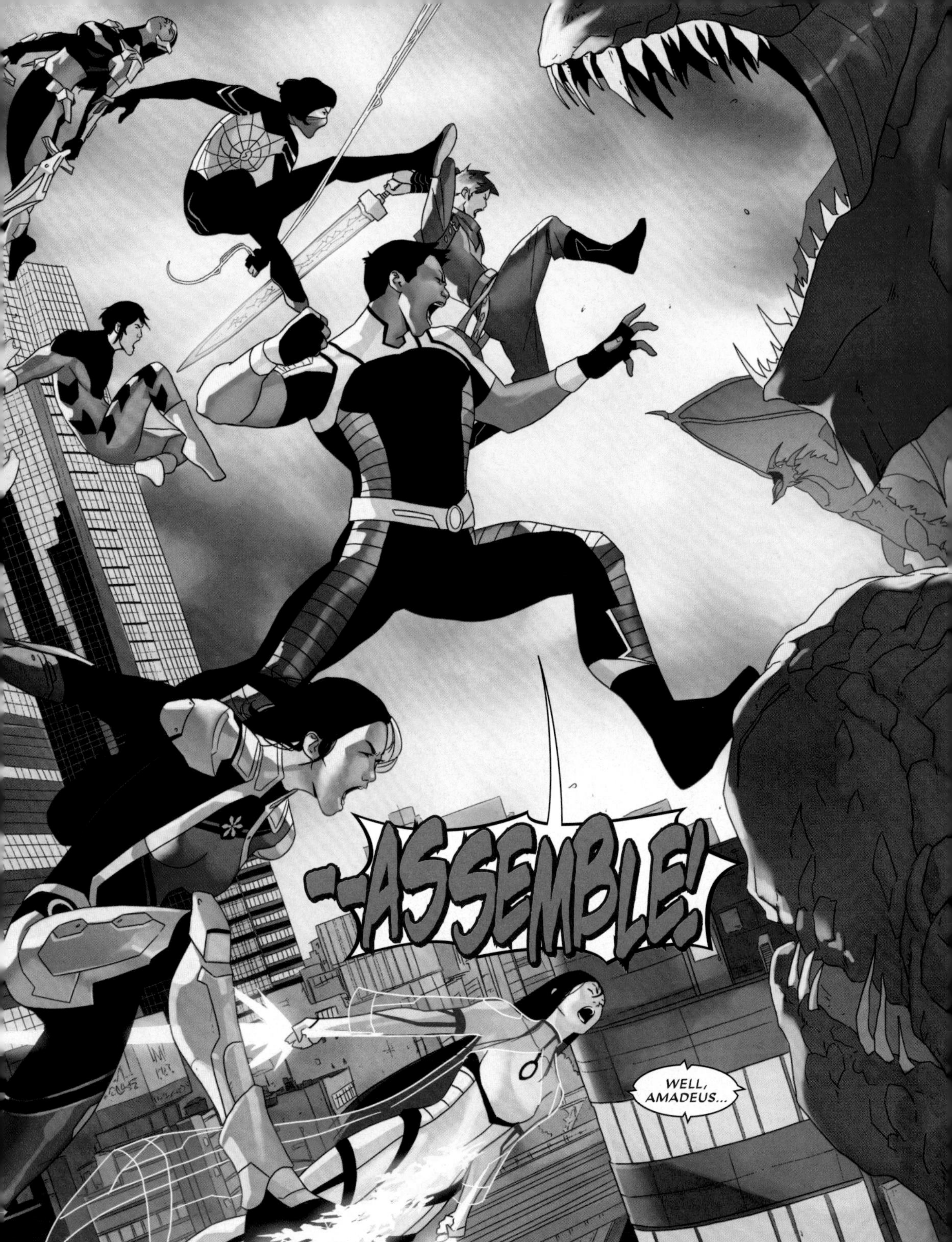
--ASSEMBLE!
WELL, AMADEUS...

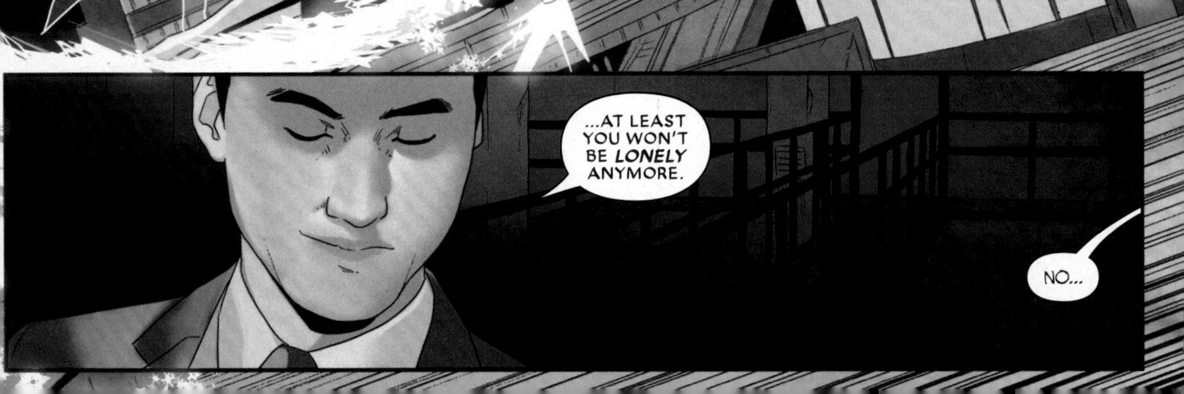
...AT LEAST YOU WON'T BE *LONELY* ANYMORE.
NO...

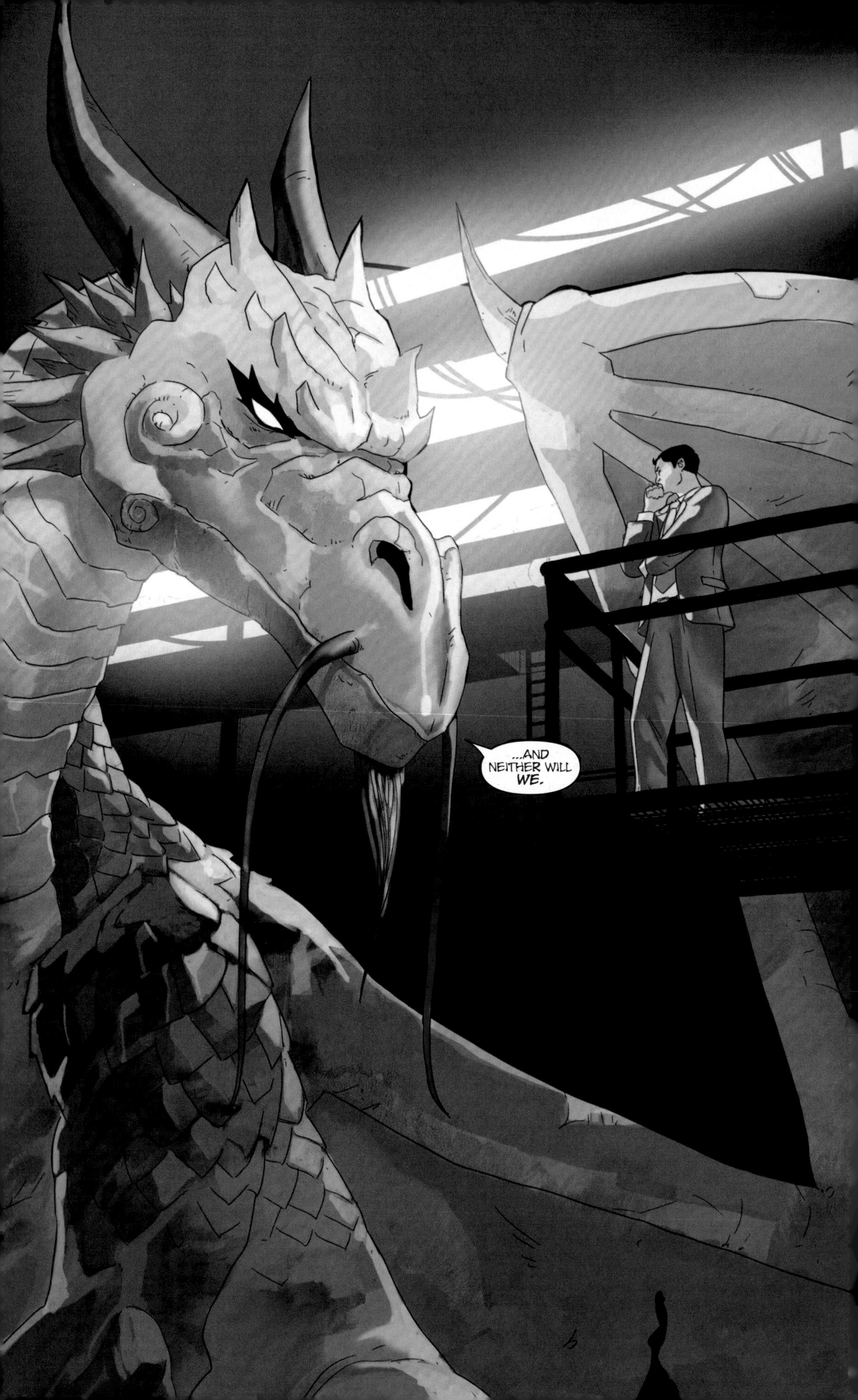
...AND NEITHER WILL WE.

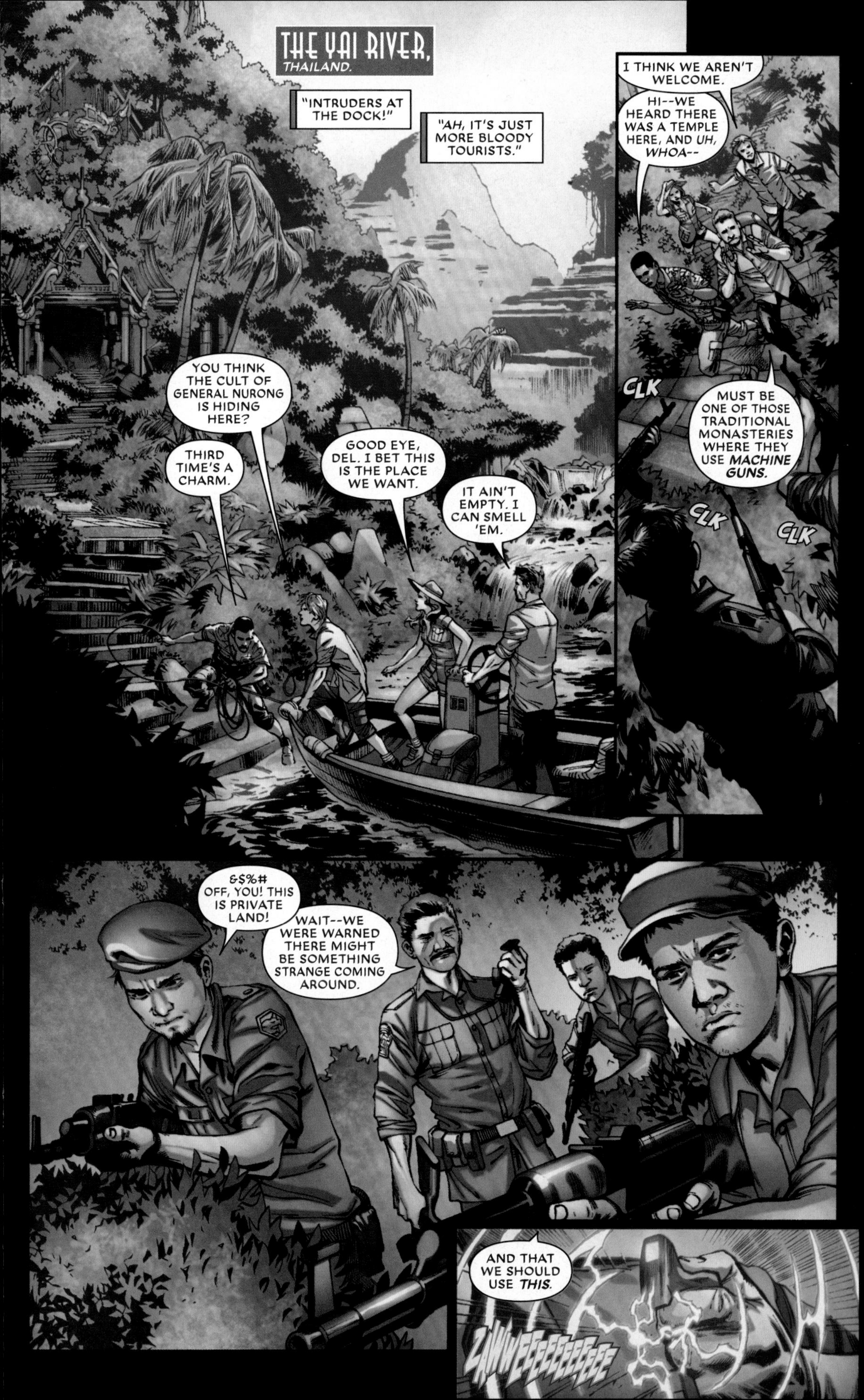
THE YAI RIVER,
THAILAND.
"INTRUDERS AT THE DOCK!"
"AH, IT'S JUST MORE BLOODY TOURISTS."
YOU THINK THE CULT OF GENERAL NURONG IS HIDING HERE?
THIRD TIME'S A CHARM.
GOOD EYE, DEL. I BET THIS IS THE PLACE WE WANT.
IT AIN'T EMPTY. I CAN SMELL 'EM.
I THINK WE AREN'T WELCOME.
HI--WE HEARD THERE WAS A TEMPLE HERE, AND UH, WHOA--
CLK
MUST BE ONE OF THOSE TRADITIONAL MONASTERIES WHERE THEY USE MACHINE GUNS.
CLK
CLK
&$%# OFF, YOU! THIS IS PRIVATE LAND!
WAIT--WE WERE WARNED THERE MIGHT BE SOMETHING STRANGE COMING AROUND.
AND THAT WE SHOULD USE THIS.
ZAWWEEEEEEEEEE

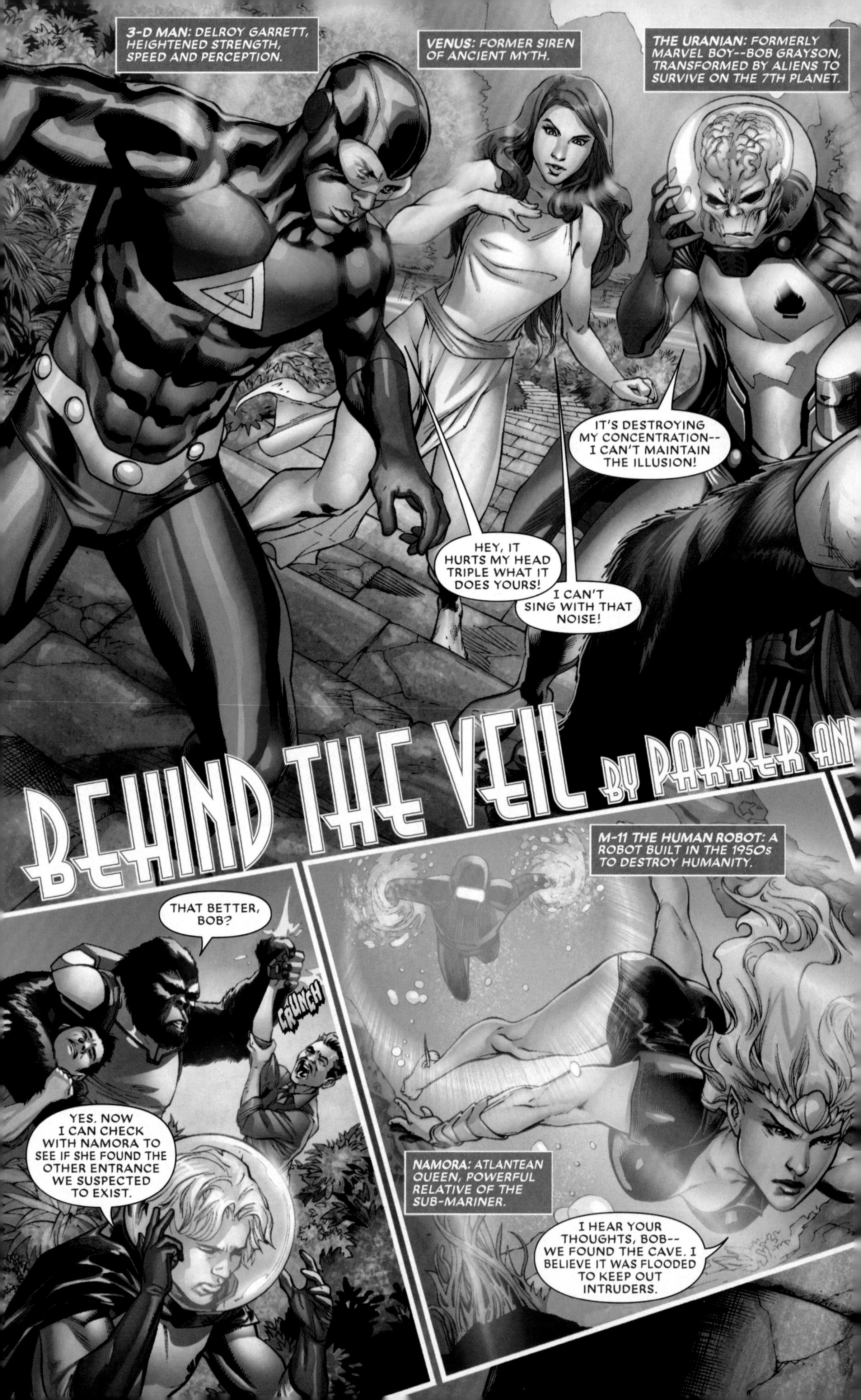
3-D MAN: DELROY GARRETT, HEIGHTENED STRENGTH, SPEED AND PERCEPTION.
VENUS: FORMER SIREN OF ANCIENT MYTH.
THE URANIAN: FORMERLY MARVEL BOY--BOB GRAYSON, TRANSFORMED BY ALIENS TO SURVIVE ON THE 7TH PLANET.
IT'S DESTROYING MY CONCENTRATION-- I CAN'T MAINTAIN THE ILLUSION!
HEY, IT HURTS MY HEAD TRIPLE WHAT IT DOES YOURS!
I CAN'T SING WITH THAT NOISE!
BEHIND THE VEIL BY PARKER AN
M-11 THE HUMAN ROBOT: A ROBOT BUILT IN THE 1950s TO DESTROY HUMANITY.
THAT BETTER, BOB?
CRUNCH
YES. NOW I CAN CHECK WITH NAMORA TO SEE IF SHE FOUND THE OTHER ENTRANCE WE SUSPECTED TO EXIST.
NAMORA: ATLANTEAN QUEEN, POWERFUL RELATIVE OF THE SUB-MARINER.
I HEAR YOUR THOUGHTS, BOB-- WE FOUND THE CAVE. I BELIEVE IT WAS FLOODED TO KEEP OUT INTRUDERS.

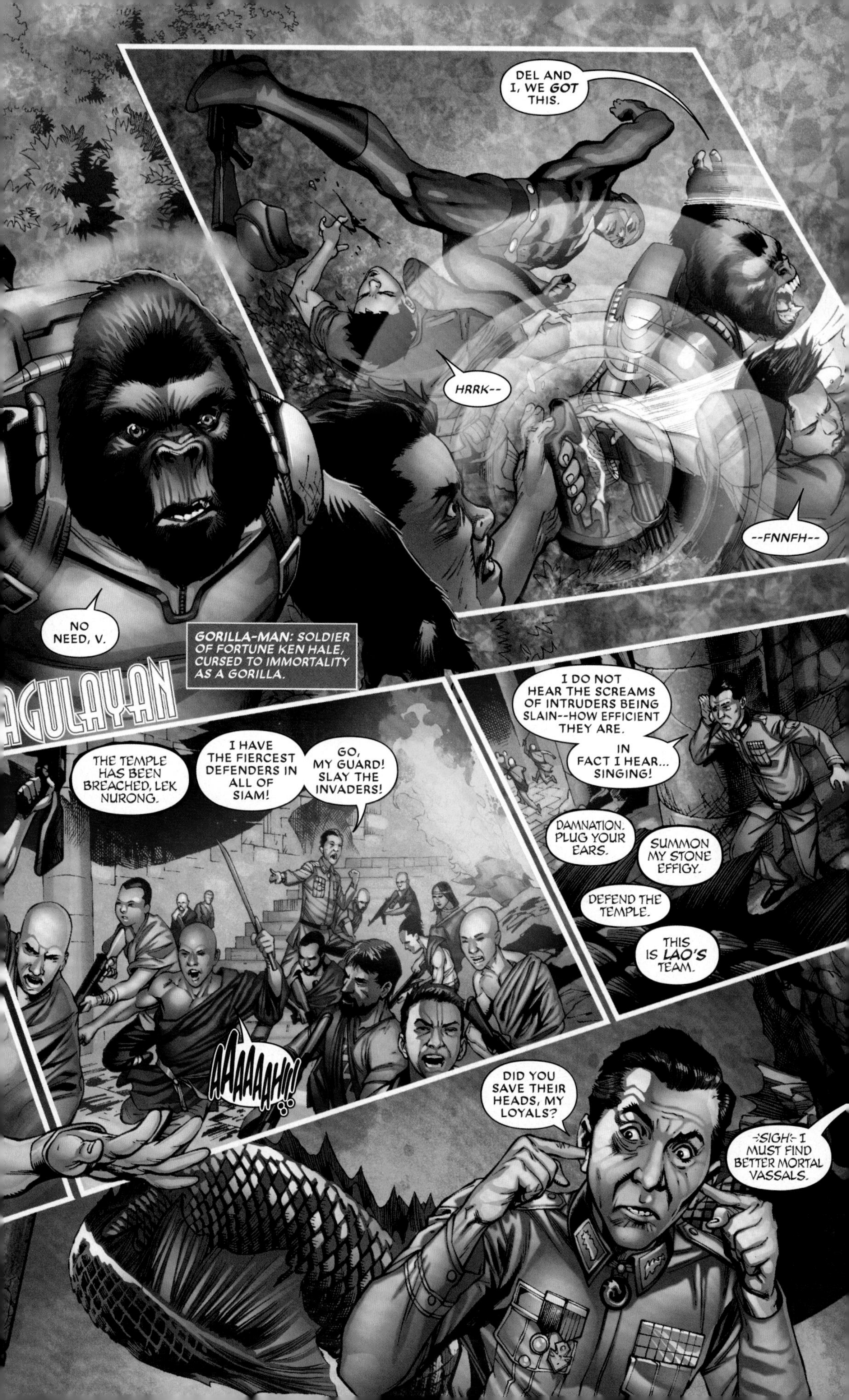
DEL AND I, WE GOT THIS.
HRRK--
--FNNFH--
NO NEED, V.
GORILLA-MAN: SOLDIER OF FORTUNE KEN HALE, CURSED TO IMMORTALITY AS A GORILLA.
AGULAYAN
THE TEMPLE HAS BEEN BREACHED, LEK NURONG.
I HAVE THE FIERCEST DEFENDERS IN ALL OF SIAM!
GO, MY GUARD! SLAY THE INVADERS!
AAAAAAHH!!
I DO NOT HEAR THE SCREAMS OF INTRUDERS BEING SLAIN--HOW EFFICIENT THEY ARE.
IN FACT I HEAR... SINGING!
DAMNATION. PLUG YOUR EARS.
SUMMON MY STONE EFFIGY.
DEFEND THE TEMPLE.
THIS IS LAO'S TEAM.
DID YOU SAVE THEIR HEADS, MY LOYALS?
-SIGH- I MUST FIND BETTER MORTAL VASSALS.

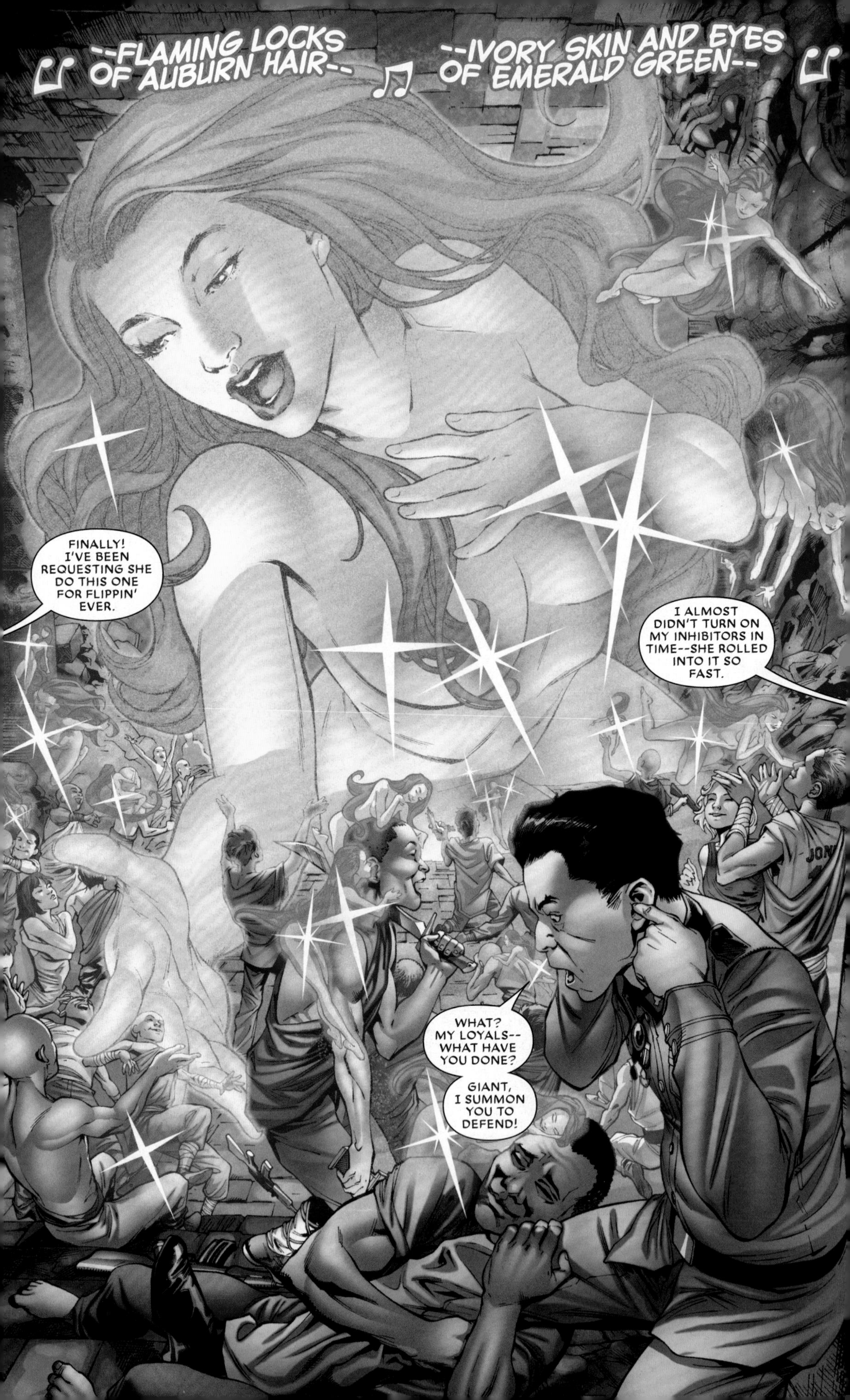
--FLAMING LOCKS OF AUBURN HAIR--
--IVORY SKIN AND EYES OF EMERALD GREEN--
FINALLY! I'VE BEEN REQUESTING SHE DO THIS ONE FOR FLIPPIN' EVER.
I ALMOST DIDN'T TURN ON MY INHIBITORS IN TIME--SHE ROLLED INTO IT SO FAST.
WHAT? MY LOYALS-- WHAT HAVE YOU DONE?
GIANT, I SUMMON YOU TO DEFEND!

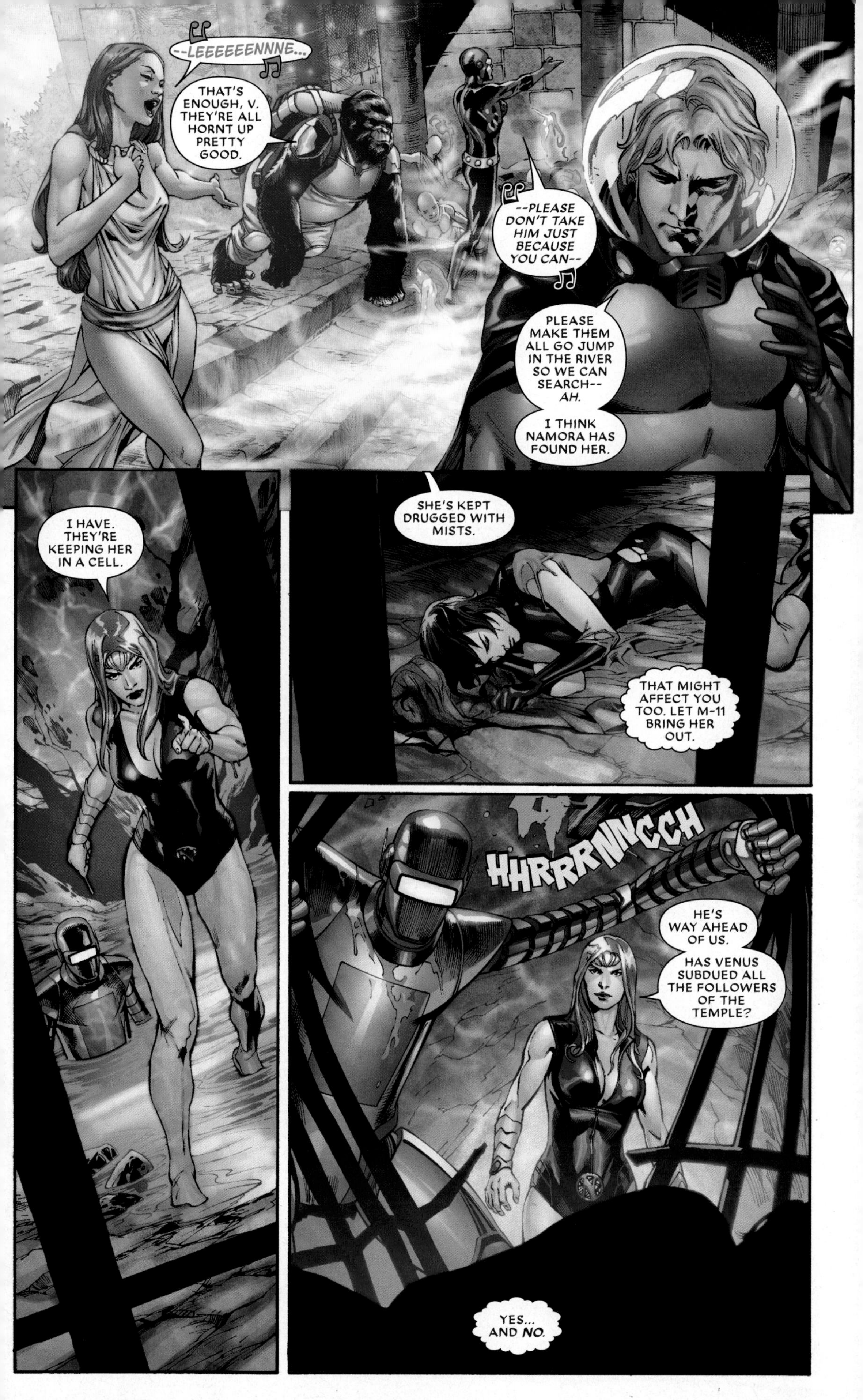
--LEEEEEEENNNE...
THAT'S ENOUGH, V. THEY'RE ALL HORNT UP PRETTY GOOD.
--PLEASE DON'T TAKE HIM JUST BECAUSE YOU CAN--
PLEASE MAKE THEM ALL GO JUMP IN THE RIVER SO WE CAN SEARCH-- AH.
I THINK NAMORA HAS FOUND HER.
I HAVE. THEY'RE KEEPING HER IN A CELL.
SHE'S KEPT DRUGGED WITH MISTS.
THAT MIGHT AFFECT YOU TOO. LET M-11 BRING HER OUT.
HHRRRNNCCH
HE'S WAY AHEAD OF US.
HAS VENUS SUBDUED ALL THE FOLLOWERS OF THE TEMPLE?
YES... AND NO.

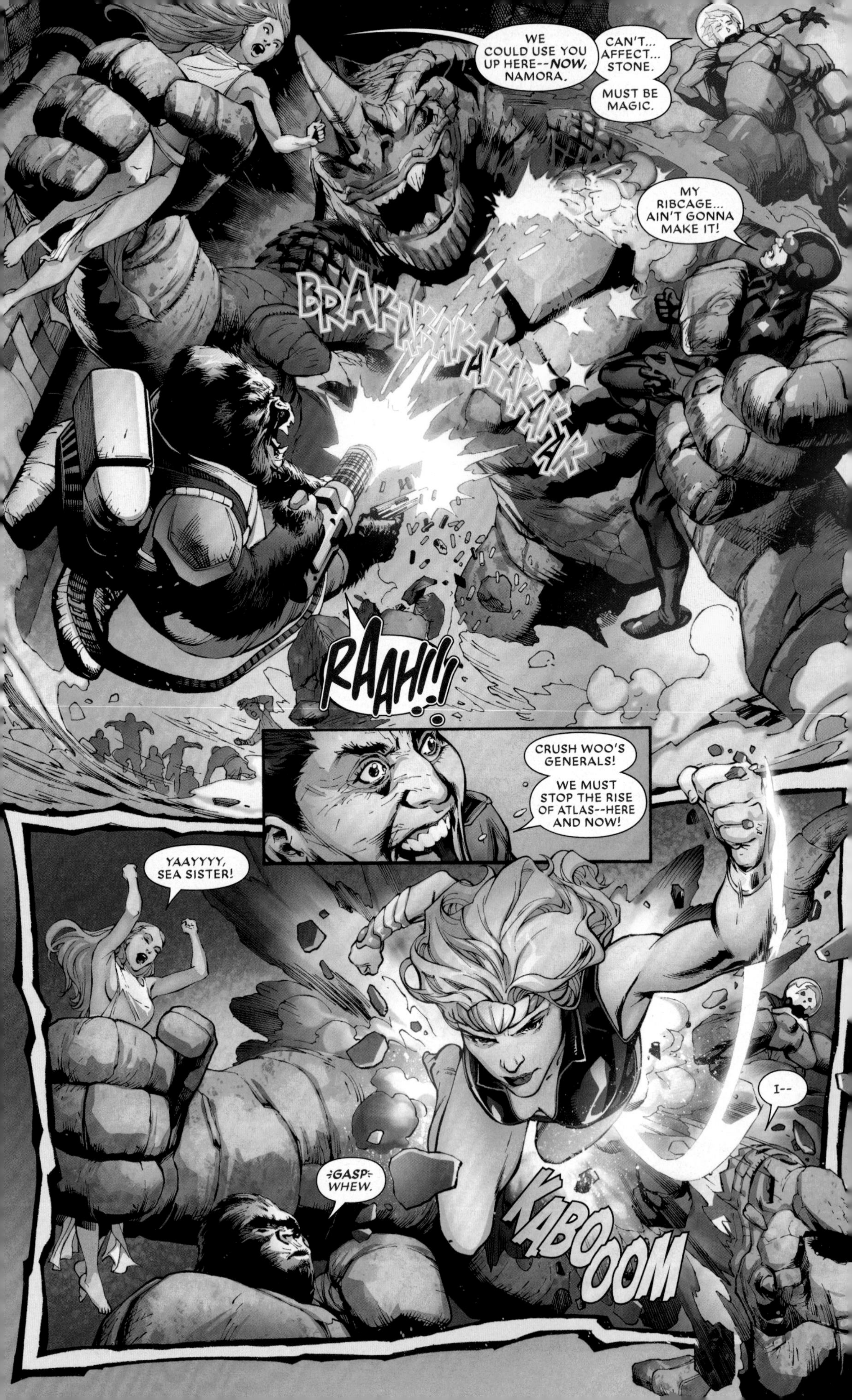

WE COULD USE YOU UP HERE--*NOW,* NAMORA.
CAN'T... AFFECT... STONE.
MUST BE MAGIC.
MY RIBCAGE... AIN'T GONNA MAKE IT!
BRAKAKAKAKAKAKAK
RAAH!!!
CRUSH WOO'S GENERALS!
WE MUST STOP THE RISE OF ATLAS--HERE AND NOW!
YAAYYYY, SEA SISTER!
I--
GASP WHEW.
KABOOOOM

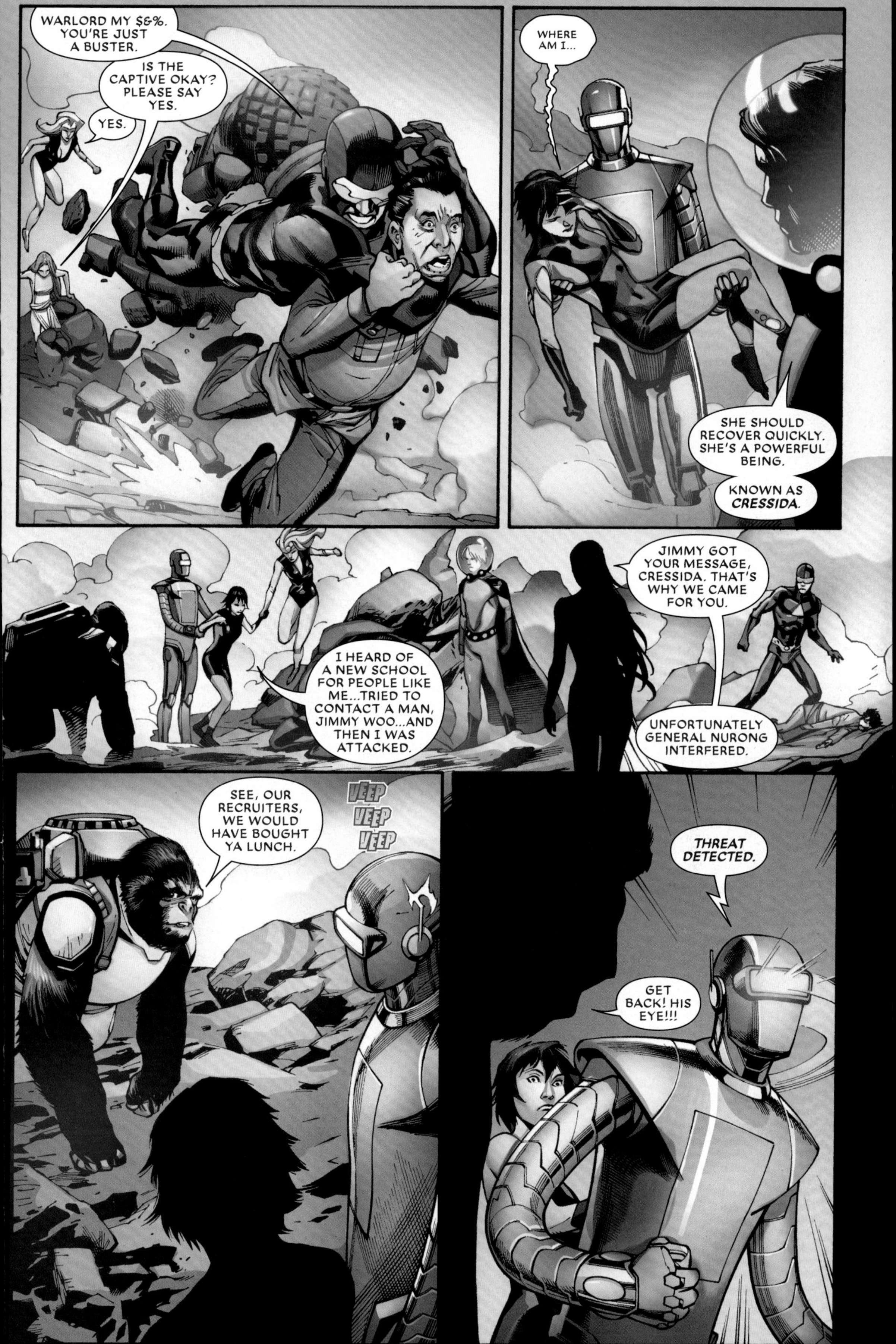
WARLORD MY $&%. YOU'RE JUST A BUSTER.
IS THE CAPTIVE OKAY? PLEASE SAY YES.
YES.
WHERE AM I...
SHE SHOULD RECOVER QUICKLY. SHE'S A POWERFUL BEING.
KNOWN AS CRESSIDA.
JIMMY GOT YOUR MESSAGE, CRESSIDA. THAT'S WHY WE CAME FOR YOU.
I HEARD OF A NEW SCHOOL FOR PEOPLE LIKE ME...TRIED TO CONTACT A MAN, JIMMY WOO...AND THEN I WAS ATTACKED.
UNFORTUNATELY GENERAL NURONG INTERFERED.
SEE, OUR RECRUITERS, WE WOULD HAVE BOUGHT YA LUNCH.
VEEP
VEEP
VEEP
THREAT DETECTED.
GET BACK! HIS EYE!!!

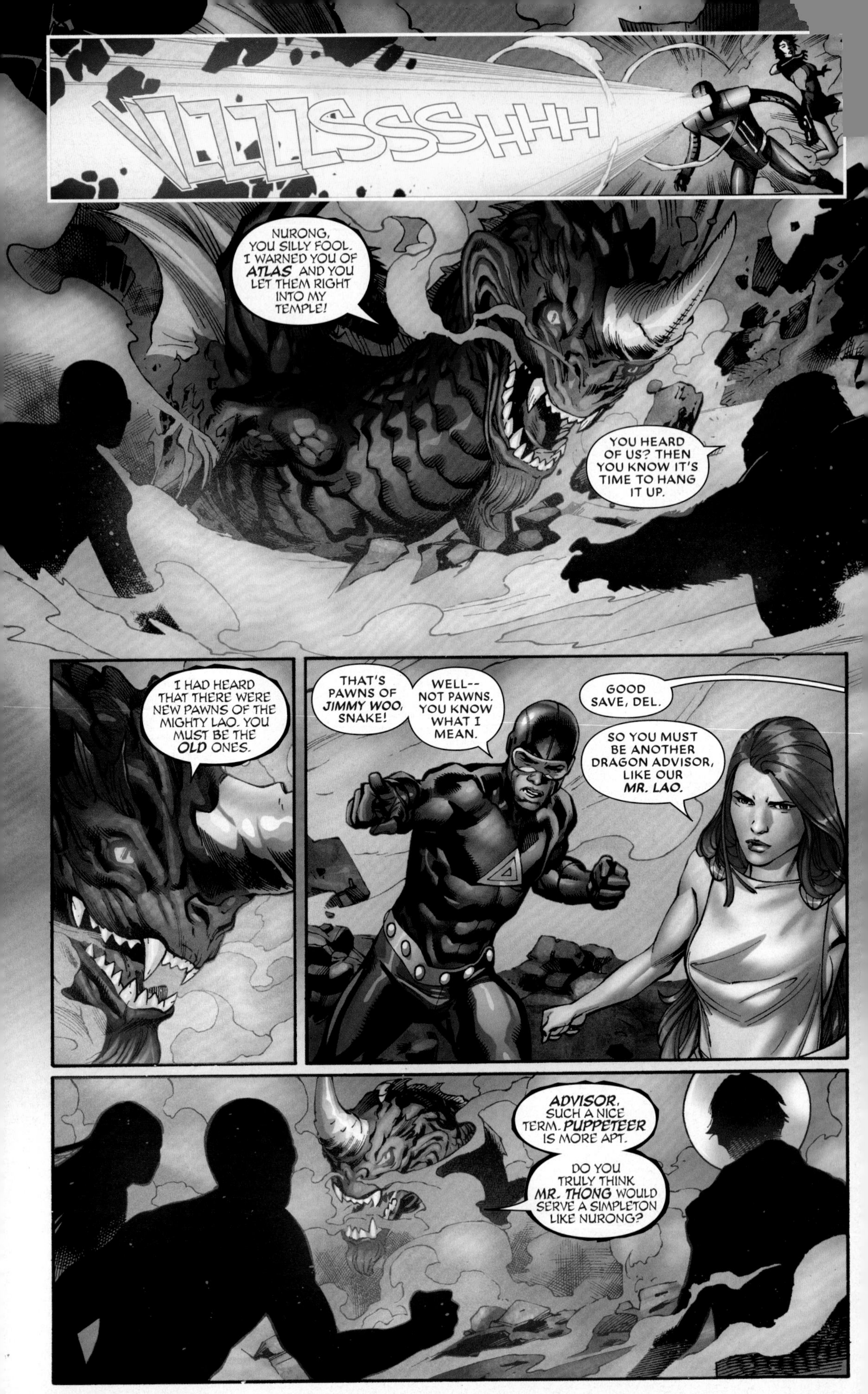
VZZZSSSHHH
NURONG, YOU SILLY FOOL. I WARNED YOU OF ATLAS AND YOU LET THEM RIGHT INTO MY TEMPLE!
YOU HEARD OF US? THEN YOU KNOW IT'S TIME TO HANG IT UP.
I HAD HEARD THAT THERE WERE NEW PAWNS OF THE MIGHTY LAO. YOU MUST BE THE OLD ONES.
THAT'S PAWNS OF JIMMY WOO, SNAKE!
WELL-- NOT PAWNS. YOU KNOW WHAT I MEAN.
GOOD SAVE, DEL.
SO YOU MUST BE ANOTHER DRAGON ADVISOR, LIKE OUR MR. LAO.
ADVISOR, SUCH A NICE TERM. PUPPETEER IS MORE APT.
DO YOU TRULY THINK MR. THONG WOULD SERVE A SIMPLETON LIKE NURONG?

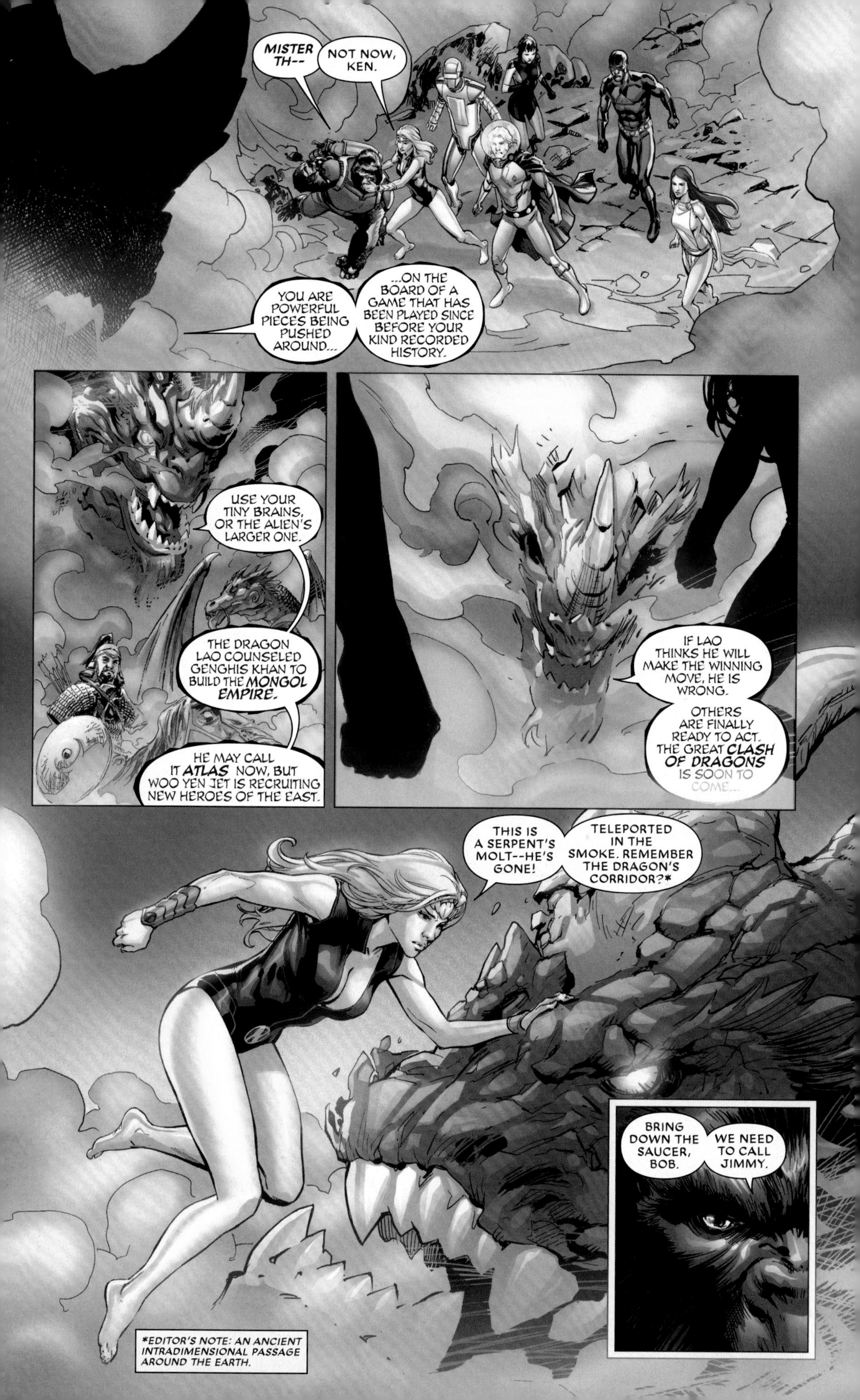
MISTER TH--
NOT NOW, KEN.
YOU ARE POWERFUL PIECES BEING PUSHED AROUND...
...ON THE BOARD OF A GAME THAT HAS BEEN PLAYED SINCE BEFORE YOUR KIND RECORDED HISTORY.
USE YOUR TINY BRAINS, OR THE ALIEN'S LARGER ONE.
THE DRAGON LAO COUNSELED GENGHIS KHAN TO BUILD THE MONGOL EMPIRE.
HE MAY CALL IT ATLAS NOW, BUT WOO YEN JET IS RECRUITING NEW HEROES OF THE EAST.
IF LAO THINKS HE WILL MAKE THE WINNING MOVE, HE IS WRONG.
OTHERS ARE FINALLY READY TO ACT. THE GREAT CLASH OF DRAGONS IS SOON TO COME...
THIS IS A SERPENT'S MOLT--HE'S GONE!
TELEPORTED IN THE SMOKE. REMEMBER THE DRAGON'S CORRIDOR?*
*EDITOR'S NOTE: AN ANCIENT INTRADIMENSIONAL PASSAGE AROUND THE EARTH.
BRING DOWN THE SAUCER, BOB.
WE NEED TO CALL JIMMY.

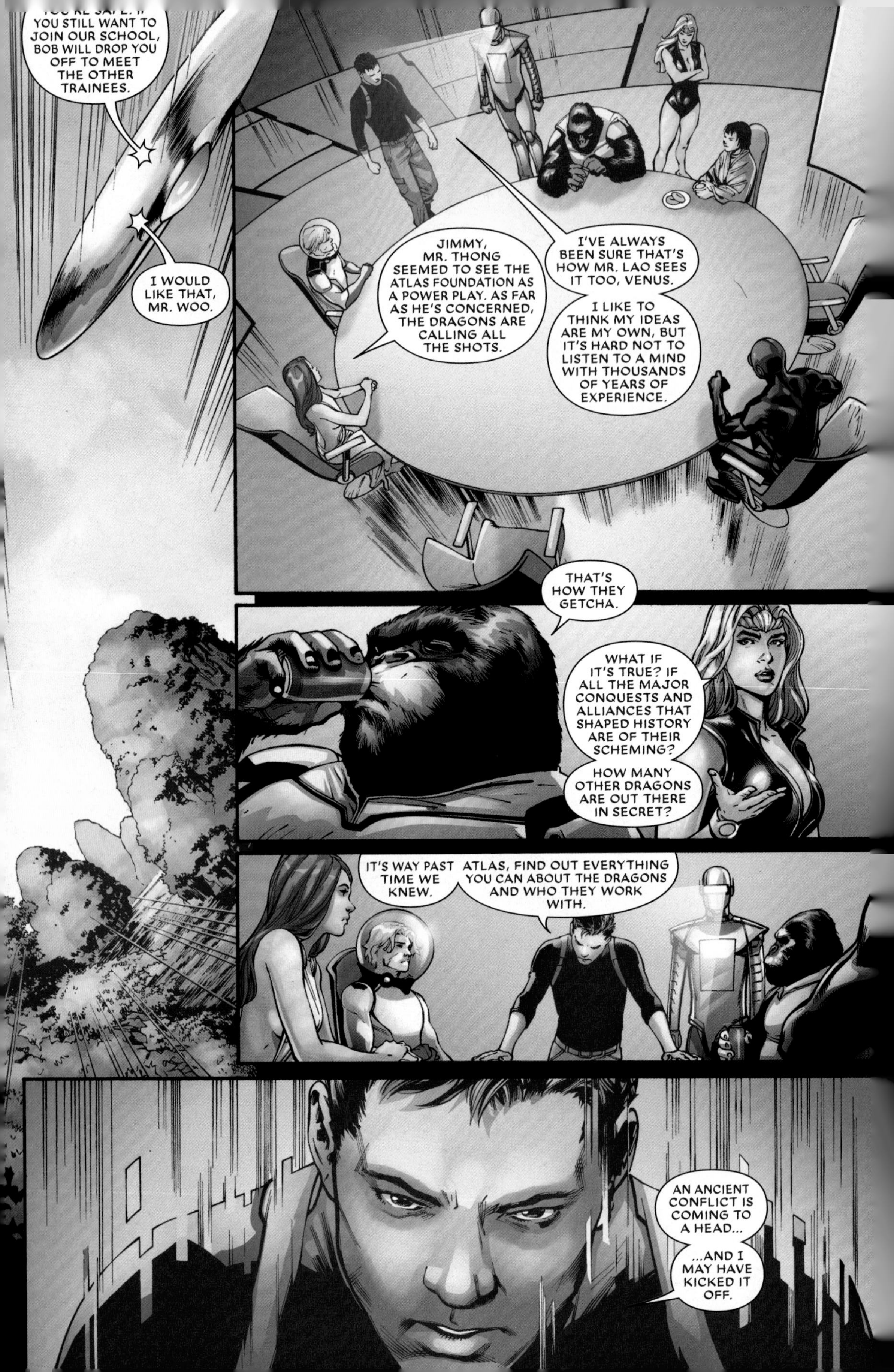
YOU STILL WANT TO JOIN OUR SCHOOL, BOB WILL DROP YOU OFF TO MEET THE OTHER TRAINEES.
I WOULD LIKE THAT, MR. WOO.
JIMMY, MR. THONG SEEMED TO SEE THE ATLAS FOUNDATION AS A POWER PLAY. AS FAR AS HE'S CONCERNED, THE DRAGONS ARE CALLING ALL THE SHOTS.
I'VE ALWAYS BEEN SURE THAT'S HOW MR. LAO SEES IT TOO, VENUS.
I LIKE TO THINK MY IDEAS ARE MY OWN, BUT IT'S HARD NOT TO LISTEN TO A MIND WITH THOUSANDS OF YEARS OF EXPERIENCE.
THAT'S HOW THEY GETCHA.
WHAT IF IT'S TRUE? IF ALL THE MAJOR CONQUESTS AND ALLIANCES THAT SHAPED HISTORY ARE OF THEIR SCHEMING?
HOW MANY OTHER DRAGONS ARE OUT THERE IN SECRET?
IT'S WAY PAST TIME WE KNEW.
ATLAS, FIND OUT EVERYTHING YOU CAN ABOUT THE DRAGONS AND WHO THEY WORK WITH.
AN ANCIENT CONFLICT IS COMING TO A HEAD...
...AND I MAY HAVE KICKED IT OFF.

TWO

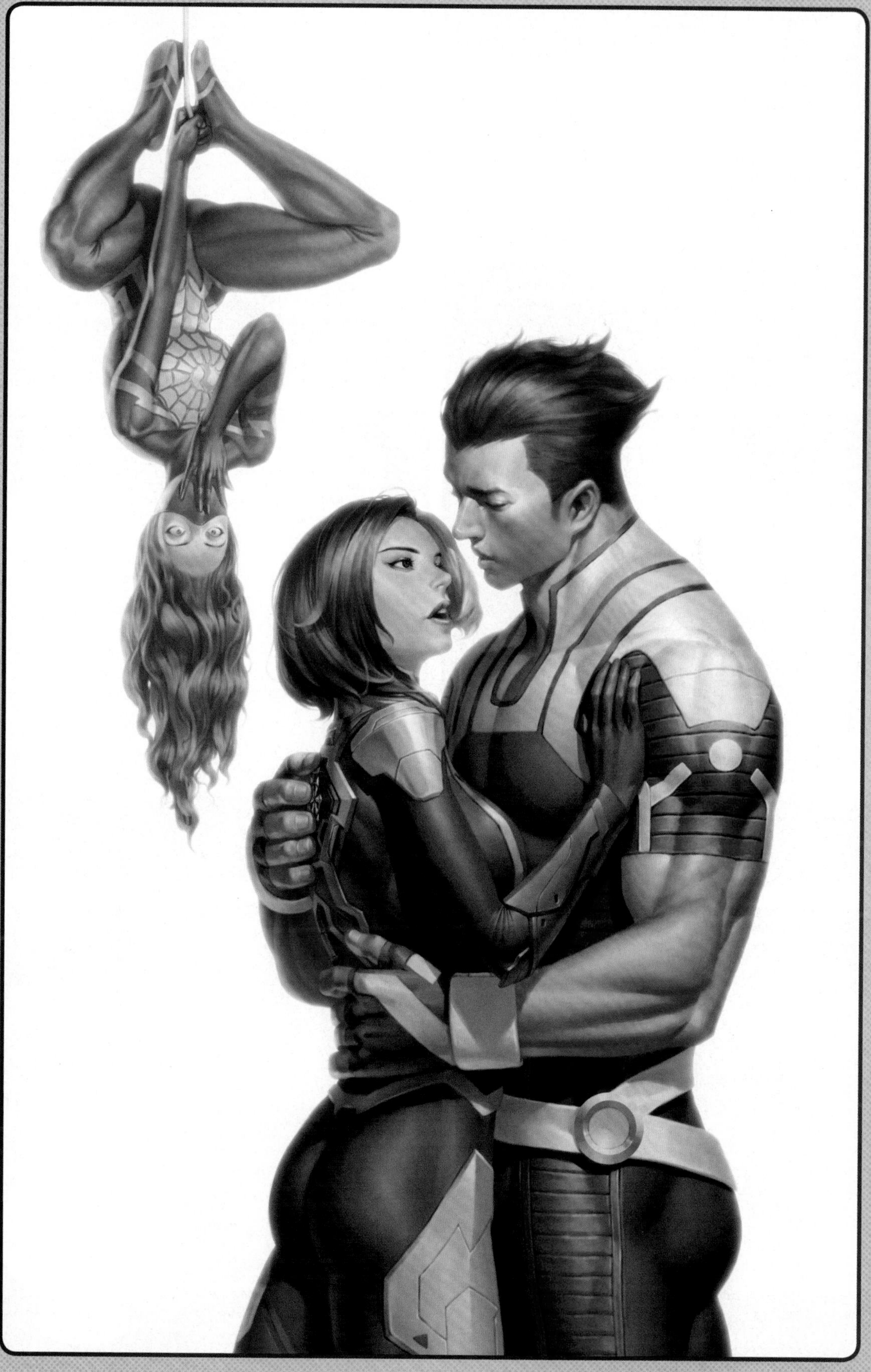

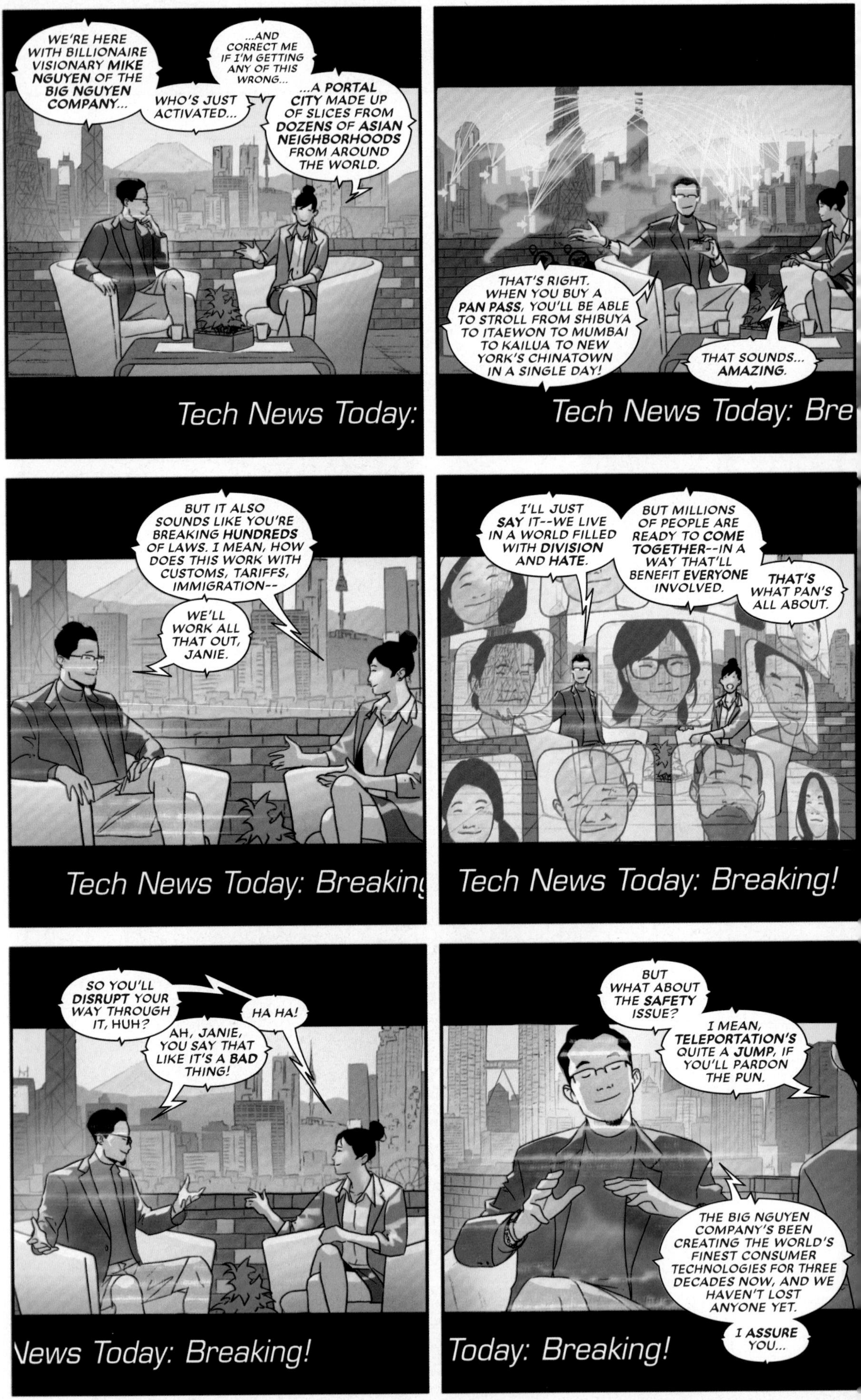
WE'RE HERE WITH BILLIONAIRE VISIONARY MIKE NGUYEN OF THE BIG NGUYEN COMPANY...
WHO'S JUST ACTIVATED...
...AND CORRECT ME IF I'M GETTING ANY OF THIS WRONG...
...A PORTAL CITY MADE UP OF SLICES FROM DOZENS OF ASIAN NEIGHBORHOODS FROM AROUND THE WORLD.
Tech News Today:
THAT'S RIGHT. WHEN YOU BUY A PAN PASS, YOU'LL BE ABLE TO STROLL FROM SHIBUYA TO ITAEWON TO MUMBAI TO KAILUA TO NEW YORK'S CHINATOWN IN A SINGLE DAY!
THAT SOUNDS... AMAZING.
Tech News Today: Bre
BUT IT ALSO SOUNDS LIKE YOU'RE BREAKING HUNDREDS OF LAWS. I MEAN, HOW DOES THIS WORK WITH CUSTOMS, TARIFFS, IMMIGRATION--
WE'LL WORK ALL THAT OUT, JANIE.
Tech News Today: Breakin
I'LL JUST SAY IT--WE LIVE IN A WORLD FILLED WITH DIVISION AND HATE.
BUT MILLIONS OF PEOPLE ARE READY TO COME TOGETHER--IN A WAY THAT'LL BENEFIT EVERYONE INVOLVED.
THAT'S WHAT PAN'S ALL ABOUT.
Tech News Today: Breaking!
SO YOU'LL DISRUPT YOUR WAY THROUGH IT, HUH?
HA HA!
AH, JANIE, YOU SAY THAT LIKE IT'S A BAD THING!
News Today: Breaking!
BUT WHAT ABOUT THE SAFETY ISSUE?
I MEAN, TELEPORTATION'S QUITE A JUMP, IF YOU'LL PARDON THE PUN.
THE BIG NGUYEN COMPANY'S BEEN CREATING THE WORLD'S FINEST CONSUMER TECHNOLOGIES FOR THREE DECADES NOW, AND WE HAVEN'T LOST ANYONE YET.
I ASSURE YOU...
Today: Breaking!

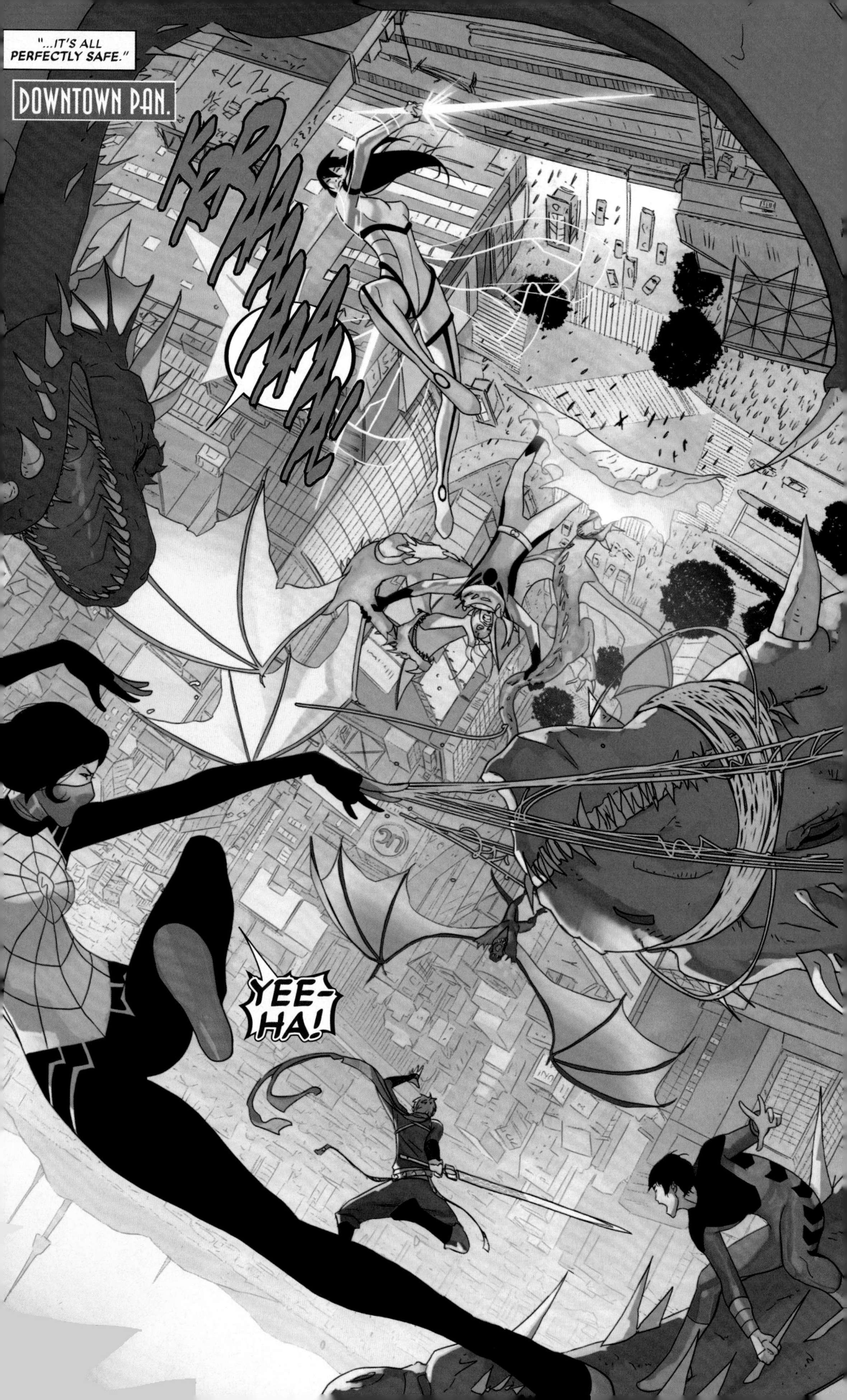
"...IT'S ALL PERFECTLY SAFE."
DOWNTOWN PAN.
KABAAAAAM!
YEE-HA!

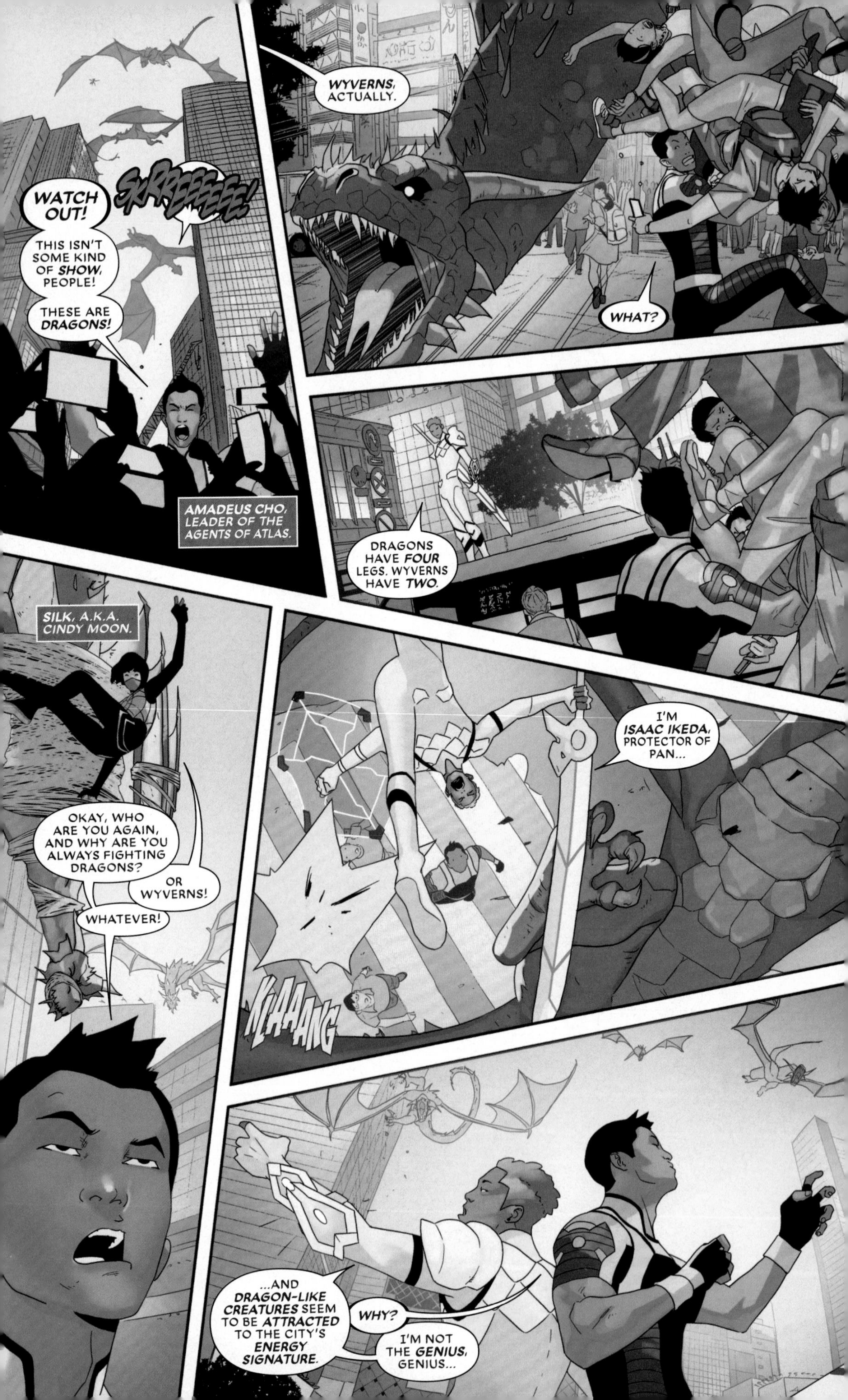

WATCH OUT!
THIS ISN'T SOME KIND OF SHOW, PEOPLE!
THESE ARE DRAGONS!
SKRREEEEEEE!
AMADEUS CHO, LEADER OF THE AGENTS OF ATLAS.
WYVERNS, ACTUALLY.
WHAT?
DRAGONS HAVE FOUR LEGS. WYVERNS HAVE TWO.
SILK, A.K.A. CINDY MOON.
OKAY, WHO ARE YOU AGAIN, AND WHY ARE YOU ALWAYS FIGHTING DRAGONS?
OR WYVERNS!
WHATEVER!
I'M ISAAC IKEDA, PROTECTOR OF PAN...
KLAAANG
...AND DRAGON-LIKE CREATURES SEEM TO BE ATTRACTED TO THE CITY'S ENERGY SIGNATURE.
WHY?
I'M NOT THE GENIUS, GENIUS...

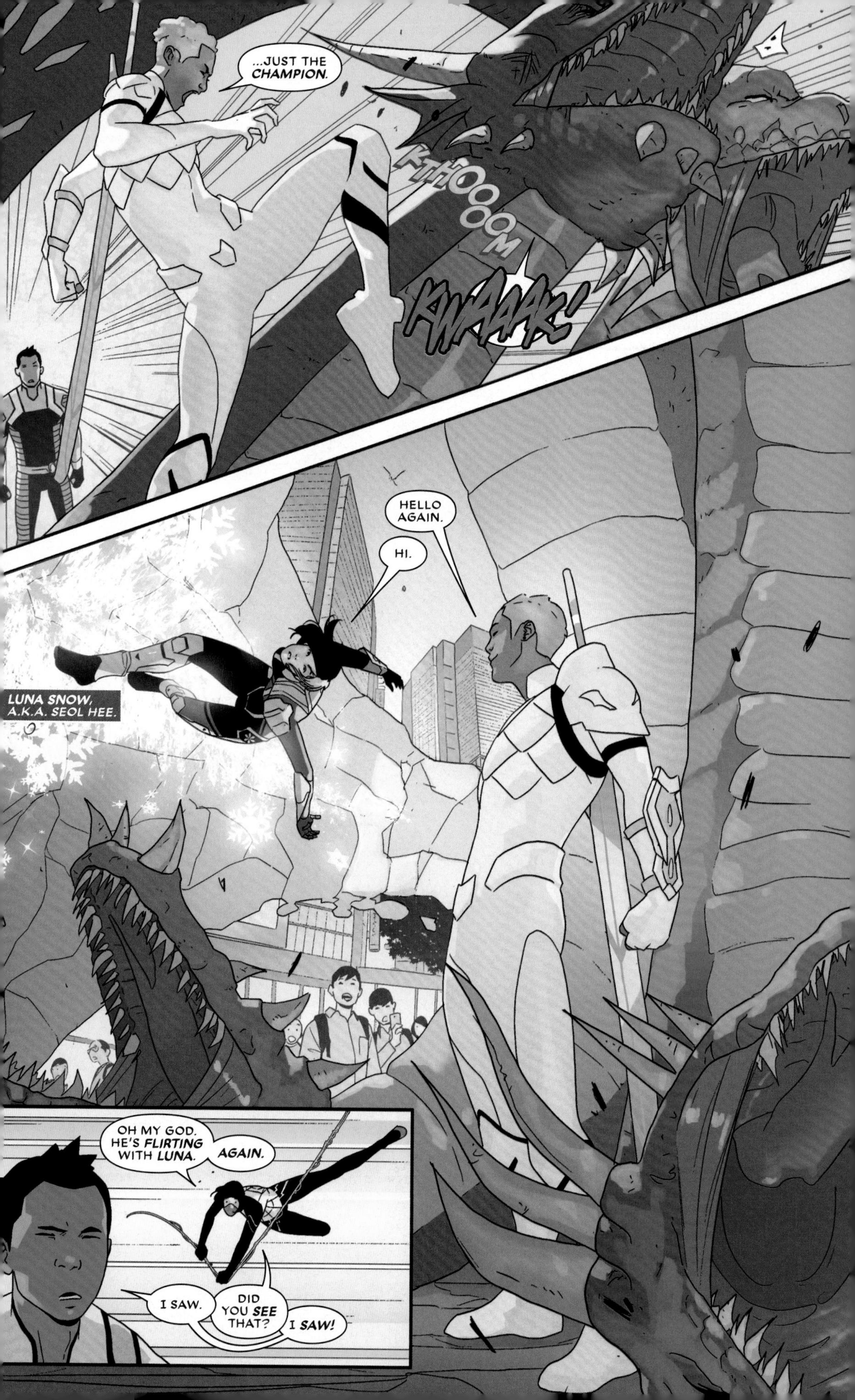
...JUST THE CHAMPION.
K-THOOOOM
KWAAAK!
HELLO AGAIN.
HI.
LUNA SNOW, A.K.A. SEOL HEE.
OH MY GOD. HE'S FLIRTING WITH LUNA.
AGAIN.
DID YOU SEE THAT?
I SAW.
I SAW!

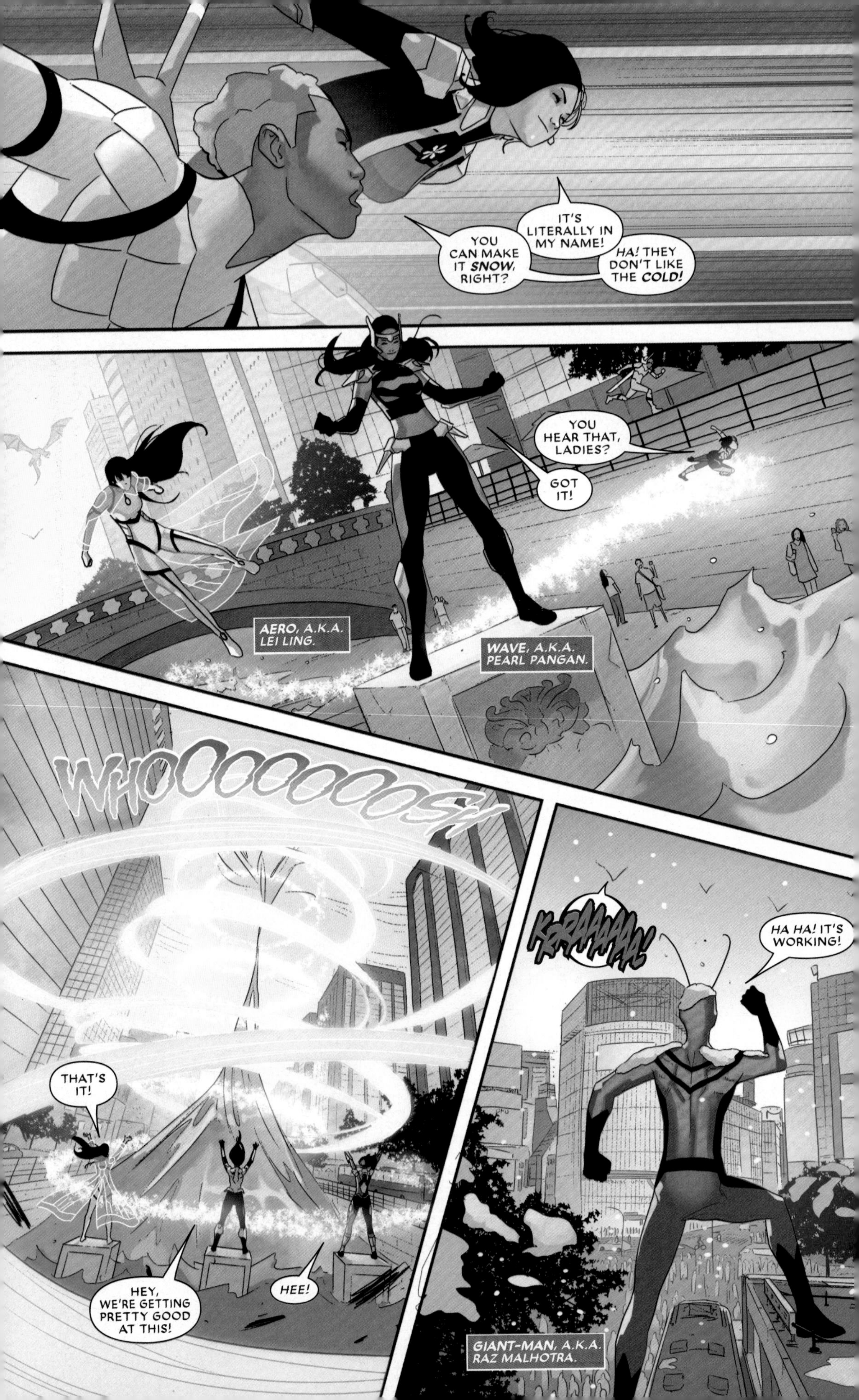
YOU CAN MAKE IT SNOW, RIGHT?
IT'S LITERALLY IN MY NAME!
HA! THEY DON'T LIKE THE COLD!
YOU HEAR THAT, LADIES?
GOT IT!
AERO, A.K.A. LEI LING.
WAVE, A.K.A. PEARL PANGAN.
WHOOOOOOOOSH
THAT'S IT!
HEY, WE'RE GETTING PRETTY GOOD AT THIS!
HEE!
KRRAAAAAA!
HA HA! IT'S WORKING!
GIANT-MAN, A.K.A. RAZ MALHOTRA.

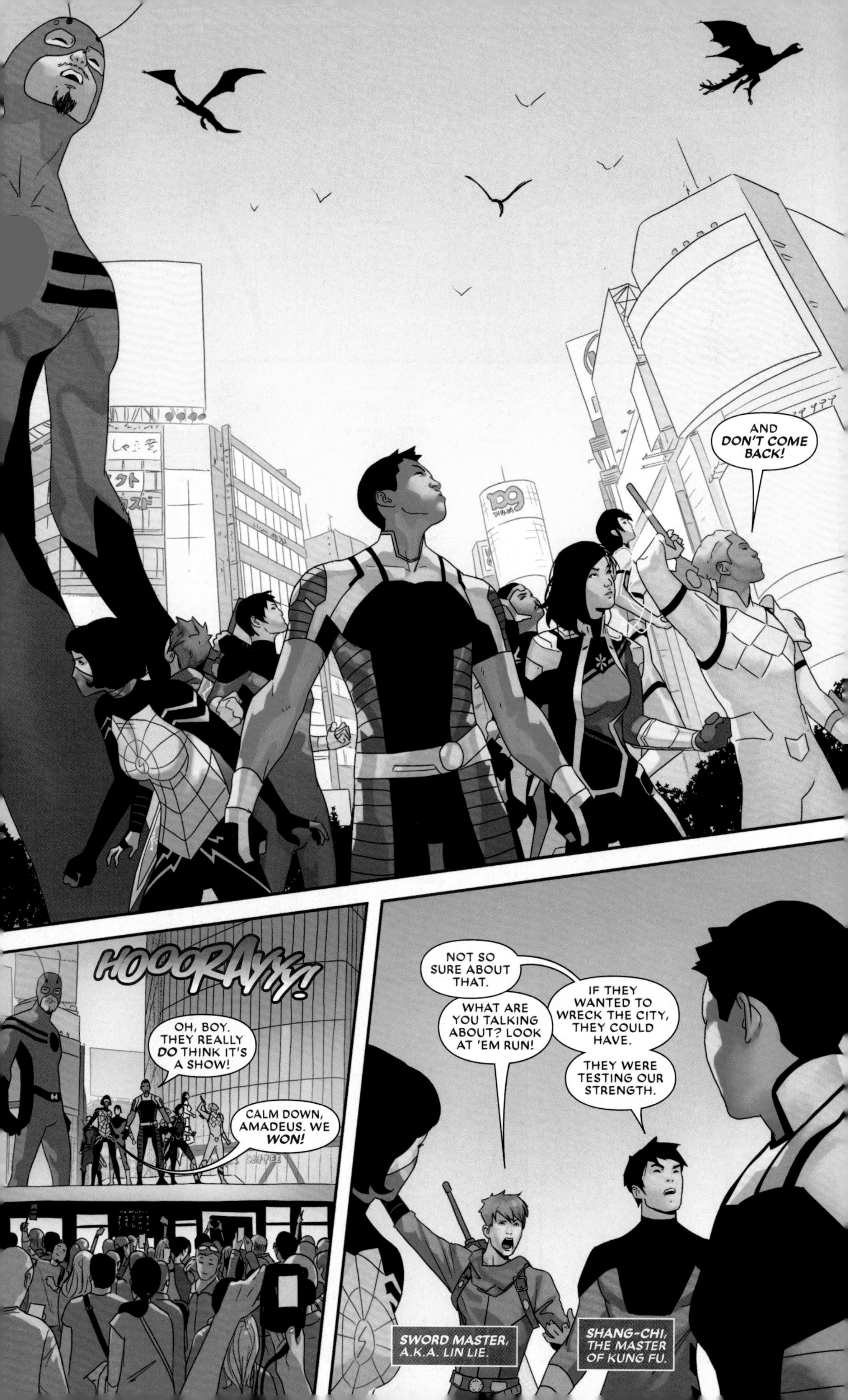
AND DON'T COME BACK!
HOOORAYYY!
OH, BOY. THEY REALLY DO THINK IT'S A SHOW!
CALM DOWN, AMADEUS. WE WON!
NOT SO SURE ABOUT THAT.
WHAT ARE YOU TALKING ABOUT? LOOK AT 'EM RUN!
IF THEY WANTED TO WRECK THE CITY, THEY COULD HAVE.
THEY WERE TESTING OUR STRENGTH.
SWORD MASTER, A.K.A. LIN LIE.
SHANG-CHI, THE MASTER OF KUNG FU.

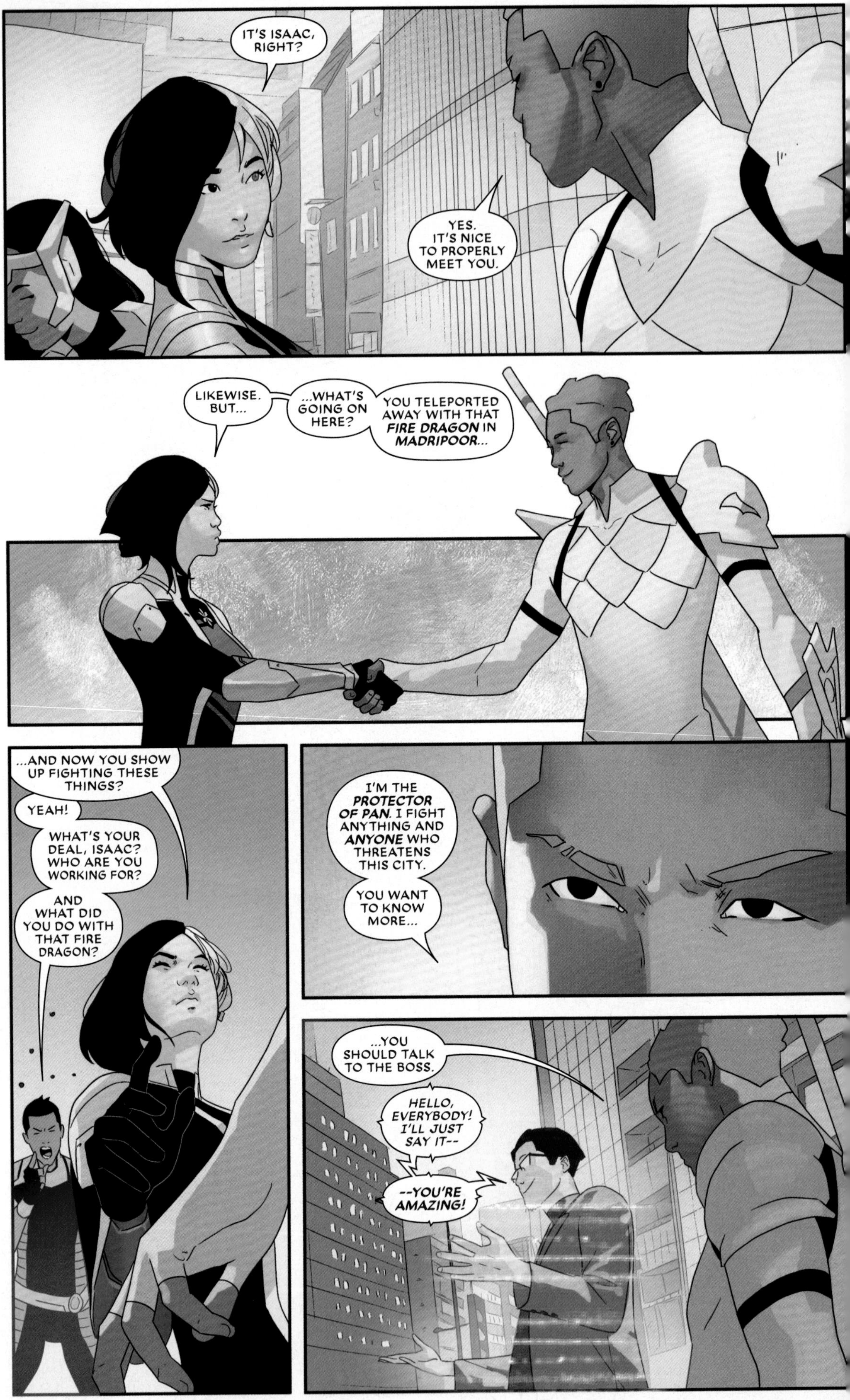
IT'S ISAAC, RIGHT?
YES. IT'S NICE TO PROPERLY MEET YOU.
LIKEWISE. BUT...
...WHAT'S GOING ON HERE?
YOU TELEPORTED AWAY WITH THAT FIRE DRAGON IN MADRIPOOR...
...AND NOW YOU SHOW UP FIGHTING THESE THINGS?
YEAH!
WHAT'S YOUR DEAL, ISAAC? WHO ARE YOU WORKING FOR?
AND WHAT DID YOU DO WITH THAT FIRE DRAGON?
I'M THE PROTECTOR OF PAN. I FIGHT ANYTHING AND ANYONE WHO THREATENS THIS CITY.
YOU WANT TO KNOW MORE...
...YOU SHOULD TALK TO THE BOSS.
HELLO, EVERYBODY! I'LL JUST SAY IT--
--YOU'RE AMAZING!

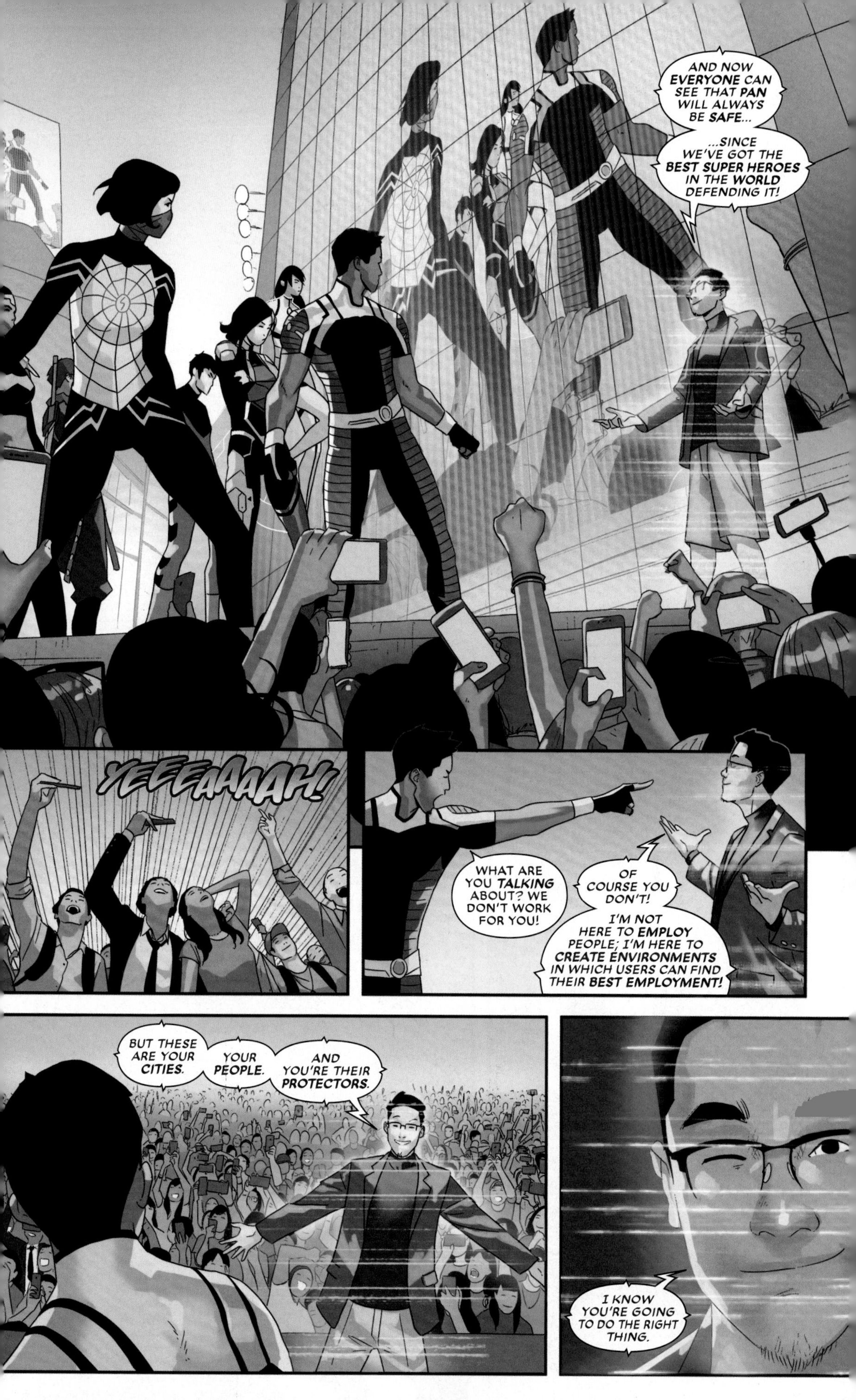
AND NOW EVERYONE CAN SEE THAT PAN WILL ALWAYS BE SAFE...
...SINCE WE'VE GOT THE BEST SUPER HEROES IN THE WORLD DEFENDING IT!
YEEEAAAAH!
WHAT ARE YOU TALKING ABOUT? WE DON'T WORK FOR YOU!
OF COURSE YOU DON'T!
I'M NOT HERE TO EMPLOY PEOPLE; I'M HERE TO CREATE ENVIRONMENTS IN WHICH USERS CAN FIND THEIR BEST EMPLOYMENT!
BUT THESE ARE YOUR CITIES.
YOUR PEOPLE.
AND YOU'RE THEIR PROTECTORS.
I KNOW YOU'RE GOING TO DO THE RIGHT THING.

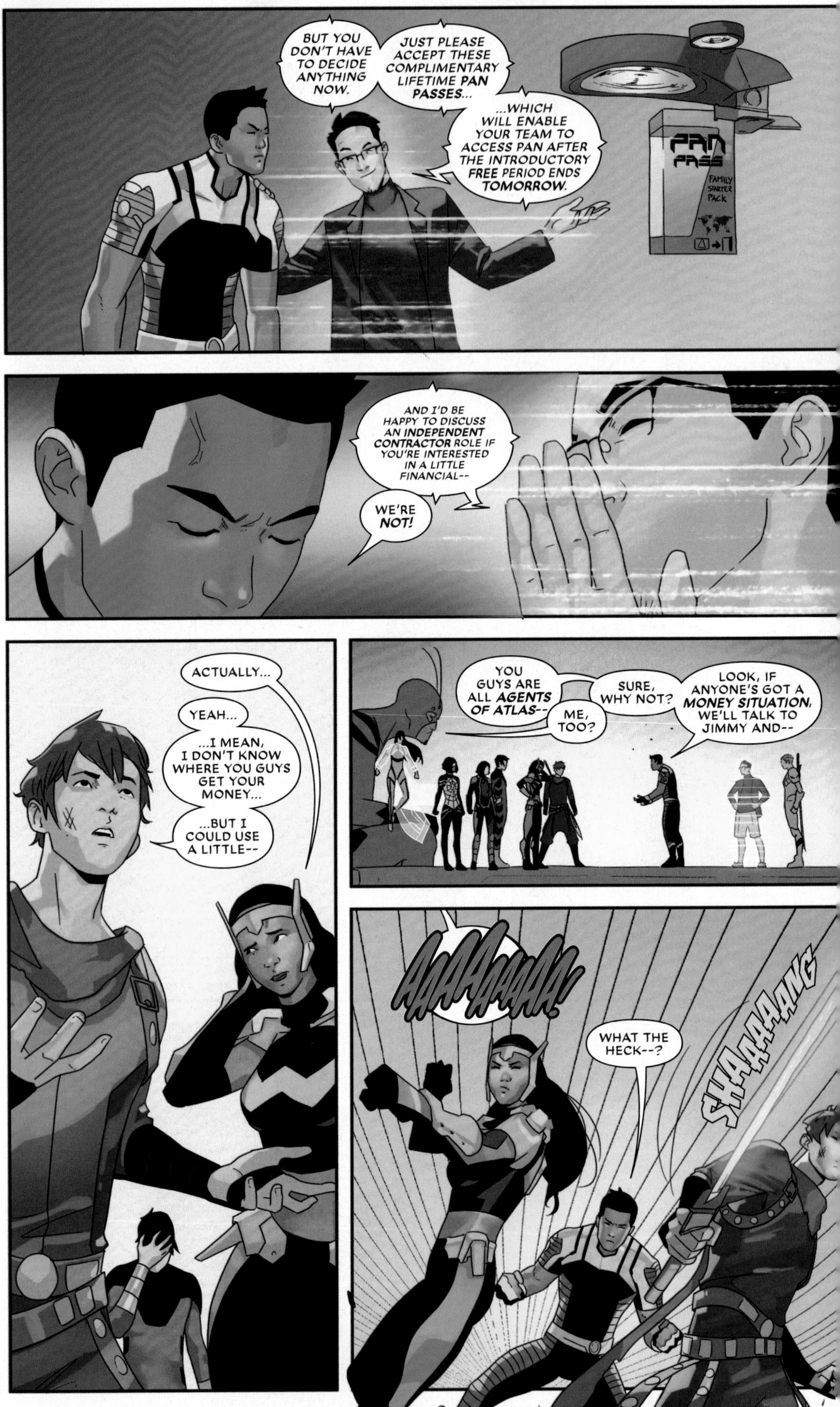
BUT YOU DON'T HAVE TO DECIDE ANYTHING NOW.
JUST PLEASE ACCEPT THESE COMPLIMENTARY LIFETIME PAN PASSES...
...WHICH WILL ENABLE YOUR TEAM TO ACCESS PAN AFTER THE INTRODUCTORY FREE PERIOD ENDS TOMORROW.
PAN PASS
FAMILY STARTER PACK
AND I'D BE HAPPY TO DISCUSS AN INDEPENDENT CONTRACTOR ROLE IF YOU'RE INTERESTED IN A LITTLE FINANCIAL--
WE'RE NOT!
ACTUALLY...
YEAH...
...I MEAN, I DON'T KNOW WHERE YOU GUYS GET YOUR MONEY...
...BUT I COULD USE A LITTLE--
YOU GUYS ARE ALL AGENTS OF ATLAS--
ME, TOO?
SURE, WHY NOT?
LOOK, IF ANYONE'S GOT A MONEY SITUATION, WE'LL TALK TO JIMMY AND--
AAAHAAAAA!
WHAT THE HECK--?
SHAAAAANG

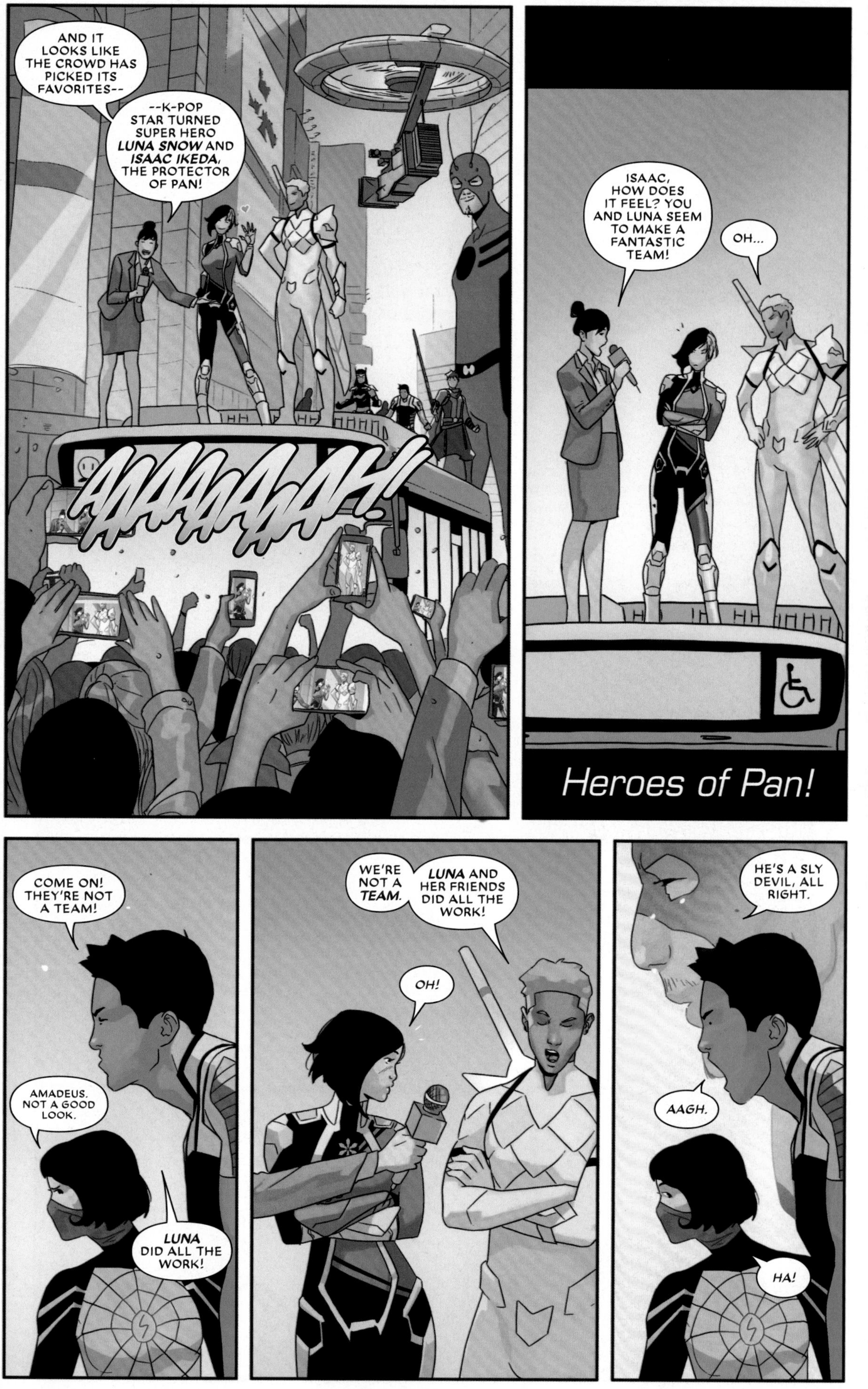
AND IT LOOKS LIKE THE CROWD HAS PICKED ITS FAVORITES--
--K-POP STAR TURNED SUPER HERO LUNA SNOW AND ISAAC IKEDA, THE PROTECTOR OF PAN!
AAAAAAAAH!
ISAAC, HOW DOES IT FEEL? YOU AND LUNA SEEM TO MAKE A FANTASTIC TEAM!
OH...
Heroes of Pan!
COME ON! THEY'RE NOT A TEAM!
AMADEUS. NOT A GOOD LOOK.
LUNA DID ALL THE WORK!
WE'RE NOT A TEAM.
LUNA AND HER FRIENDS DID ALL THE WORK!
OH!
HE'S A SLY DEVIL, ALL RIGHT.
AAGH.
HA!

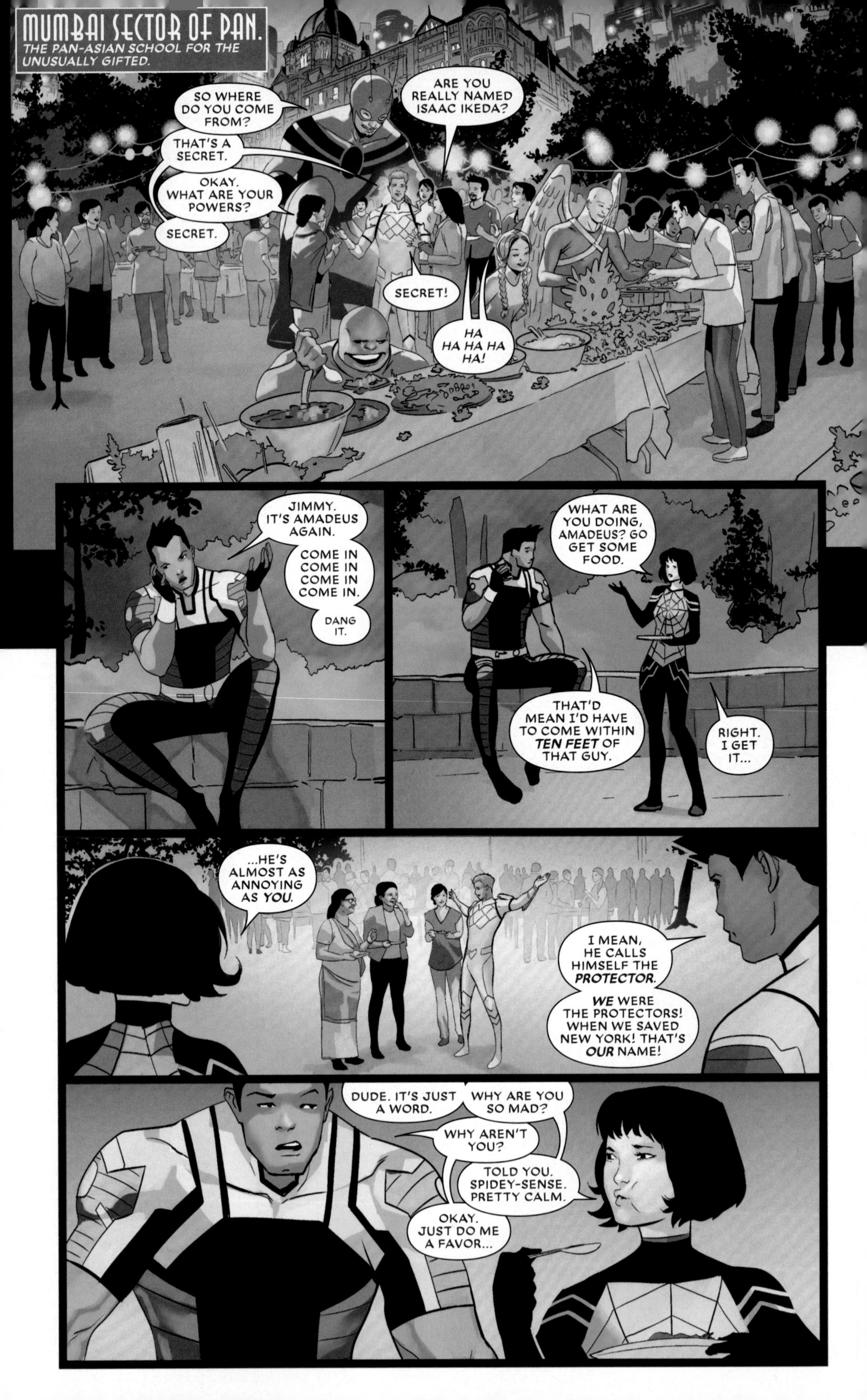
MUMBAI SECTOR OF PAN.
THE PAN-ASIAN SCHOOL FOR THE UNUSUALLY GIFTED.
SO WHERE DO YOU COME FROM?
THAT'S A SECRET.
OKAY. WHAT ARE YOUR POWERS?
SECRET.
ARE YOU REALLY NAMED ISAAC IKEDA?
SECRET!
HA HA HA HA HA!
JIMMY. IT'S AMADEUS AGAIN.
COME IN COME IN COME IN COME IN.
DANG IT.
WHAT ARE YOU DOING, AMADEUS? GO GET SOME FOOD.
THAT'D MEAN I'D HAVE TO COME WITHIN TEN FEET OF THAT GUY.
RIGHT. I GET IT...
...HE'S ALMOST AS ANNOYING AS YOU.
I MEAN, HE CALLS HIMSELF THE PROTECTOR.
WE WERE THE PROTECTORS! WHEN WE SAVED NEW YORK! THAT'S OUR NAME!
DUDE. IT'S JUST A WORD.
WHY ARE YOU SO MAD?
WHY AREN'T YOU?
TOLD YOU. SPIDEY-SENSE. PRETTY CALM.
OKAY. JUST DO ME A FAVOR...

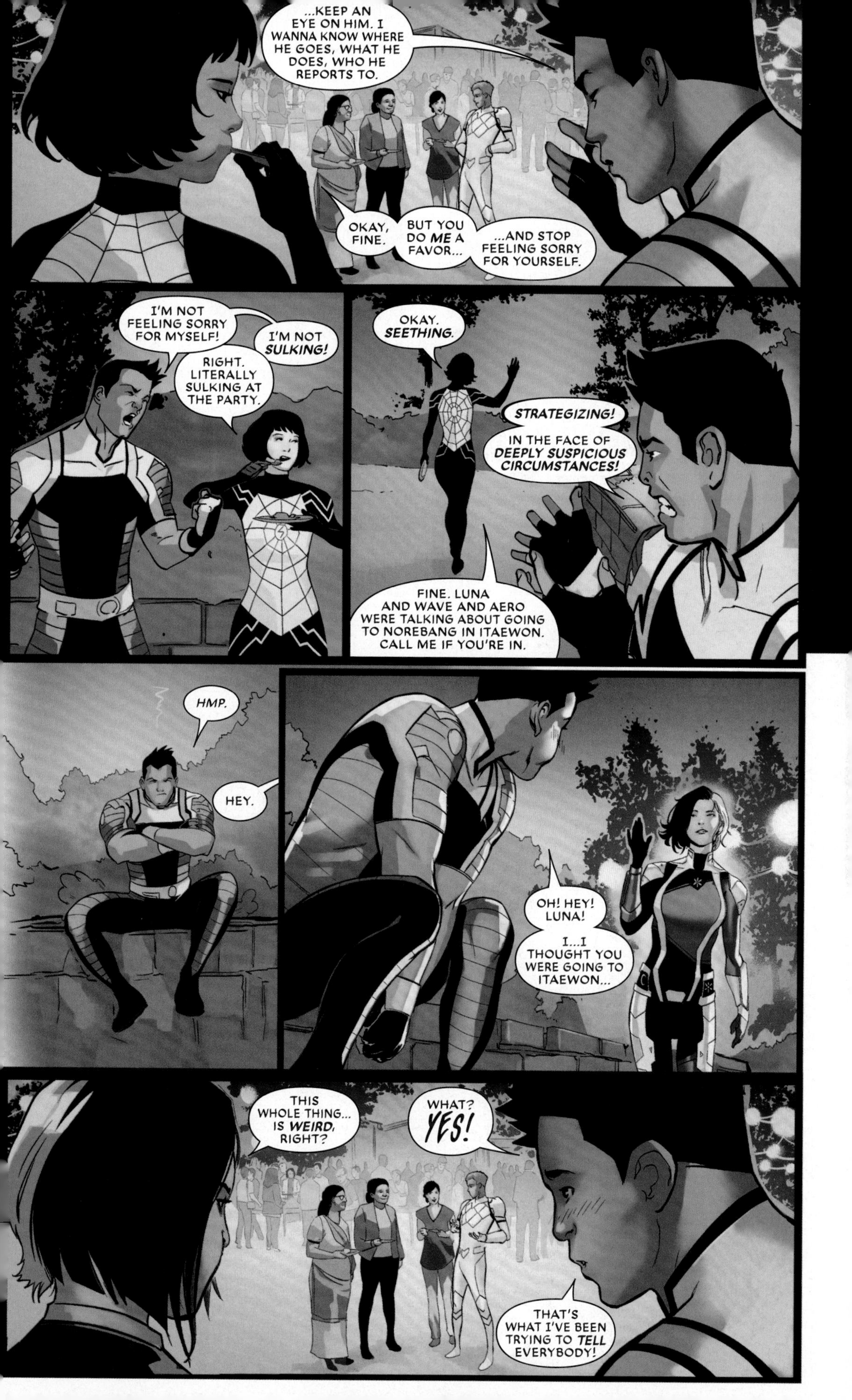
...KEEP AN EYE ON HIM. I WANNA KNOW WHERE HE GOES, WHAT HE DOES, WHO HE REPORTS TO.
OKAY, FINE.
BUT YOU DO *ME* A FAVOR...
...AND STOP FEELING SORRY FOR YOURSELF.
I'M NOT FEELING SORRY FOR MYSELF!
I'M NOT *SULKING!*
RIGHT. LITERALLY SULKING AT THE PARTY.
OKAY. *SEETHING.*
STRATEGIZING!
IN THE FACE OF *DEEPLY SUSPICIOUS CIRCUMSTANCES!*
FINE. LUNA AND WAVE AND AERO WERE TALKING ABOUT GOING TO NOREBANG IN ITAEWON. CALL ME IF YOU'RE IN.
HMP.
HEY.
OH! HEY! LUNA!
I...I THOUGHT YOU WERE GOING TO ITAEWON...
THIS WHOLE THING... IS *WEIRD,* RIGHT?
WHAT? *YES!*
THAT'S WHAT I'VE BEEN TRYING TO *TELL* EVERYBODY!

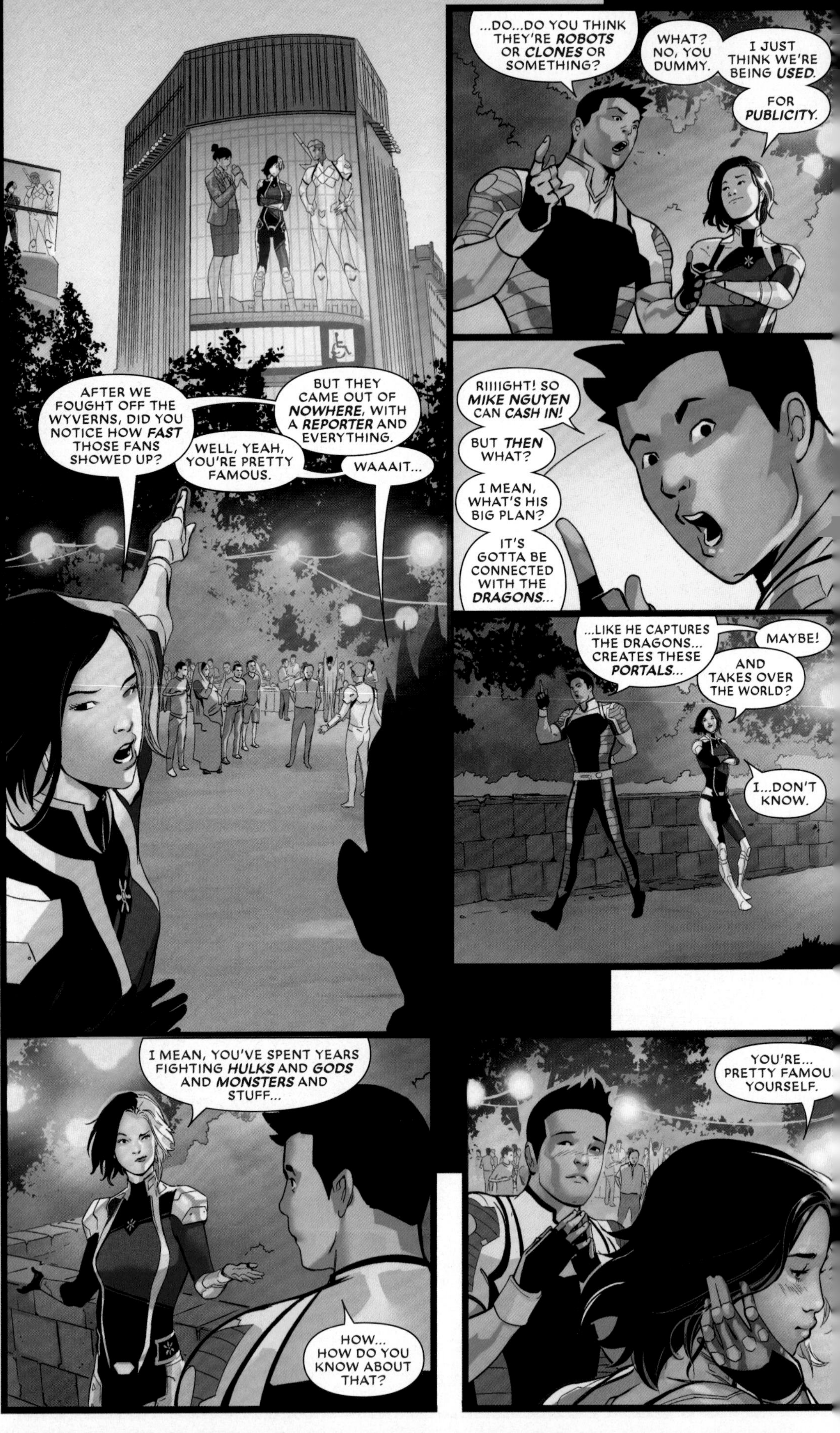
AFTER WE FOUGHT OFF THE WYVERNS, DID YOU NOTICE HOW FAST THOSE FANS SHOWED UP?
BUT THEY CAME OUT OF NOWHERE, WITH A REPORTER AND EVERYTHING.
WELL, YEAH, YOU'RE PRETTY FAMOUS.
WAAAIT...
...DO...DO YOU THINK THEY'RE ROBOTS OR CLONES OR SOMETHING?
WHAT? NO, YOU DUMMY.
I JUST THINK WE'RE BEING USED.
FOR PUBLICITY.
RIIIIGHT! SO MIKE NGUYEN CAN CASH IN!
BUT THEN WHAT?
I MEAN, WHAT'S HIS BIG PLAN?
IT'S GOTTA BE CONNECTED WITH THE DRAGONS...
...LIKE HE CAPTURES THE DRAGONS... CREATES THESE PORTALS...
MAYBE!
AND TAKES OVER THE WORLD?
I...DON'T KNOW.
I MEAN, YOU'VE SPENT YEARS FIGHTING HULKS AND GODS AND MONSTERS AND STUFF...
HOW... HOW DO YOU KNOW ABOUT THAT?
YOU'RE... PRETTY FAMOU YOURSELF.

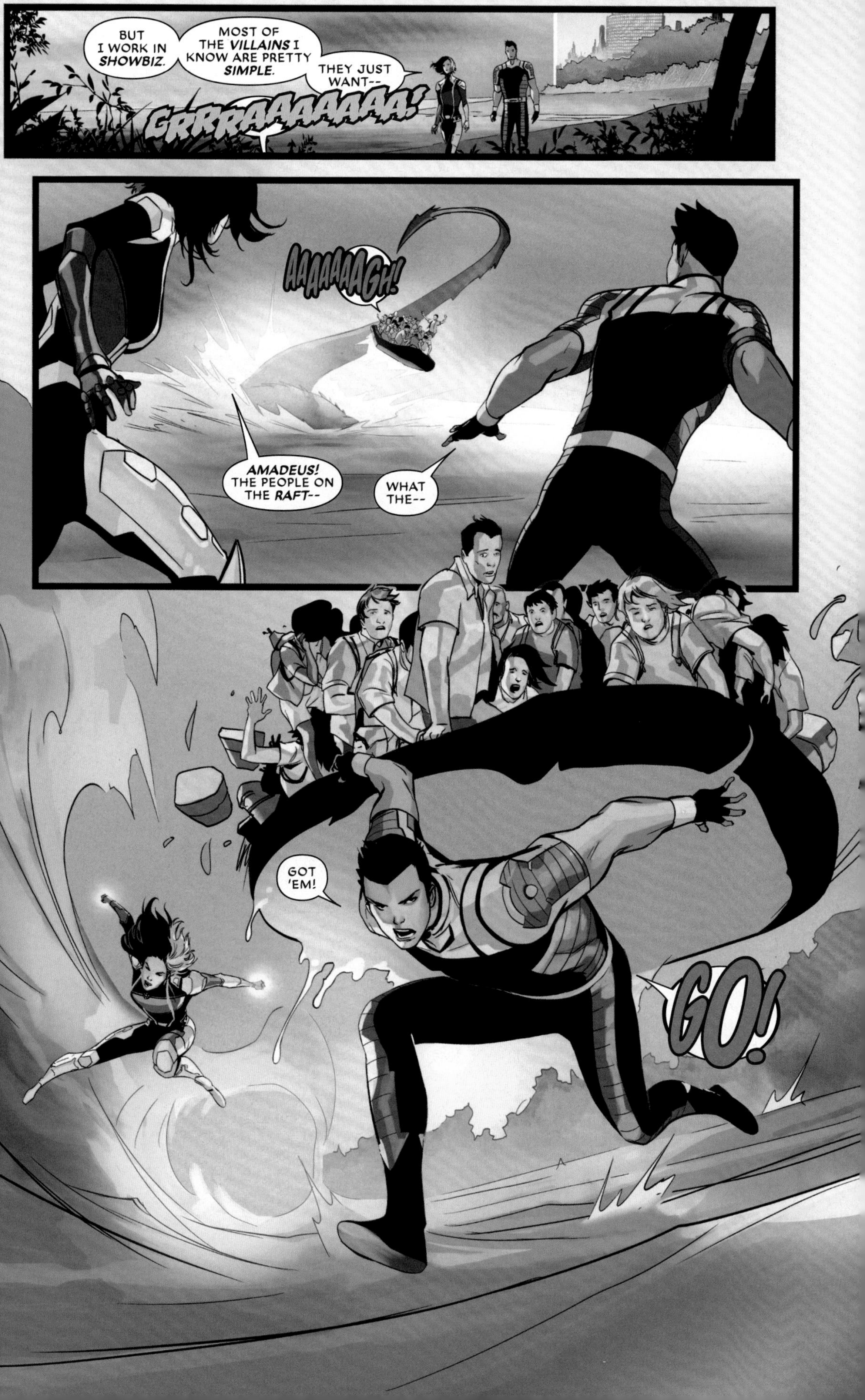
BUT I WORK IN SHOWBIZ.
MOST OF THE VILLAINS I KNOW ARE PRETTY SIMPLE.
THEY JUST WANT--
GRRRAAAAAAAA!
AAAAAAAGH!
AMADEUS! THE PEOPLE ON THE RAFT--
WHAT THE--
GOT 'EM!
GO!

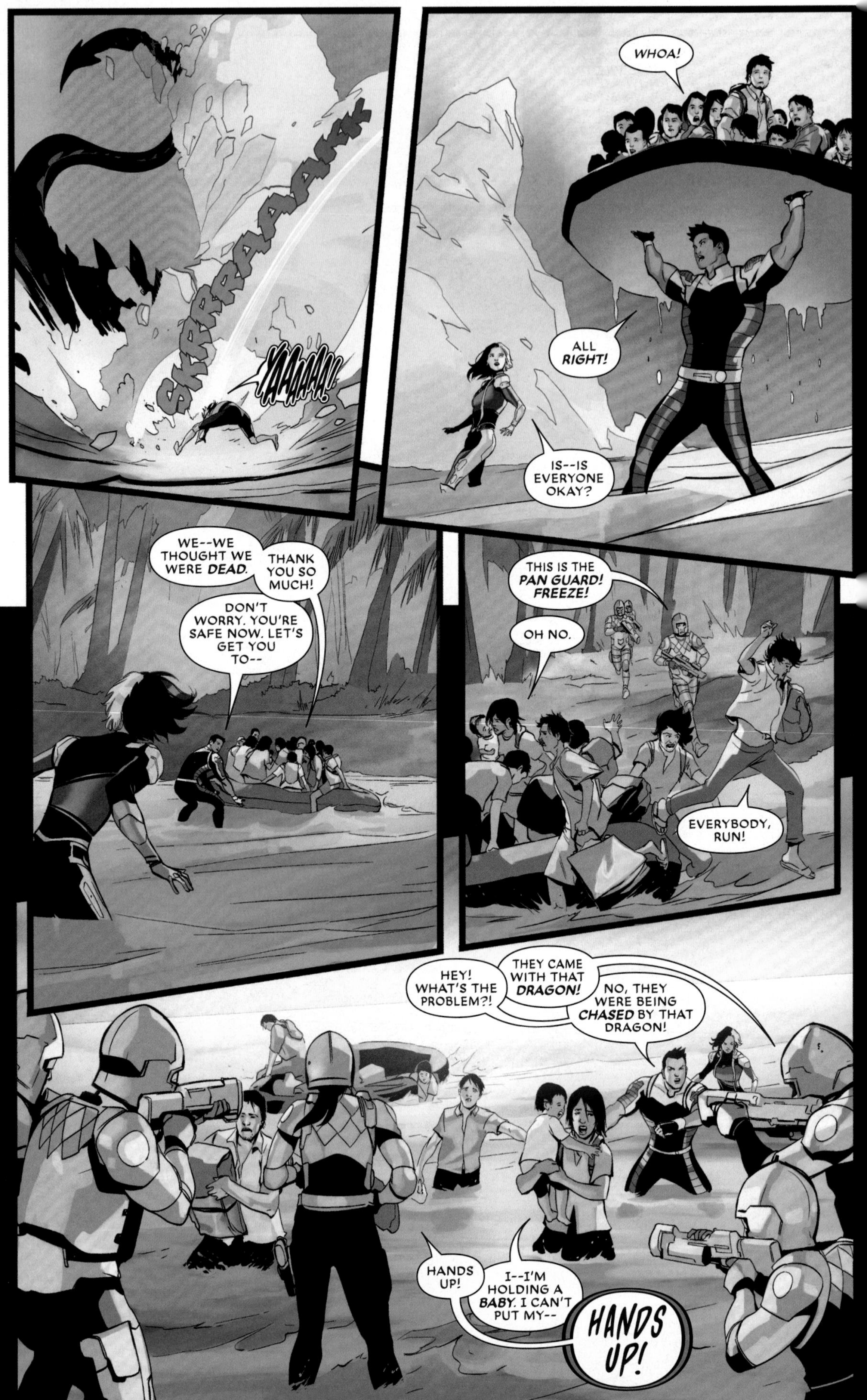
SKRRAAAKK
YAAAAAA!
WHOA!
ALL RIGHT!
IS--IS EVERYONE OKAY?
WE--WE THOUGHT WE WERE DEAD.
THANK YOU SO MUCH!
DON'T WORRY. YOU'RE SAFE NOW. LET'S GET YOU TO--
THIS IS THE PAN GUARD! FREEZE!
OH NO.
EVERYBODY, RUN!
HEY! WHAT'S THE PROBLEM?!
THEY CAME WITH THAT DRAGON!
NO, THEY WERE BEING CHASED BY THAT DRAGON!
HANDS UP!
I--I'M HOLDING A BABY. I CAN'T PUT MY--
HANDS UP!

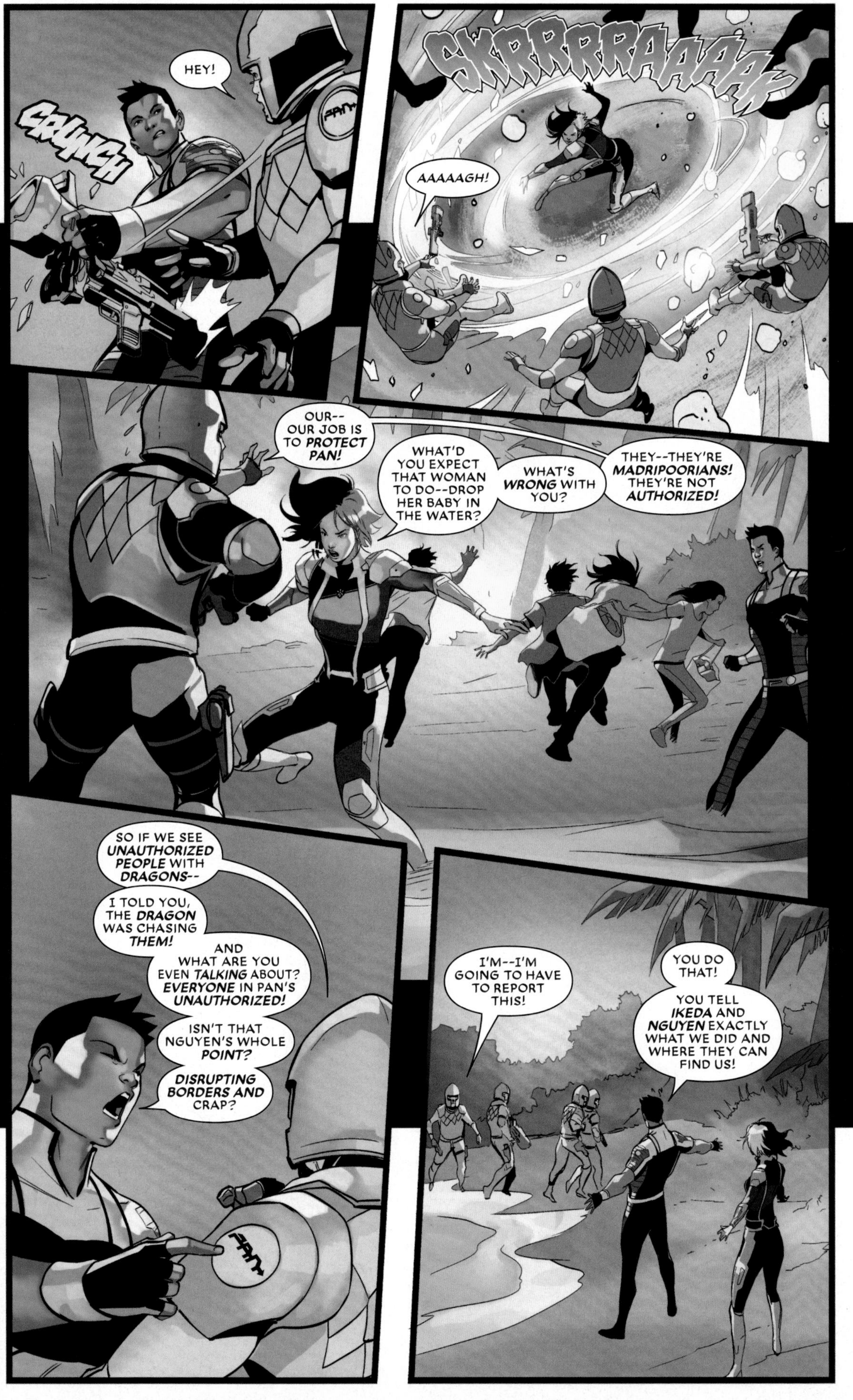
HEY!
CRUNCH
PAN
SKRRRRAAAAK
AAAAAGH!
OUR-- OUR JOB IS TO PROTECT PAN!
WHAT'D YOU EXPECT THAT WOMAN TO DO--DROP HER BABY IN THE WATER?
WHAT'S WRONG WITH YOU?
THEY--THEY'RE MADRIPOORIANS! THEY'RE NOT AUTHORIZED!
SO IF WE SEE UNAUTHORIZED PEOPLE WITH DRAGONS--
I TOLD YOU, THE DRAGON WAS CHASING THEM!
AND WHAT ARE YOU EVEN TALKING ABOUT? EVERYONE IN PAN'S UNAUTHORIZED!
ISN'T THAT NGUYEN'S WHOLE POINT?
DISRUPTING BORDERS AND CRAP?
PAN
I'M--I'M GOING TO HAVE TO REPORT THIS!
YOU DO THAT!
YOU TELL IKEDA AND NGUYEN EXACTLY WHAT WE DID AND WHERE THEY CAN FIND US!

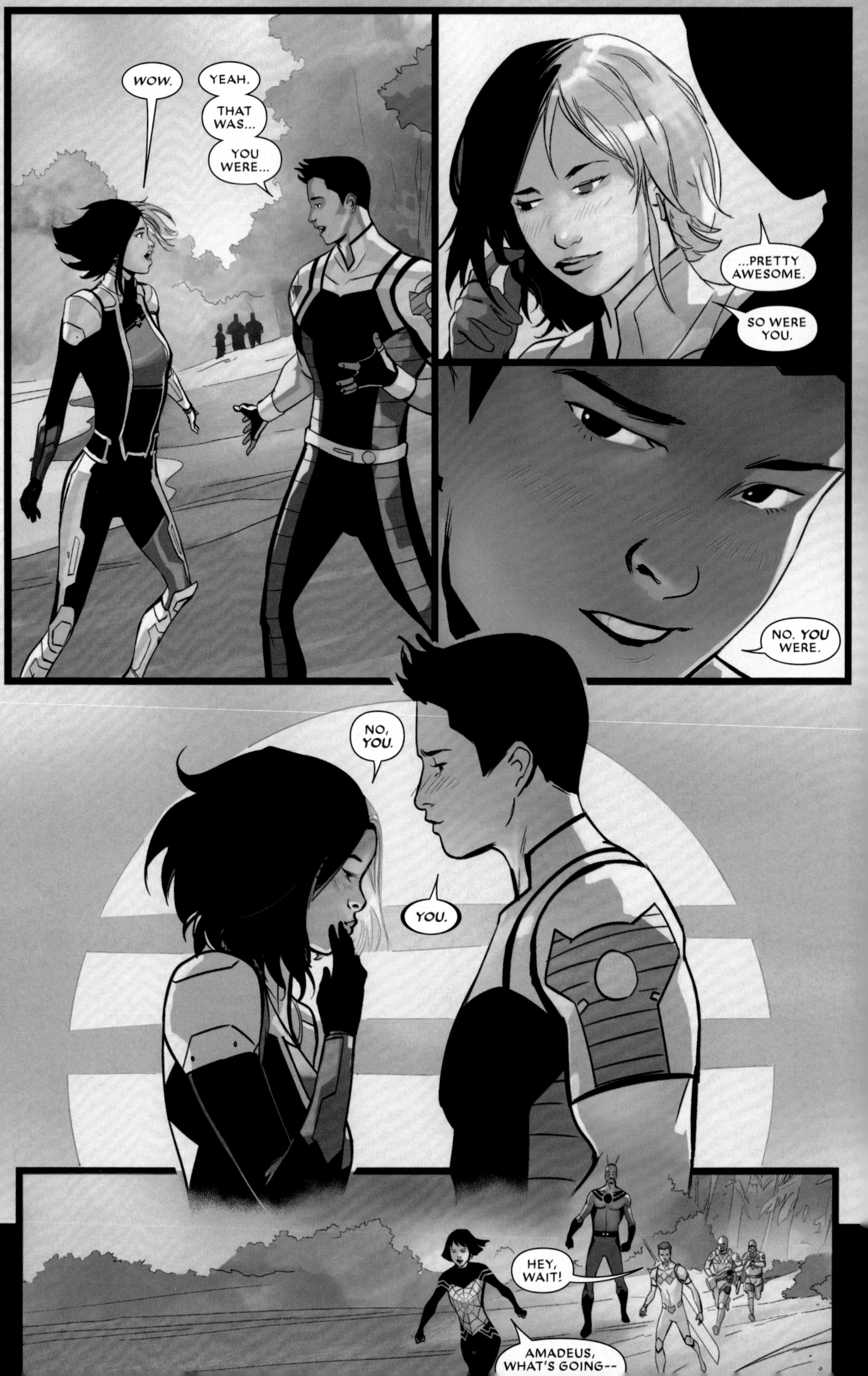
WOW.
YEAH.
THAT WAS...
YOU WERE...
...PRETTY AWESOME.
SO WERE YOU.
NO. YOU WERE.
NO, YOU.
YOU.
HEY, WAIT!
AMADEUS, WHAT'S GOING--

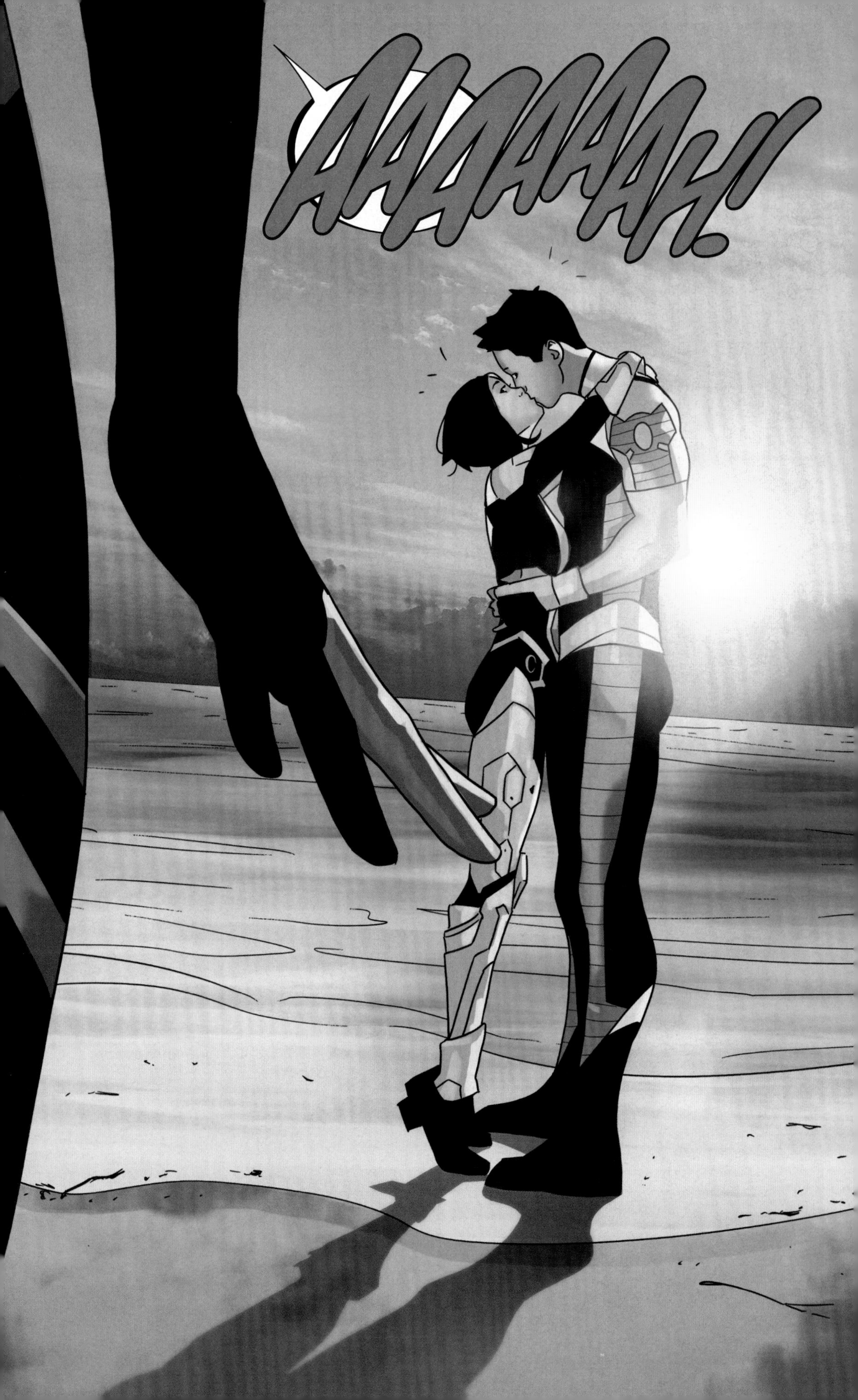
AAAAAAAH!

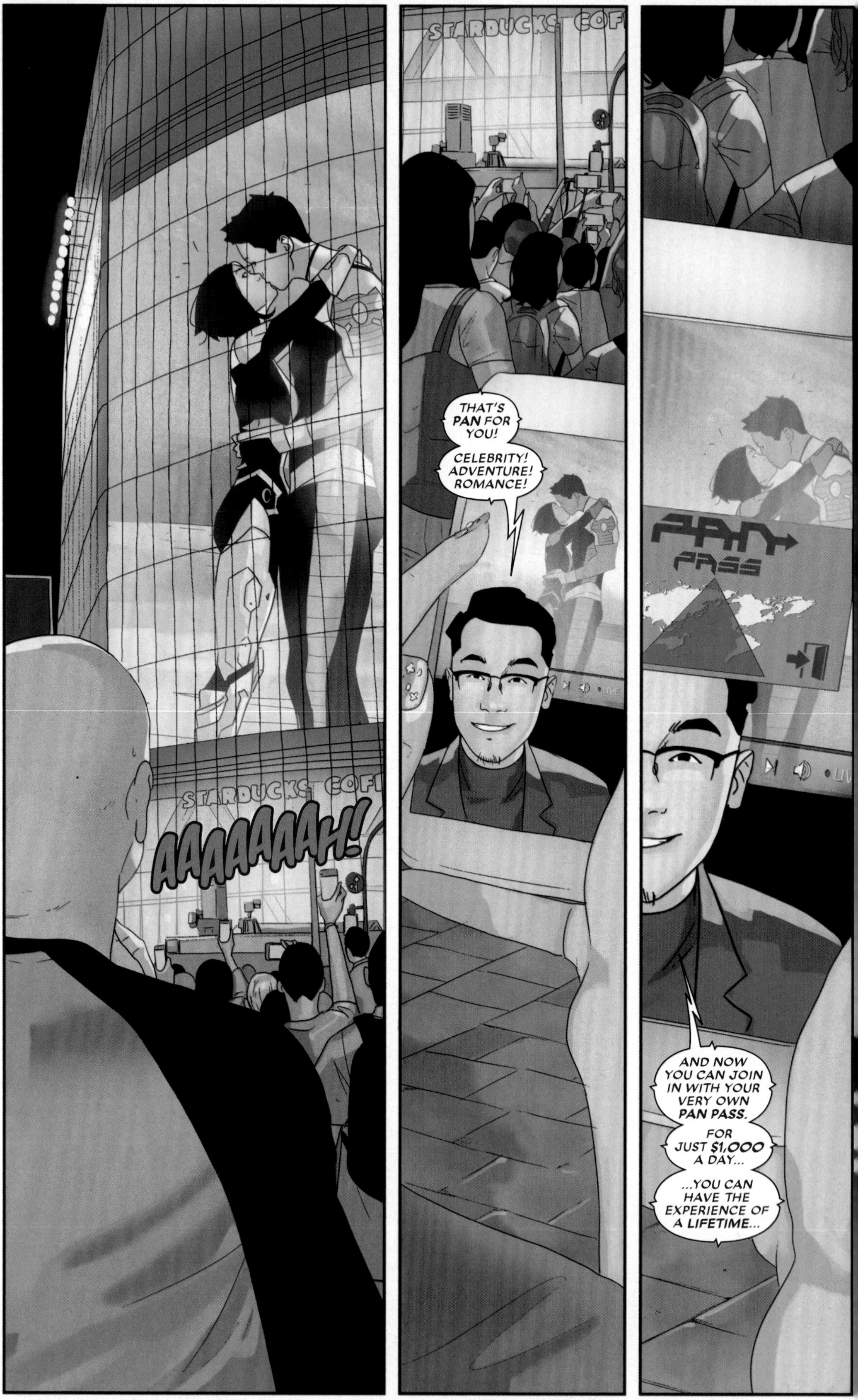
STARBUCKS COFFEE
AAAAAAAH!
THAT'S PAN FOR YOU!
CELEBRITY! ADVENTURE! ROMANCE!
PAN PASS
AND NOW YOU CAN JOIN IN WITH YOUR VERY OWN PAN PASS.
FOR JUST $1,000 A DAY...
...YOU CAN HAVE THE EXPERIENCE OF A LIFETIME...

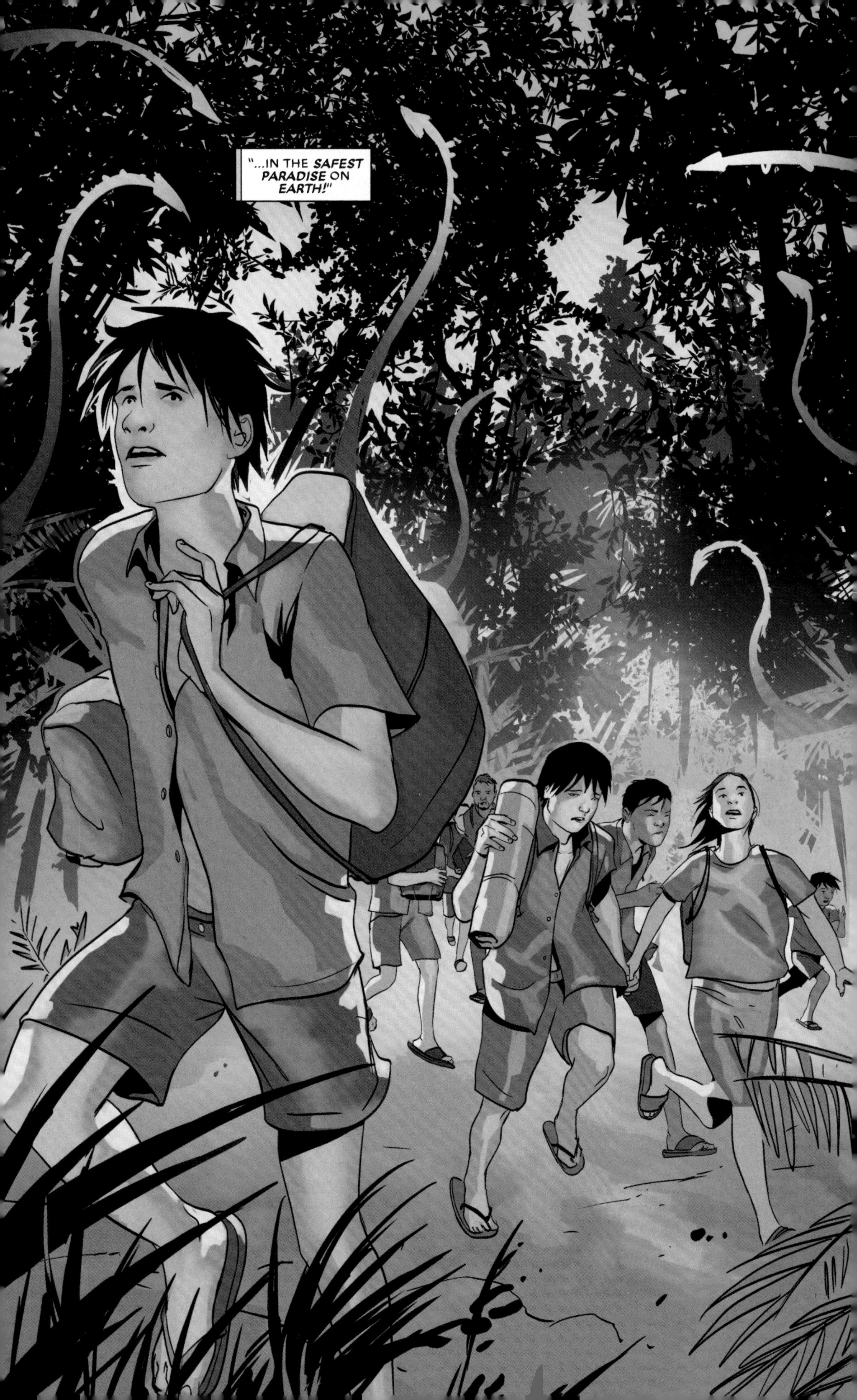
"...IN THE *SAFEST PARADISE* ON *EARTH!*"

THREE

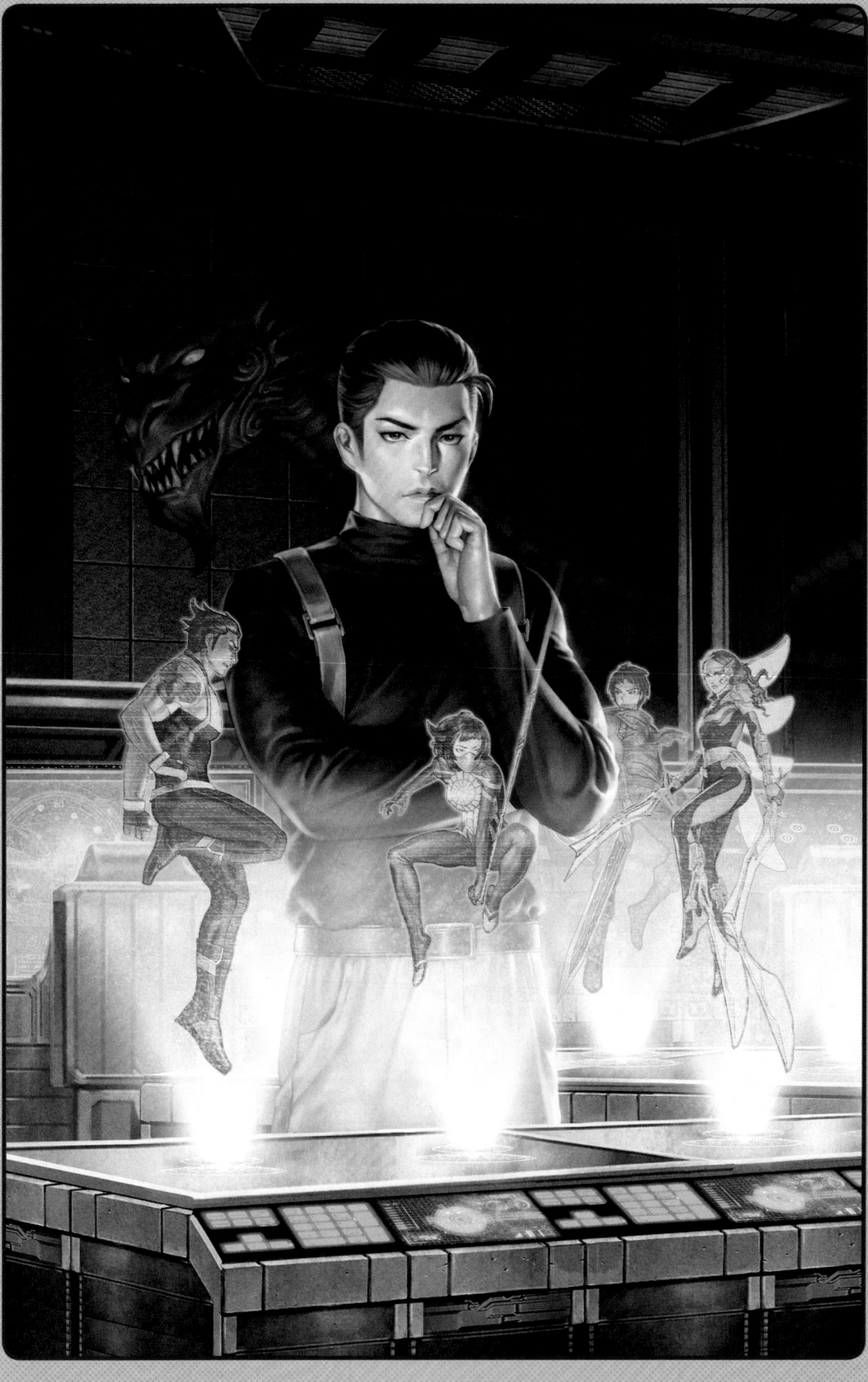

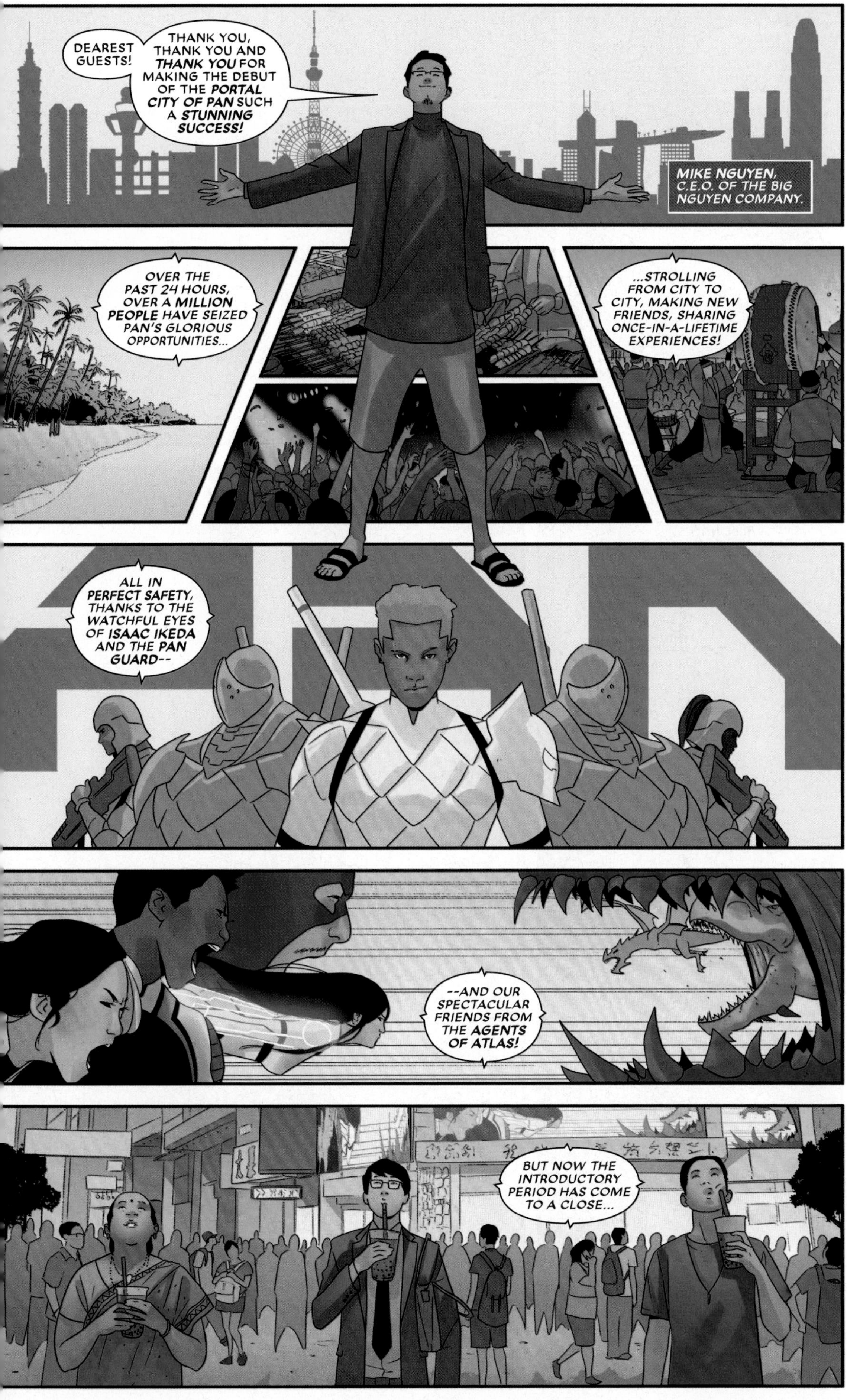
DEAREST GUESTS!
THANK YOU, THANK YOU AND THANK YOU FOR MAKING THE DEBUT OF THE PORTAL CITY OF PAN SUCH A STUNNING SUCCESS!
MIKE NGUYEN, C.E.O. OF THE BIG NGUYEN COMPANY.
OVER THE PAST 24 HOURS, OVER A MILLION PEOPLE HAVE SEIZED PAN'S GLORIOUS OPPORTUNITIES...
...STROLLING FROM CITY TO CITY, MAKING NEW FRIENDS, SHARING ONCE-IN-A-LIFETIME EXPERIENCES!
ALL IN PERFECT SAFETY, THANKS TO THE WATCHFUL EYES OF ISAAC IKEDA AND THE PAN GUARD--
--AND OUR SPECTACULAR FRIENDS FROM THE AGENTS OF ATLAS!
BUT NOW THE INTRODUCTORY PERIOD HAS COME TO A CLOSE...

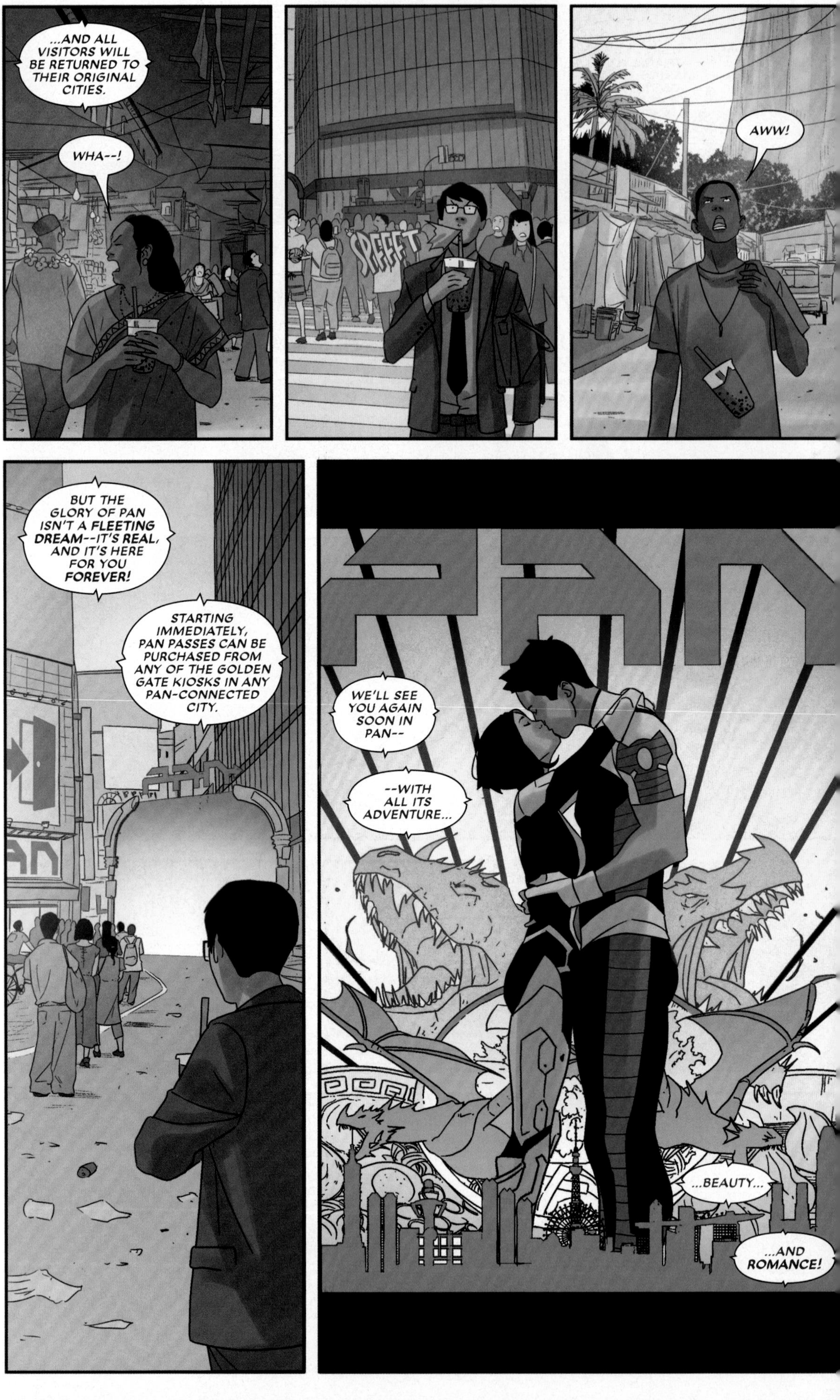
...AND ALL VISITORS WILL BE RETURNED TO THEIR ORIGINAL CITIES.
WHA--!
SPFFFT
AWW!
BUT THE GLORY OF PAN ISN'T A **FLEETING DREAM**--IT'S **REAL**, AND IT'S HERE FOR YOU **FOREVER!**
STARTING IMMEDIATELY, PAN PASSES CAN BE PURCHASED FROM ANY OF THE GOLDEN GATE KIOSKS IN ANY PAN-CONNECTED CITY.
WE'LL SEE YOU AGAIN SOON IN PAN--
--WITH ALL ITS ADVENTURE...
...BEAUTY...
...AND **ROMANCE!**

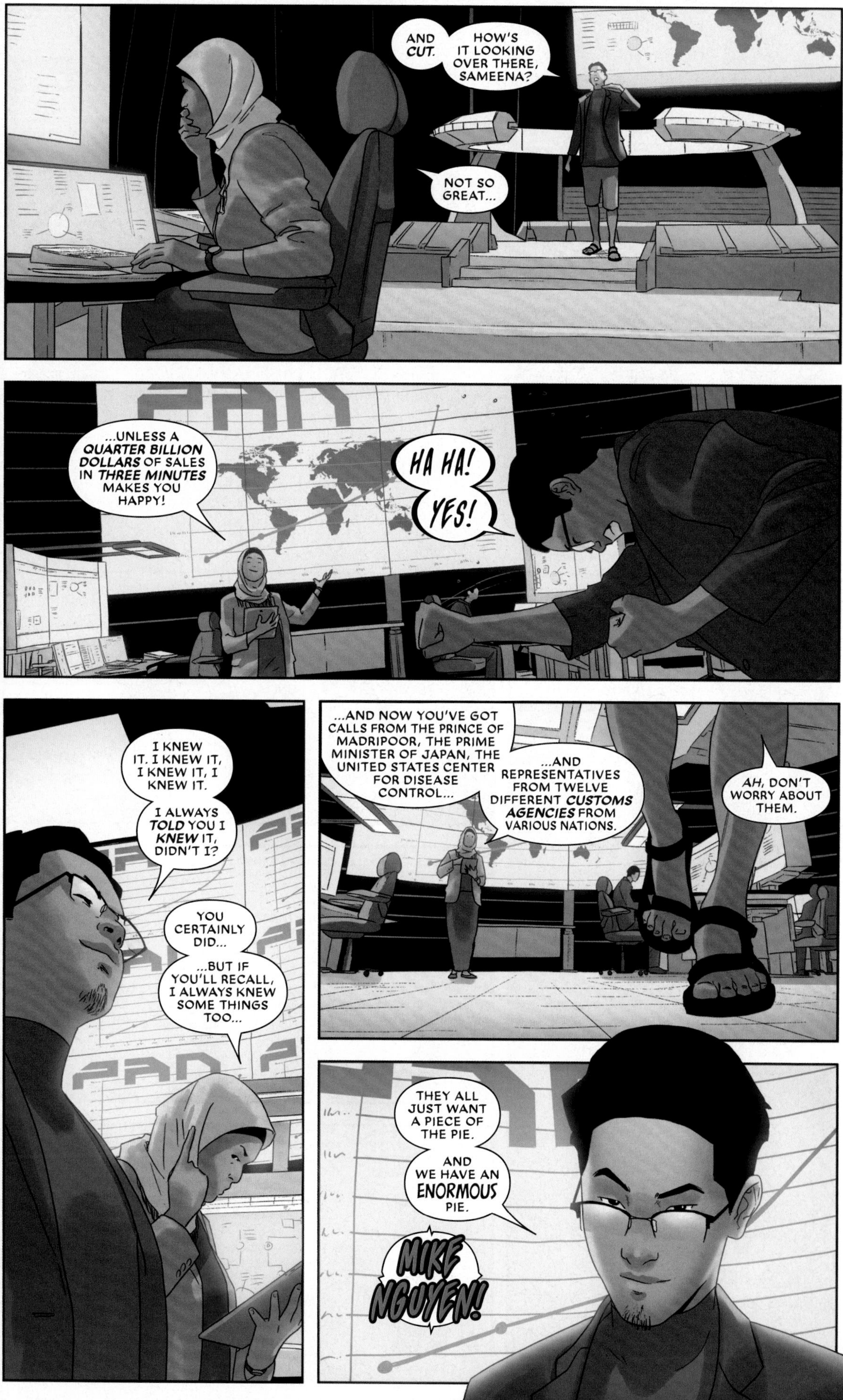
AND CUT.
HOW'S IT LOOKING OVER THERE, SAMEENA?
NOT SO GREAT...
...UNLESS A QUARTER BILLION DOLLARS OF SALES IN THREE MINUTES MAKES YOU HAPPY!
HA HA!
YES!
I KNEW IT. I KNEW IT, I KNEW IT, I KNEW IT.
I ALWAYS TOLD YOU I KNEW IT, DIDN'T I?
YOU CERTAINLY DID...
...BUT IF YOU'LL RECALL, I ALWAYS KNEW SOME THINGS TOO...
...AND NOW YOU'VE GOT CALLS FROM THE PRINCE OF MADRIPOOR, THE PRIME MINISTER OF JAPAN, THE UNITED STATES CENTER FOR DISEASE CONTROL...
...AND REPRESENTATIVES FROM TWELVE DIFFERENT CUSTOMS AGENCIES FROM VARIOUS NATIONS.
AH, DON'T WORRY ABOUT THEM.
THEY ALL JUST WANT A PIECE OF THE PIE.
AND WE HAVE AN ENORMOUS PIE.
MIKE NGUYEN!

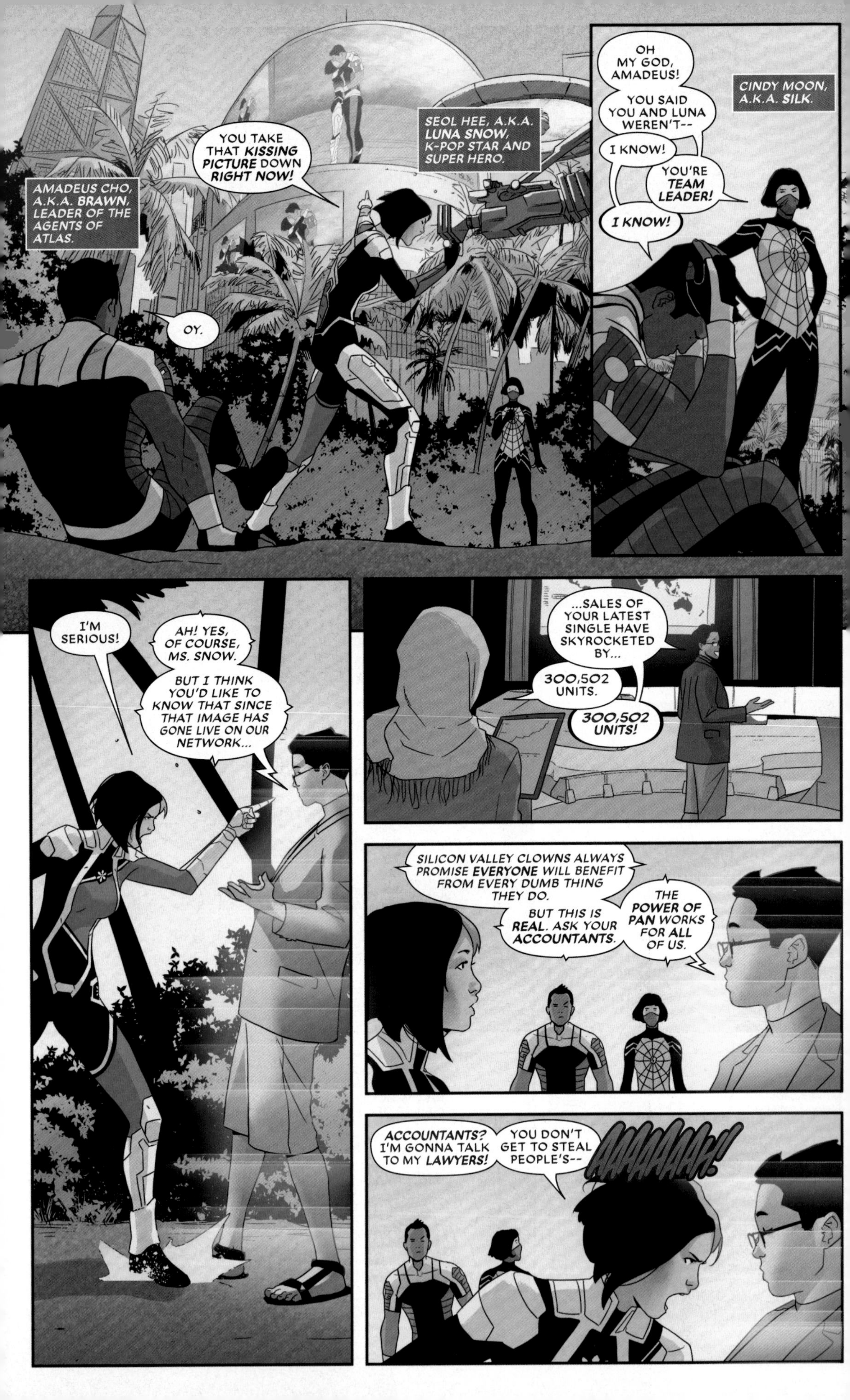
YOU TAKE THAT KISSING PICTURE DOWN RIGHT NOW!
SEOL HEE, A.K.A. LUNA SNOW, K-POP STAR AND SUPER HERO.
AMADEUS CHO, A.K.A. BRAWN, LEADER OF THE AGENTS OF ATLAS.
OY.
OH MY GOD, AMADEUS!
YOU SAID YOU AND LUNA WEREN'T--
I KNOW!
YOU'RE TEAM LEADER!
I KNOW!
CINDY MOON, A.K.A. SILK.
I'M SERIOUS!
AH! YES, OF COURSE, MS. SNOW.
BUT I THINK YOU'D LIKE TO KNOW THAT SINCE THAT IMAGE HAS GONE LIVE ON OUR NETWORK...
...SALES OF YOUR LATEST SINGLE HAVE SKYROCKETED BY...
300,502 UNITS.
300,502 UNITS!
SILICON VALLEY CLOWNS ALWAYS PROMISE EVERYONE WILL BENEFIT FROM EVERY DUMB THING THEY DO.
BUT THIS IS REAL. ASK YOUR ACCOUNTANTS.
THE POWER OF PAN WORKS FOR ALL OF US.
ACCOUNTANTS? I'M GONNA TALK TO MY LAWYERS!
YOU DON'T GET TO STEAL PEOPLE'S--
AAAAAAAH!

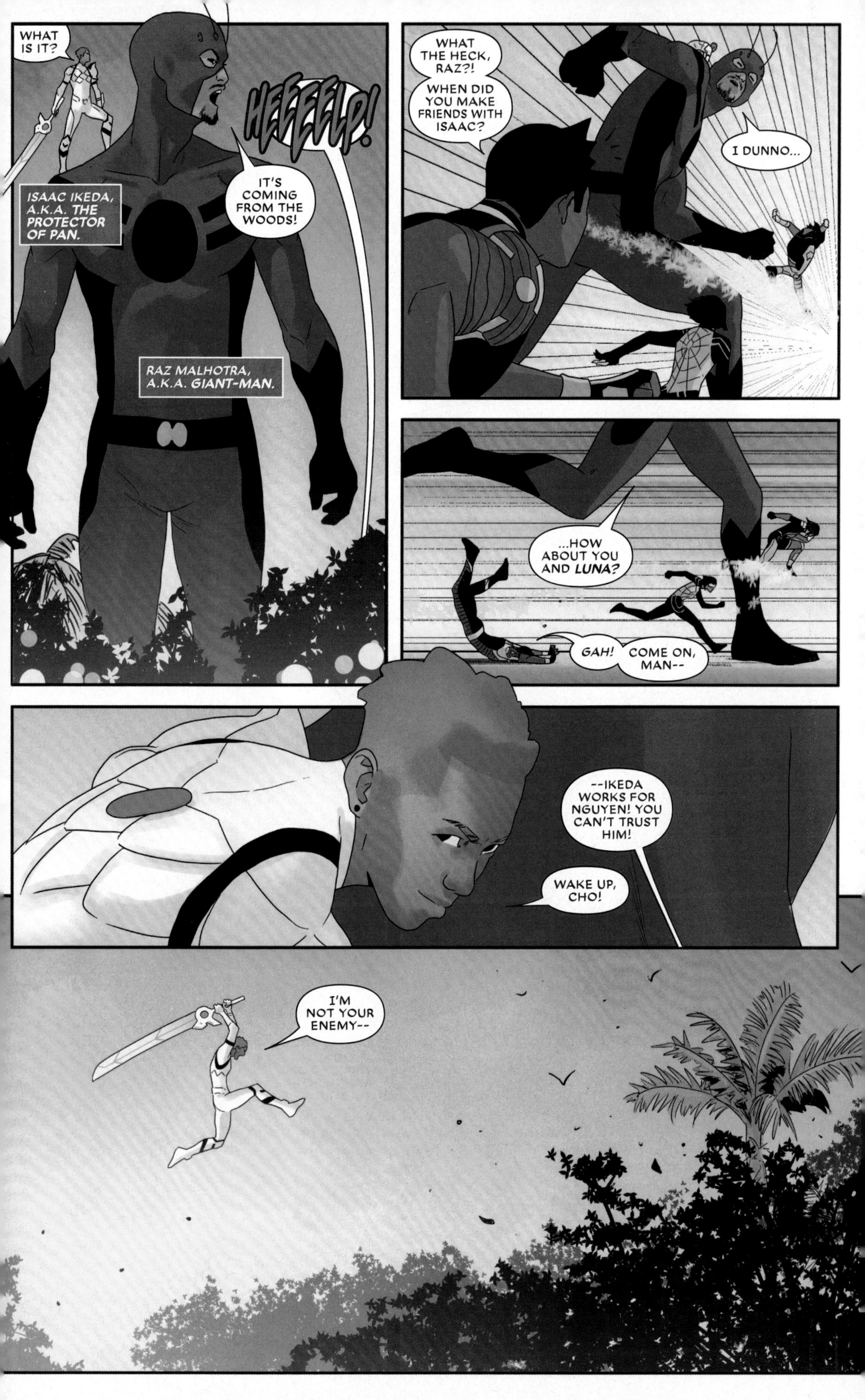
WHAT IS IT?
HEEEELP!
IT'S COMING FROM THE WOODS!
ISAAC IKEDA, A.K.A. THE PROTECTOR OF PAN.
RAZ MALHOTRA, A.K.A. GIANT-MAN.
WHAT THE HECK, RAZ?!
WHEN DID YOU MAKE FRIENDS WITH ISAAC?
I DUNNO...
...HOW ABOUT YOU AND LUNA?
GAH!
COME ON, MAN--
--IKEDA WORKS FOR NGUYEN! YOU CAN'T TRUST HIM!
WAKE UP, CHO!
I'M NOT YOUR ENEMY--

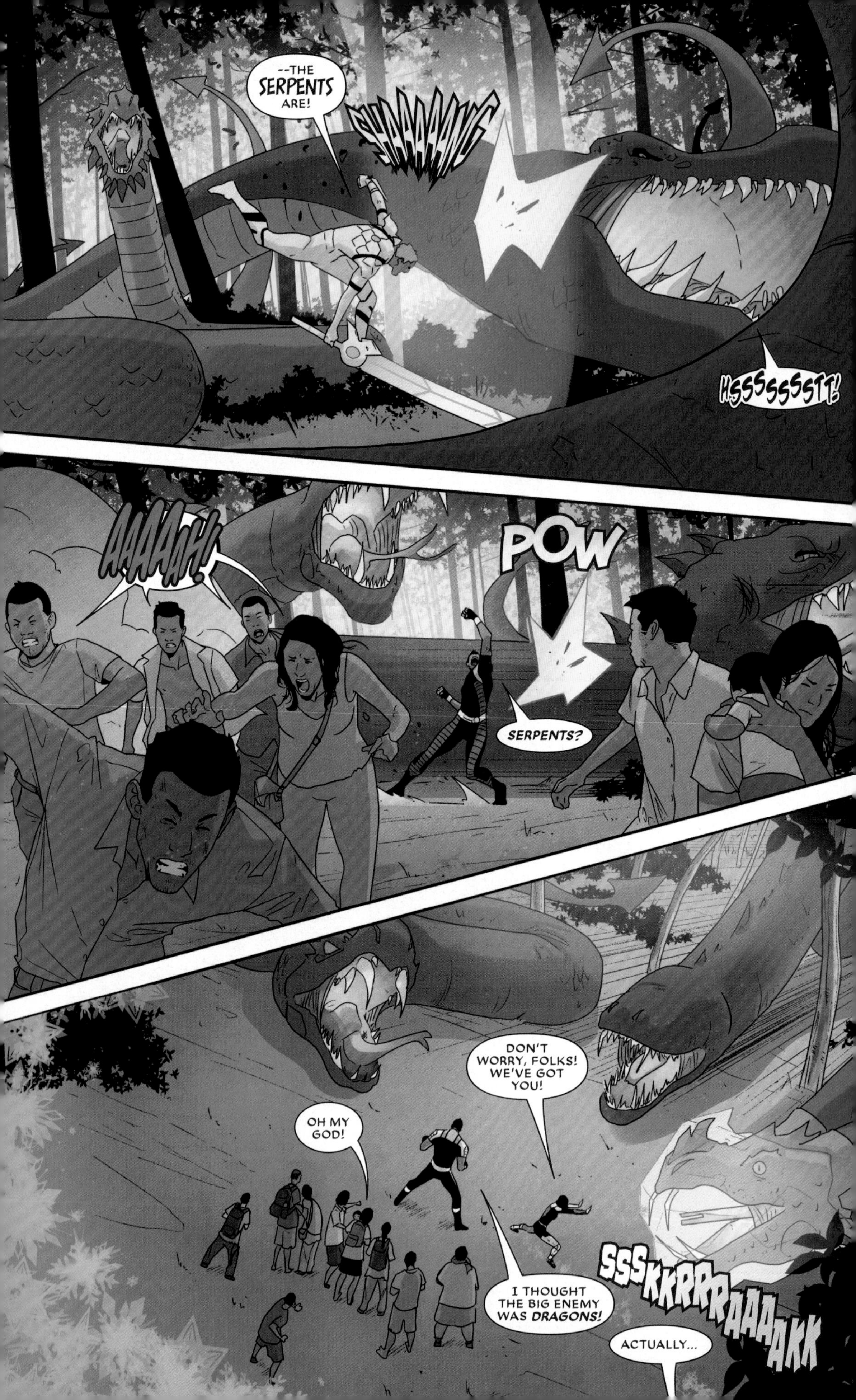
--THE SERPENTS ARE!
SHAAAAANG
HSSSSSSSTT!
AAAAAH!
POW
SERPENTS?
DON'T WORRY, FOLKS! WE'VE GOT YOU!
OH MY GOD!
I THOUGHT THE BIG ENEMY WAS DRAGONS!
SSSKKRRRAAAAKK
ACTUALLY...

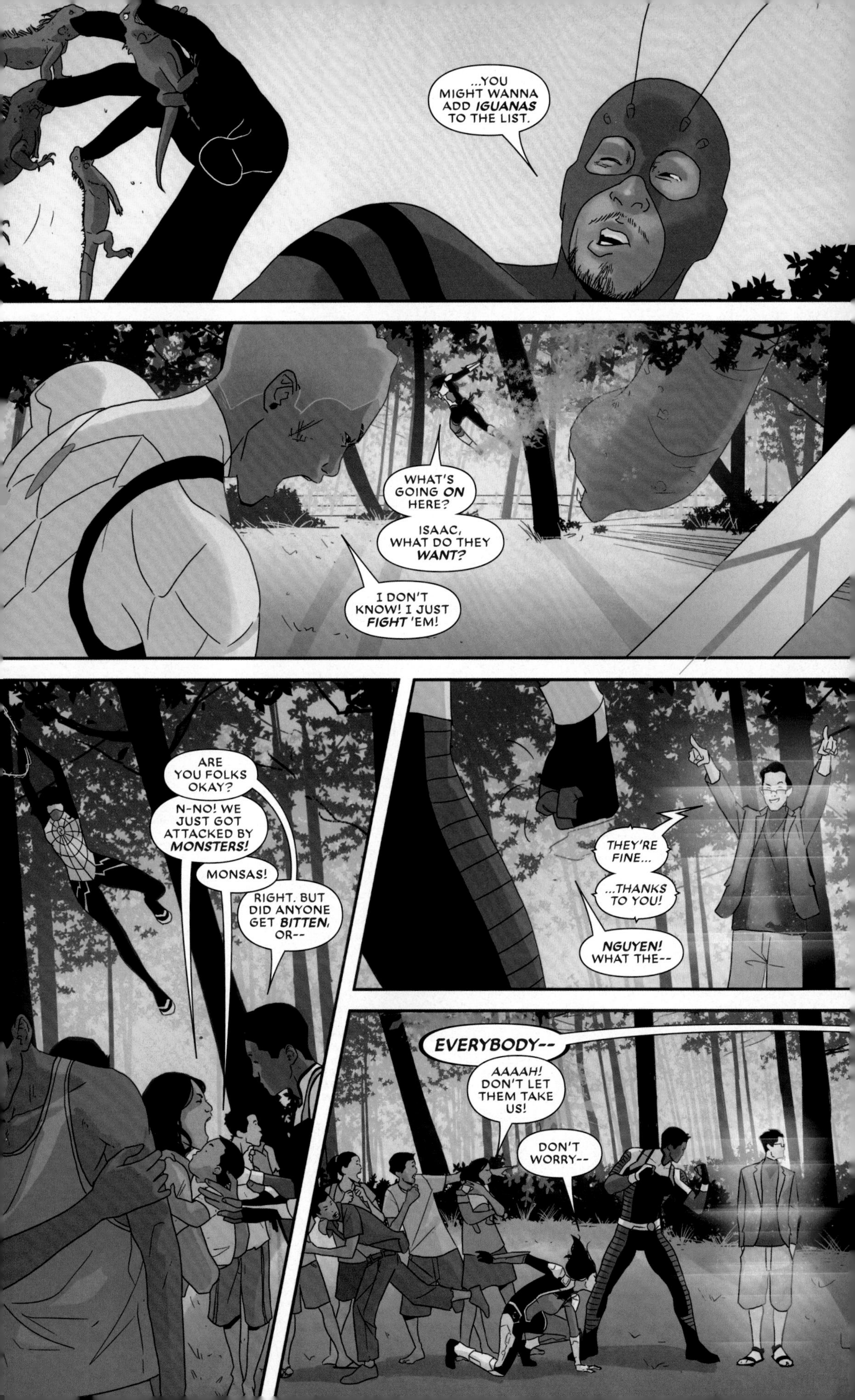
...YOU MIGHT WANNA ADD IGUANAS TO THE LIST.
WHAT'S GOING ON HERE?
ISAAC, WHAT DO THEY WANT?
I DON'T KNOW! I JUST FIGHT 'EM!
ARE YOU FOLKS OKAY?
N-NO! WE JUST GOT ATTACKED BY MONSTERS!
MONSAS!
RIGHT. BUT DID ANYONE GET BITTEN, OR--
THEY'RE FINE...
...THANKS TO YOU!
NGUYEN! WHAT THE--
EVERYBODY--
AAAAH! DON'T LET THEM TAKE US!
DON'T WORRY--

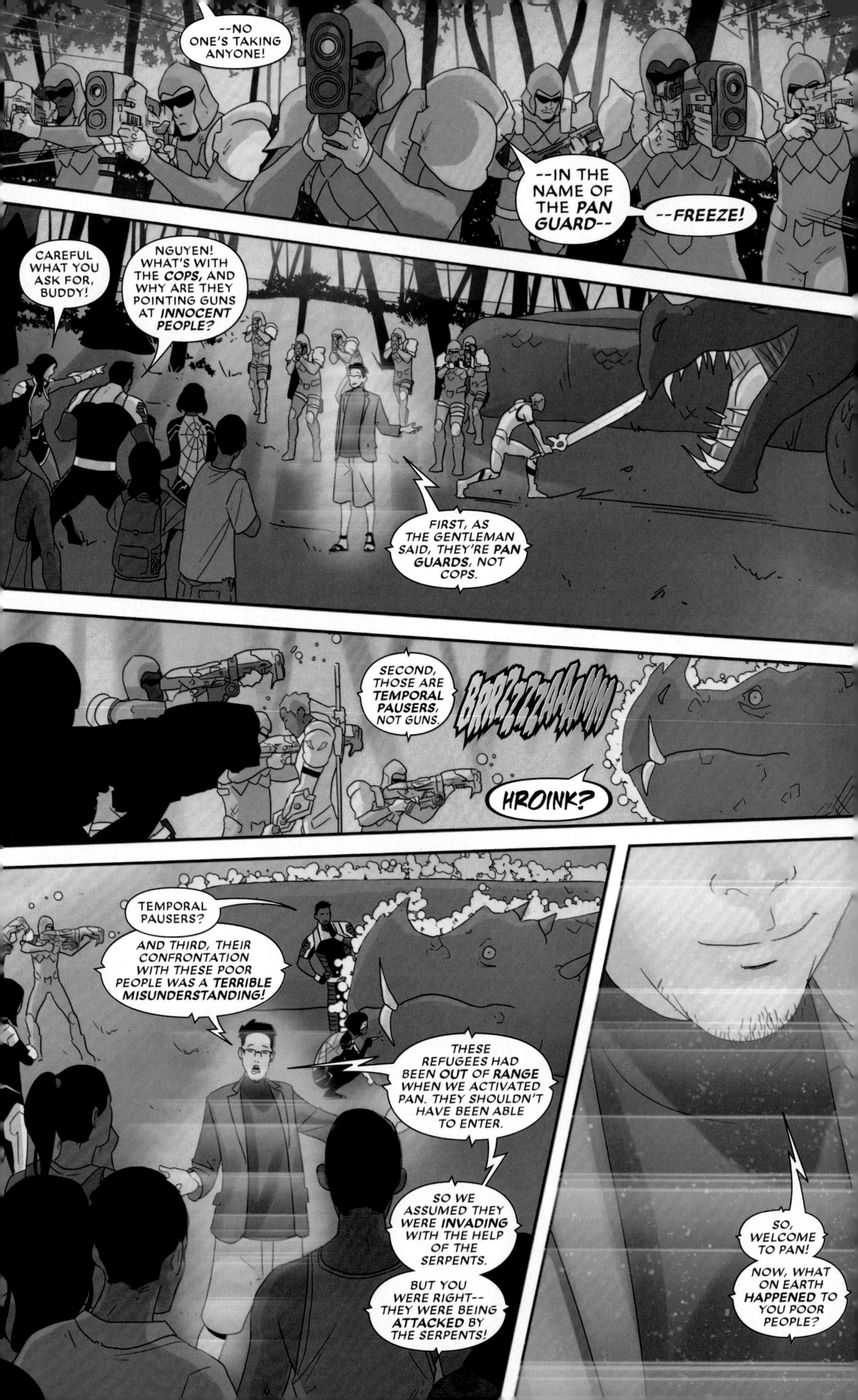
--NO ONE'S TAKING ANYONE!
--IN THE NAME OF THE PAN GUARD--
--FREEZE!
CAREFUL WHAT YOU ASK FOR, BUDDY!
NGUYEN! WHAT'S WITH THE COPS, AND WHY ARE THEY POINTING GUNS AT INNOCENT PEOPLE?
FIRST, AS THE GENTLEMAN SAID, THEY'RE PAN GUARDS, NOT COPS.
SECOND, THOSE ARE TEMPORAL PAUSERS, NOT GUNS.
BRRZZZZAAAMM
HROINK?
TEMPORAL PAUSERS?
AND THIRD, THEIR CONFRONTATION WITH THESE POOR PEOPLE WAS A TERRIBLE MISUNDERSTANDING!
THESE REFUGEES HAD BEEN OUT OF RANGE WHEN WE ACTIVATED PAN. THEY SHOULDN'T HAVE BEEN ABLE TO ENTER.
SO WE ASSUMED THEY WERE INVADING WITH THE HELP OF THE SERPENTS.
BUT YOU WERE RIGHT-- THEY WERE BEING ATTACKED BY THE SERPENTS!
SO, WELCOME TO PAN!
NOW, WHAT ON EARTH HAPPENED TO YOU POOR PEOPLE?

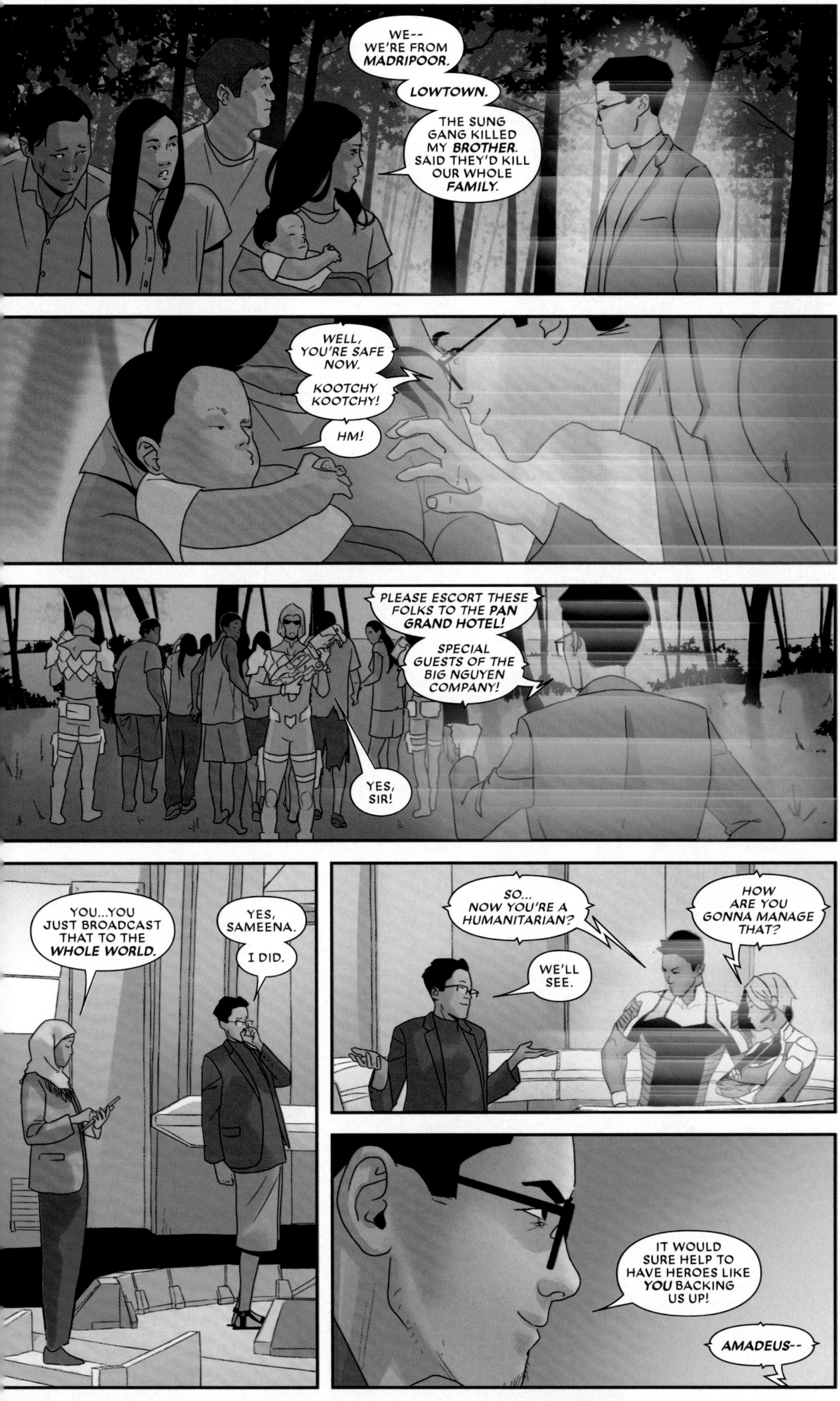
WE-- WE'RE FROM MADRIPOOR.
LOWTOWN.
THE SUNG GANG KILLED MY BROTHER. SAID THEY'D KILL OUR WHOLE FAMILY.
WELL, YOU'RE SAFE NOW.
KOOTCHY KOOTCHY!
HM!
PLEASE ESCORT THESE FOLKS TO THE PAN GRAND HOTEL!
SPECIAL GUESTS OF THE BIG NGUYEN COMPANY!
YES, SIR!
YOU...YOU JUST BROADCAST THAT TO THE WHOLE WORLD.
YES, SAMEENA.
I DID.
SO... NOW YOU'RE A HUMANITARIAN?
HOW ARE YOU GONNA MANAGE THAT?
WE'LL SEE.
IT WOULD SURE HELP TO HAVE HEROES LIKE YOU BACKING US UP!
AMADEUS--

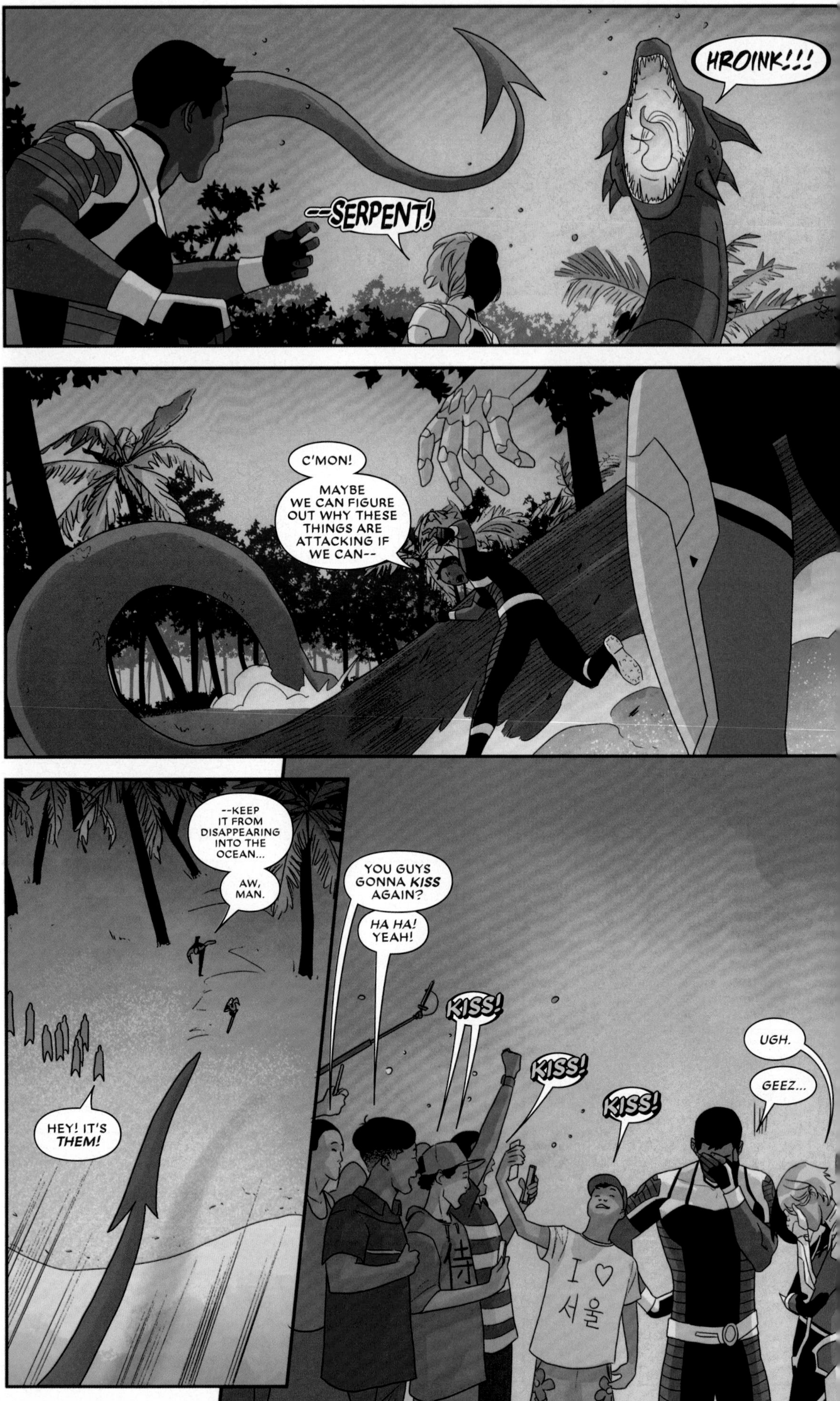
HROINK!!!
--SERPENT!
C'MON!
MAYBE WE CAN FIGURE OUT WHY THESE THINGS ARE ATTACKING IF WE CAN--
--KEEP IT FROM DISAPPEARING INTO THE OCEAN...
AW, MAN.
HEY! IT'S *THEM!*
YOU GUYS GONNA *KISS* AGAIN?
HA HA! YEAH!
KISS!
KISS!
KISS!
UGH.
GEEZ...
I ♡ 서울

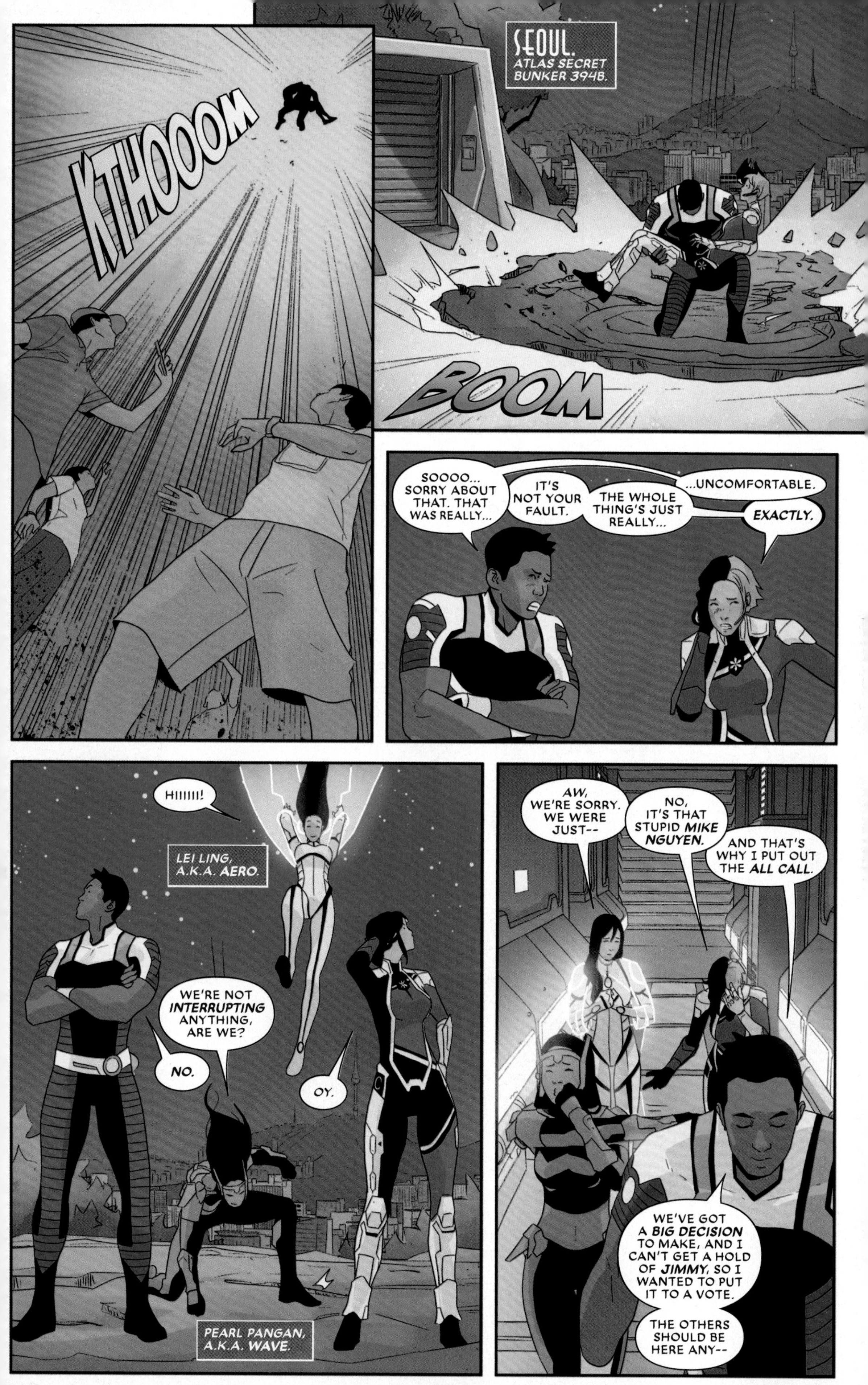
KTHOOOM
SEOUL.
ATLAS SECRET BUNKER 394B.
BOOM
SOOOO... SORRY ABOUT THAT. THAT WAS REALLY...
...UNCOMFORTABLE.
IT'S NOT YOUR FAULT.
THE WHOLE THING'S JUST REALLY...
EXACTLY.
HIIIIII!
LEI LING, A.K.A. AERO.
WE'RE NOT INTERRUPTING ANYTHING, ARE WE?
NO.
OY.
PEARL PANGAN, A.K.A. WAVE.
AW, WE'RE SORRY. WE WERE JUST--
NO, IT'S THAT STUPID MIKE NGUYEN.
AND THAT'S WHY I PUT OUT THE ALL CALL.
WE'VE GOT A BIG DECISION TO MAKE, AND I CAN'T GET A HOLD OF JIMMY, SO I WANTED TO PUT IT TO A VOTE.
THE OTHERS SHOULD BE HERE ANY--

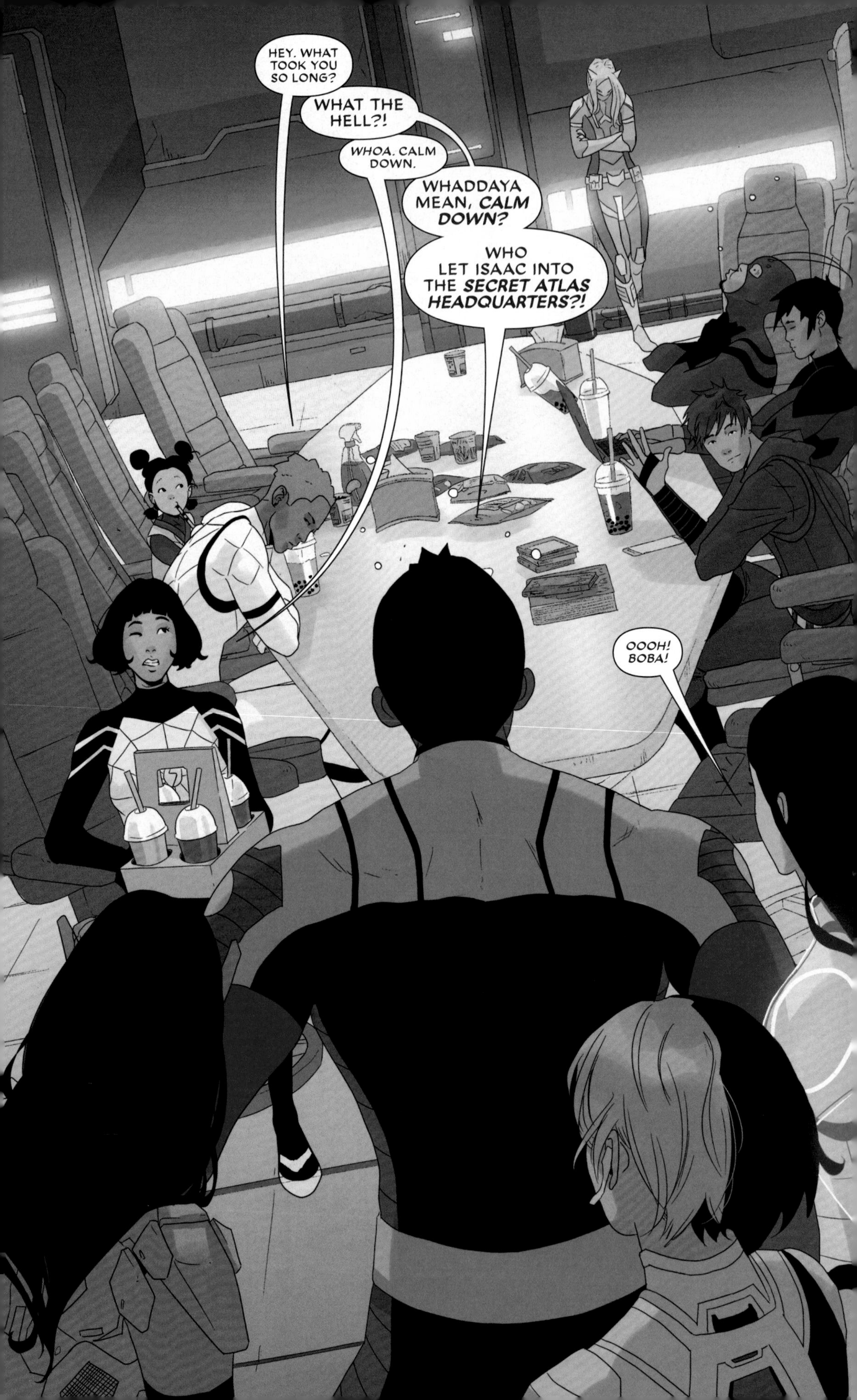
HEY. WHAT TOOK YOU SO LONG?
WHAT THE HELL?!
WHOA. CALM DOWN.
WHADDAYA MEAN, CALM DOWN?
WHO LET ISAAC INTO THE SECRET ATLAS HEADQUARTERS?!
OOOH! BOBA!

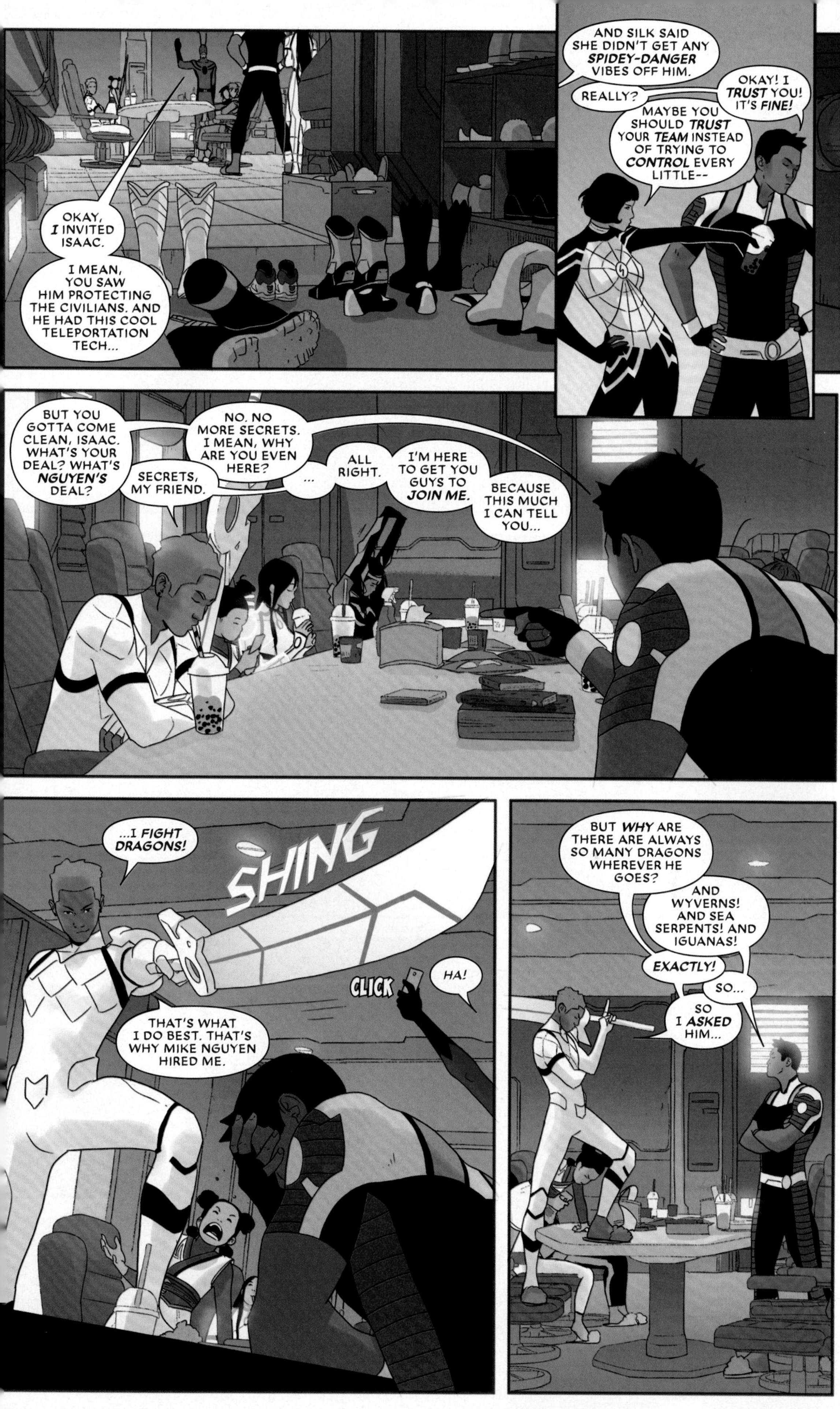
OKAY, I INVITED ISAAC.
I MEAN, YOU SAW HIM PROTECTING THE CIVILIANS. AND HE HAD THIS COOL TELEPORTATION TECH...
AND SILK SAID SHE DIDN'T GET ANY SPIDEY-DANGER VIBES OFF HIM.
REALLY?
OKAY! I TRUST YOU! IT'S FINE!
MAYBE YOU SHOULD TRUST YOUR TEAM INSTEAD OF TRYING TO CONTROL EVERY LITTLE--
BUT YOU GOTTA COME CLEAN, ISAAC. WHAT'S YOUR DEAL? WHAT'S NGUYEN'S DEAL?
SECRETS, MY FRIEND.
NO. NO MORE SECRETS. I MEAN, WHY ARE YOU EVEN HERE?
...
ALL RIGHT.
I'M HERE TO GET YOU GUYS TO JOIN ME.
BECAUSE THIS MUCH I CAN TELL YOU...
...I FIGHT DRAGONS!
SHING
CLICK
HA!
THAT'S WHAT I DO BEST. THAT'S WHY MIKE NGUYEN HIRED ME.
BUT WHY ARE THERE ARE ALWAYS SO MANY DRAGONS WHEREVER HE GOES?
AND WYVERNS! AND SEA SERPENTS! AND IGUANAS!
EXACTLY!
SO...
SO I ASKED HIM...

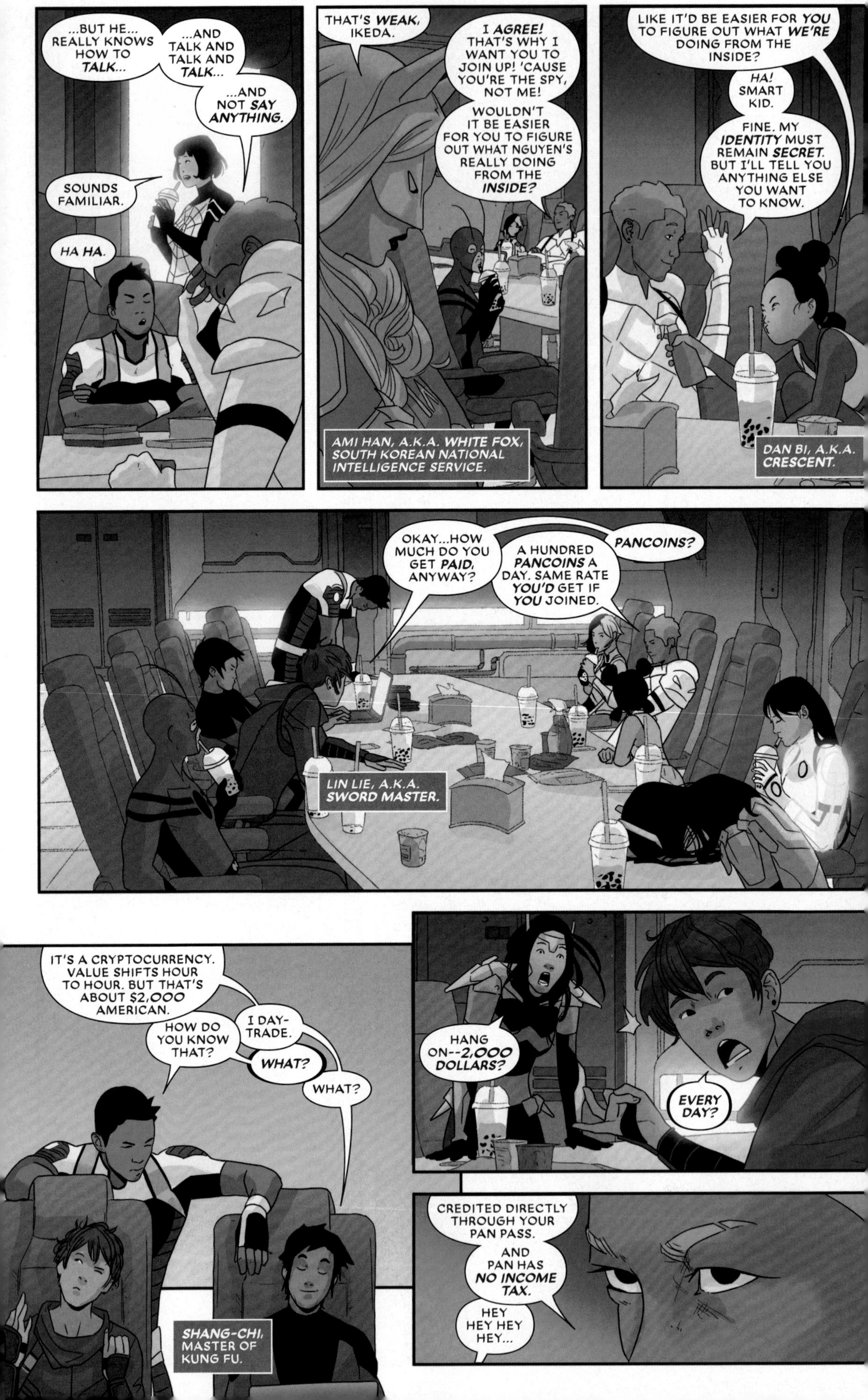
...BUT HE... REALLY KNOWS HOW TO TALK...
...AND TALK AND TALK AND TALK...
...AND NOT SAY ANYTHING.
SOUNDS FAMILIAR.
HA HA.
THAT'S WEAK, IKEDA.
I AGREE! THAT'S WHY I WANT YOU TO JOIN UP! 'CAUSE YOU'RE THE SPY, NOT ME!
WOULDN'T IT BE EASIER FOR YOU TO FIGURE OUT WHAT NGUYEN'S REALLY DOING FROM THE INSIDE?
AMI HAN, A.K.A. WHITE FOX, SOUTH KOREAN NATIONAL INTELLIGENCE SERVICE.
LIKE IT'D BE EASIER FOR YOU TO FIGURE OUT WHAT WE'RE DOING FROM THE INSIDE?
HA! SMART KID.
FINE. MY IDENTITY MUST REMAIN SECRET. BUT I'LL TELL YOU ANYTHING ELSE YOU WANT TO KNOW.
DAN BI, A.K.A. CRESCENT.
OKAY...HOW MUCH DO YOU GET PAID, ANYWAY?
A HUNDRED PANCOINS A DAY. SAME RATE YOU'D GET IF YOU JOINED.
PANCOINS?
LIN LIE, A.K.A. SWORD MASTER.
IT'S A CRYPTOCURRENCY. VALUE SHIFTS HOUR TO HOUR. BUT THAT'S ABOUT $2,000 AMERICAN.
HOW DO YOU KNOW THAT?
I DAY-TRADE.
WHAT?
WHAT?
SHANG-CHI, MASTER OF KUNG FU.
HANG ON--2,000 DOLLARS?
EVERY DAY?
CREDITED DIRECTLY THROUGH YOUR PAN PASS.
AND PAN HAS NO INCOME TAX.
HEY HEY HEY HEY...

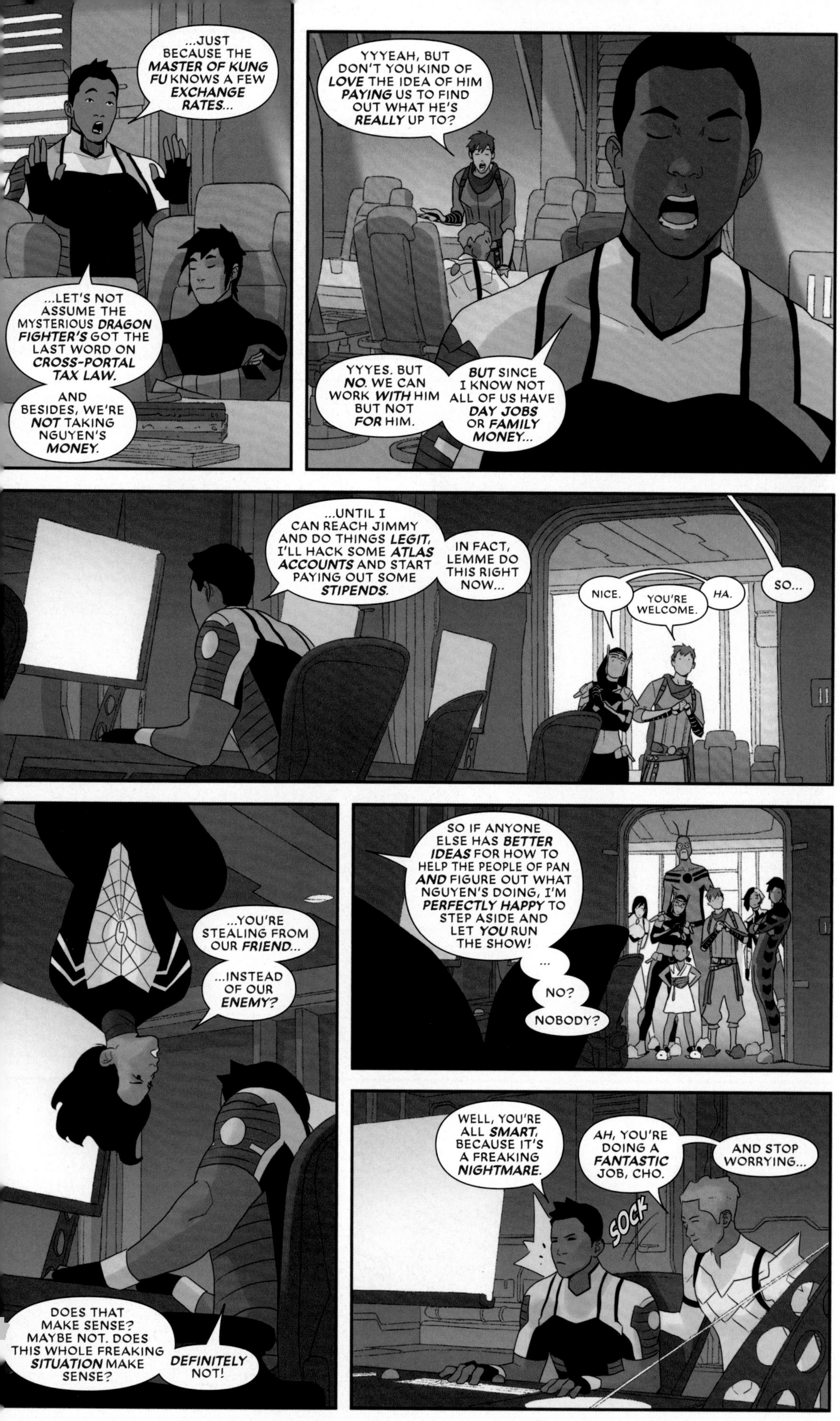
...JUST BECAUSE THE MASTER OF KUNG FU KNOWS A FEW EXCHANGE RATES...
...LET'S NOT ASSUME THE MYSTERIOUS DRAGON FIGHTER'S GOT THE LAST WORD ON CROSS-PORTAL TAX LAW.
AND BESIDES, WE'RE NOT TAKING NGUYEN'S MONEY.
YYYEAH, BUT DON'T YOU KIND OF LOVE THE IDEA OF HIM PAYING US TO FIND OUT WHAT HE'S REALLY UP TO?
YYYES. BUT NO. WE CAN WORK WITH HIM BUT NOT FOR HIM.
BUT SINCE I KNOW NOT ALL OF US HAVE DAY JOBS OR FAMILY MONEY...
...UNTIL I CAN REACH JIMMY AND DO THINGS LEGIT, I'LL HACK SOME ATLAS ACCOUNTS AND START PAYING OUT SOME STIPENDS.
IN FACT, LEMME DO THIS RIGHT NOW...
NICE.
YOU'RE WELCOME.
HA.
SO...
...YOU'RE STEALING FROM OUR FRIEND...
...INSTEAD OF OUR ENEMY?
DOES THAT MAKE SENSE? MAYBE NOT. DOES THIS WHOLE FREAKING SITUATION MAKE SENSE?
DEFINITELY NOT!
SO IF ANYONE ELSE HAS BETTER IDEAS FOR HOW TO HELP THE PEOPLE OF PAN AND FIGURE OUT WHAT NGUYEN'S DOING, I'M PERFECTLY HAPPY TO STEP ASIDE AND LET YOU RUN THE SHOW!
...
NO?
NOBODY?
WELL, YOU'RE ALL SMART, BECAUSE IT'S A FREAKING NIGHTMARE.
AH, YOU'RE DOING A FANTASTIC JOB, CHO.
AND STOP WORRYING...
SOCK

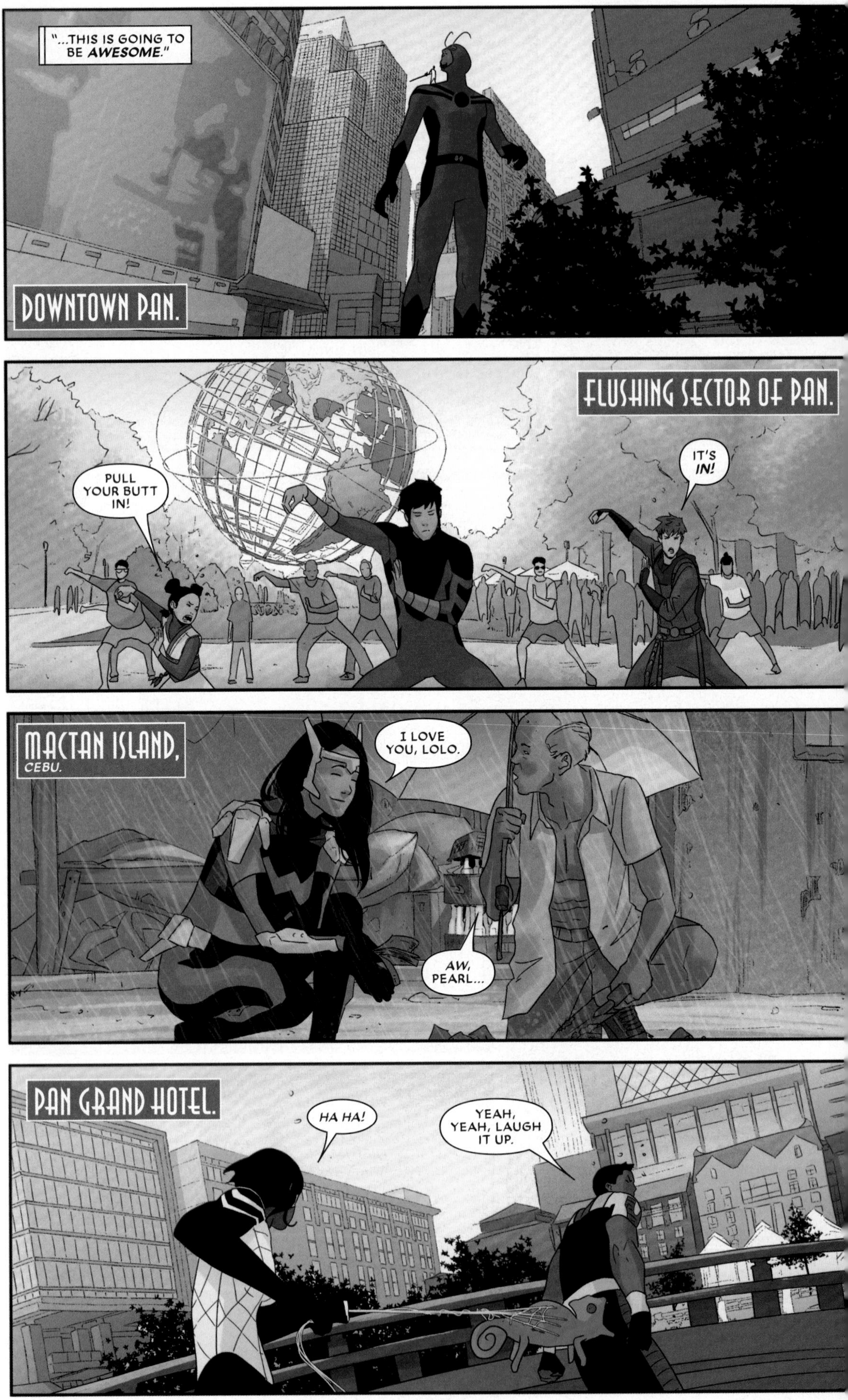
"...THIS IS GOING TO BE AWESOME."
DOWNTOWN PAN.
FLUSHING SECTOR OF PAN.
PULL YOUR BUTT IN!
IT'S IN!
MACTAN ISLAND, CEBU.
I LOVE YOU, LOLO.
AW, PEARL...
PAN GRAND HOTEL.
HA HA!
YEAH, YEAH, LAUGH IT UP.

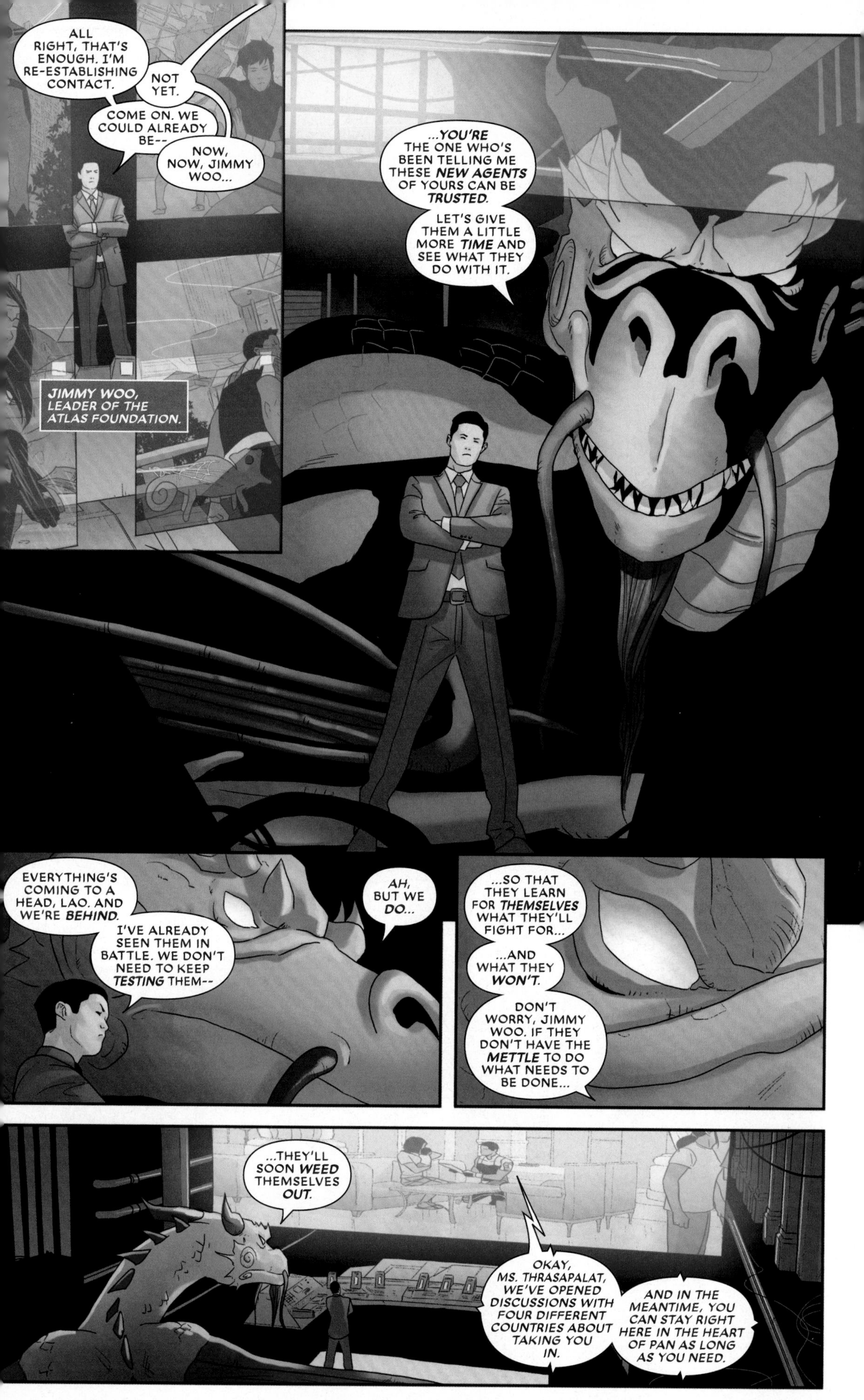
ALL RIGHT, THAT'S ENOUGH. I'M RE-ESTABLISHING CONTACT.
NOT YET.
COME ON. WE COULD ALREADY BE--
NOW, NOW, JIMMY WOO...
JIMMY WOO, LEADER OF THE ATLAS FOUNDATION.
...YOU'RE THE ONE WHO'S BEEN TELLING ME THESE NEW AGENTS OF YOURS CAN BE TRUSTED.
LET'S GIVE THEM A LITTLE MORE TIME AND SEE WHAT THEY DO WITH IT.
EVERYTHING'S COMING TO A HEAD, LAO. AND WE'RE BEHIND.
I'VE ALREADY SEEN THEM IN BATTLE. WE DON'T NEED TO KEEP TESTING THEM--
AH, BUT WE DO...
...SO THAT THEY LEARN FOR THEMSELVES WHAT THEY'LL FIGHT FOR...
...AND WHAT THEY WON'T.
DON'T WORRY, JIMMY WOO. IF THEY DON'T HAVE THE METTLE TO DO WHAT NEEDS TO BE DONE...
...THEY'LL SOON WEED THEMSELVES OUT.
OKAY, MS. THRASAPALAT, WE'VE OPENED DISCUSSIONS WITH FOUR DIFFERENT COUNTRIES ABOUT TAKING YOU IN.
AND IN THE MEANTIME, YOU CAN STAY RIGHT HERE IN THE HEART OF PAN AS LONG AS YOU NEED.

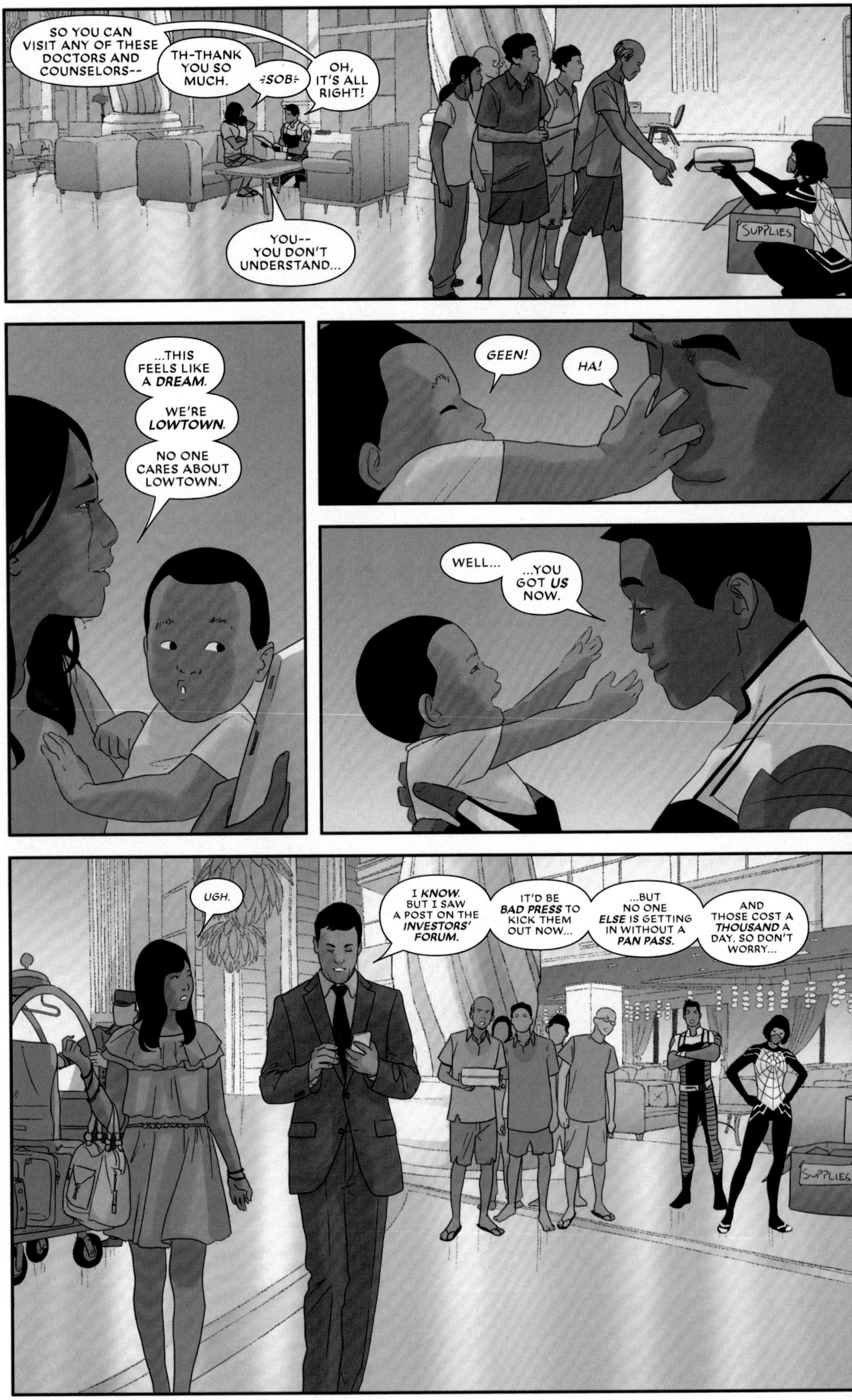
SO YOU CAN VISIT ANY OF THESE DOCTORS AND COUNSELORS--
TH-THANK YOU SO MUCH.
-SOB-
OH, IT'S ALL RIGHT!
YOU-- YOU DON'T UNDERSTAND...
SUPPLIES
...THIS FEELS LIKE A DREAM.
WE'RE LOWTOWN.
NO ONE CARES ABOUT LOWTOWN.
GEEN!
HA!
WELL...
...YOU GOT US NOW.
UGH.
I KNOW. BUT I SAW A POST ON THE INVESTORS' FORUM.
IT'D BE BAD PRESS TO KICK THEM OUT NOW...
...BUT NO ONE ELSE IS GETTING IN WITHOUT A PAN PASS.
AND THOSE COST A THOUSAND A DAY. SO DON'T WORRY...
SUPPLIES

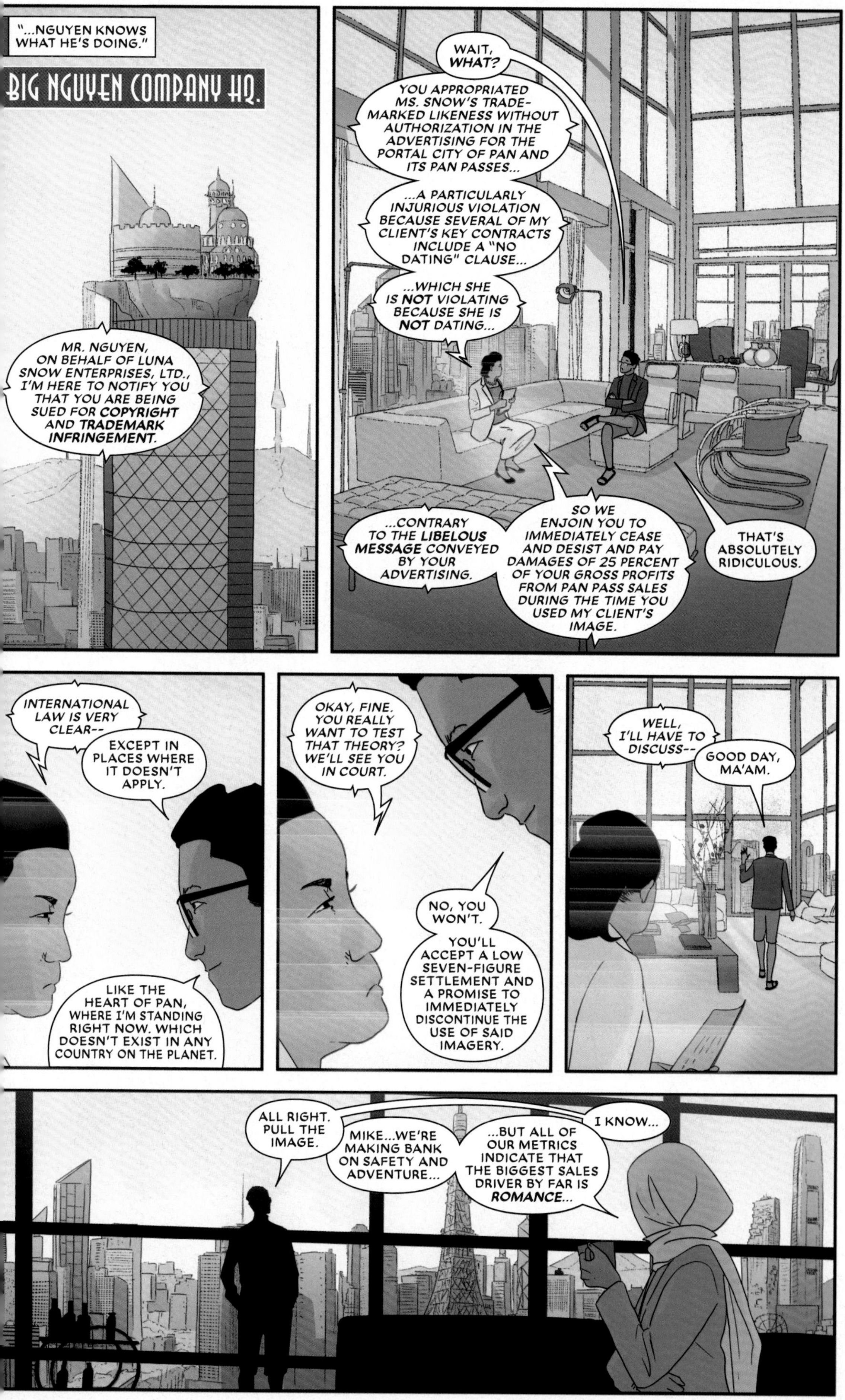

"...NGUYEN KNOWS WHAT HE'S DOING."
BIG NGUYEN COMPANY HQ.
MR. NGUYEN, ON BEHALF OF LUNA SNOW ENTERPRISES, LTD., I'M HERE TO NOTIFY YOU THAT YOU ARE BEING SUED FOR COPYRIGHT AND TRADEMARK INFRINGEMENT.
WAIT, WHAT?
YOU APPROPRIATED MS. SNOW'S TRADE-MARKED LIKENESS WITHOUT AUTHORIZATION IN THE ADVERTISING FOR THE PORTAL CITY OF PAN AND ITS PAN PASSES...
...A PARTICULARLY INJURIOUS VIOLATION BECAUSE SEVERAL OF MY CLIENT'S KEY CONTRACTS INCLUDE A "NO DATING" CLAUSE...
...WHICH SHE IS NOT VIOLATING BECAUSE SHE IS NOT DATING...
...CONTRARY TO THE LIBELOUS MESSAGE CONVEYED BY YOUR ADVERTISING.
SO WE ENJOIN YOU TO IMMEDIATELY CEASE AND DESIST AND PAY DAMAGES OF 25 PERCENT OF YOUR GROSS PROFITS FROM PAN PASS SALES DURING THE TIME YOU USED MY CLIENT'S IMAGE.
THAT'S ABSOLUTELY RIDICULOUS.
INTERNATIONAL LAW IS VERY CLEAR--
EXCEPT IN PLACES WHERE IT DOESN'T APPLY.
LIKE THE HEART OF PAN, WHERE I'M STANDING RIGHT NOW. WHICH DOESN'T EXIST IN ANY COUNTRY ON THE PLANET.
OKAY, FINE. YOU REALLY WANT TO TEST THAT THEORY? WE'LL SEE YOU IN COURT.
NO, YOU WON'T.
YOU'LL ACCEPT A LOW SEVEN-FIGURE SETTLEMENT AND A PROMISE TO IMMEDIATELY DISCONTINUE THE USE OF SAID IMAGERY.
WELL, I'LL HAVE TO DISCUSS--
GOOD DAY, MA'AM.
ALL RIGHT. PULL THE IMAGE.
MIKE...WE'RE MAKING BANK ON SAFETY AND ADVENTURE...
I KNOW...
...BUT ALL OF OUR METRICS INDICATE THAT THE BIGGEST SALES DRIVER BY FAR IS ROMANCE...

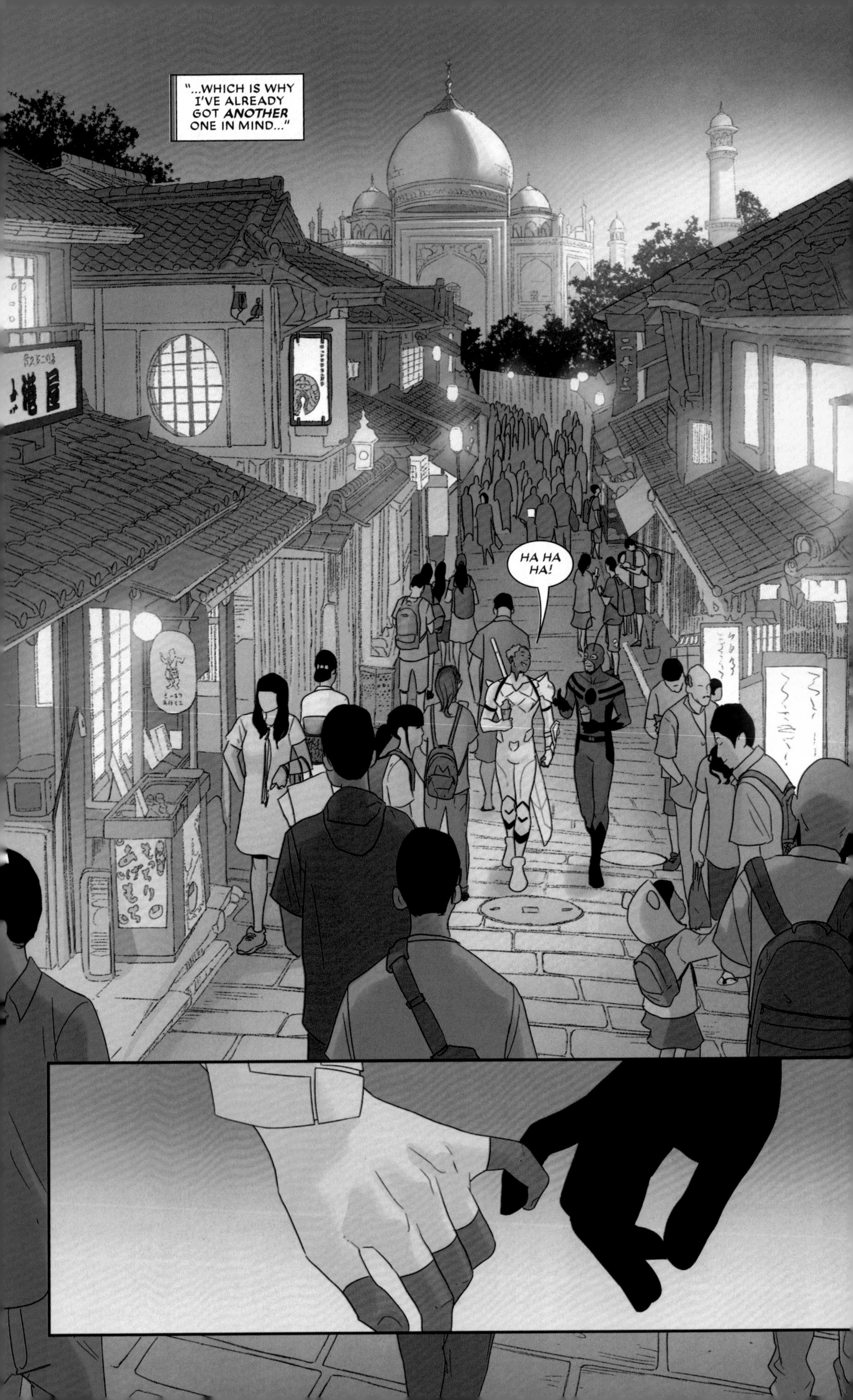
"...WHICH IS WHY I'VE ALREADY GOT ANOTHER ONE IN MIND..."
HA HA HA!

FOUR

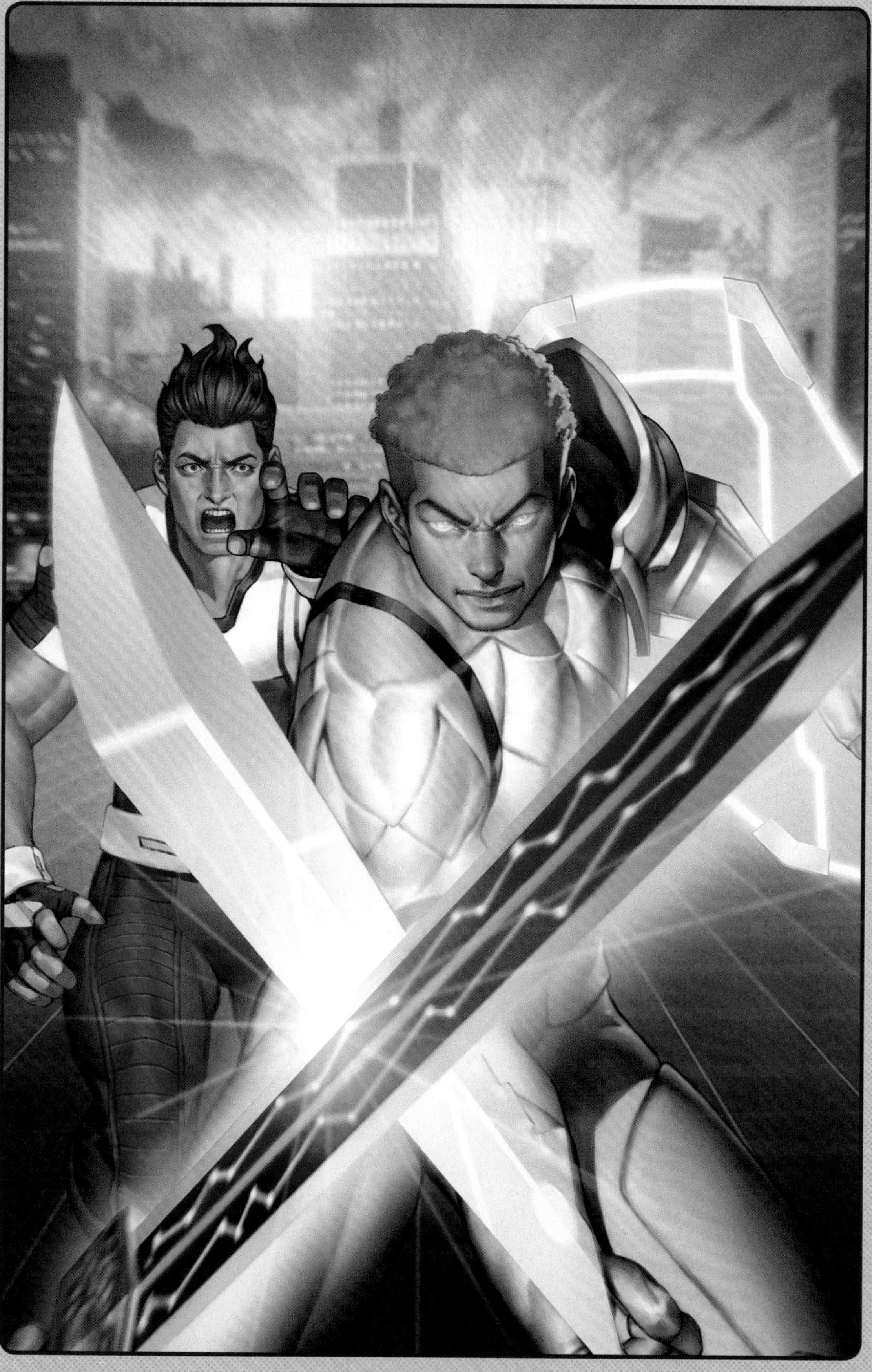

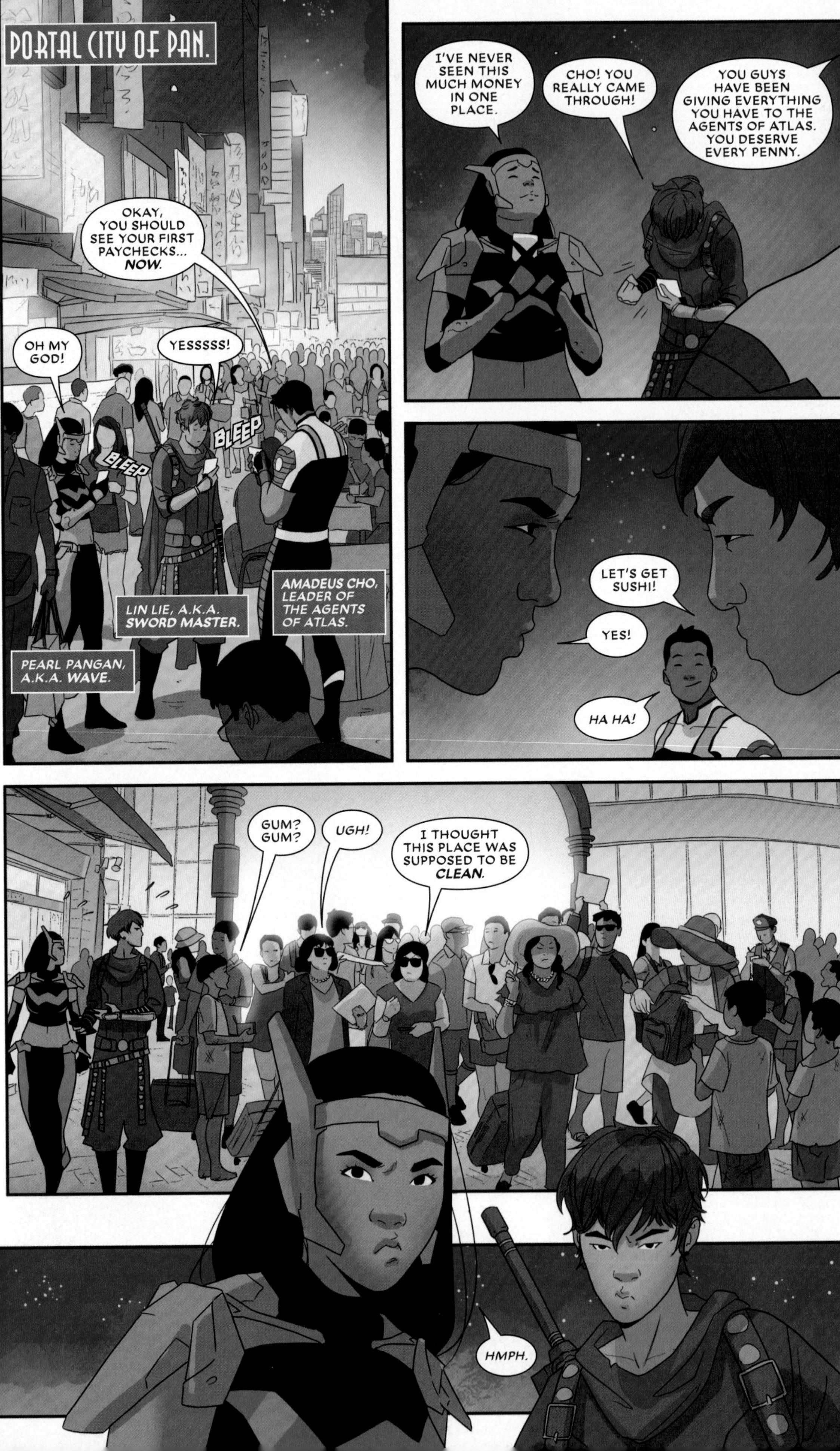
PORTAL CITY OF PAN.
OKAY, YOU SHOULD SEE YOUR FIRST PAYCHECKS... NOW.
OH MY GOD!
YESSSSS!
BLEEP
BLEEP
LIN LIE, A.K.A. SWORD MASTER.
AMADEUS CHO, LEADER OF THE AGENTS OF ATLAS.
PEARL PANGAN, A.K.A. WAVE.
I'VE NEVER SEEN THIS MUCH MONEY IN ONE PLACE.
CHO! YOU REALLY CAME THROUGH!
YOU GUYS HAVE BEEN GIVING EVERYTHING YOU HAVE TO THE AGENTS OF ATLAS. YOU DESERVE EVERY PENNY.
LET'S GET SUSHI!
YES!
HA HA!
GUM? GUM?
UGH!
I THOUGHT THIS PLACE WAS SUPPOSED TO BE CLEAN.
HMPH.

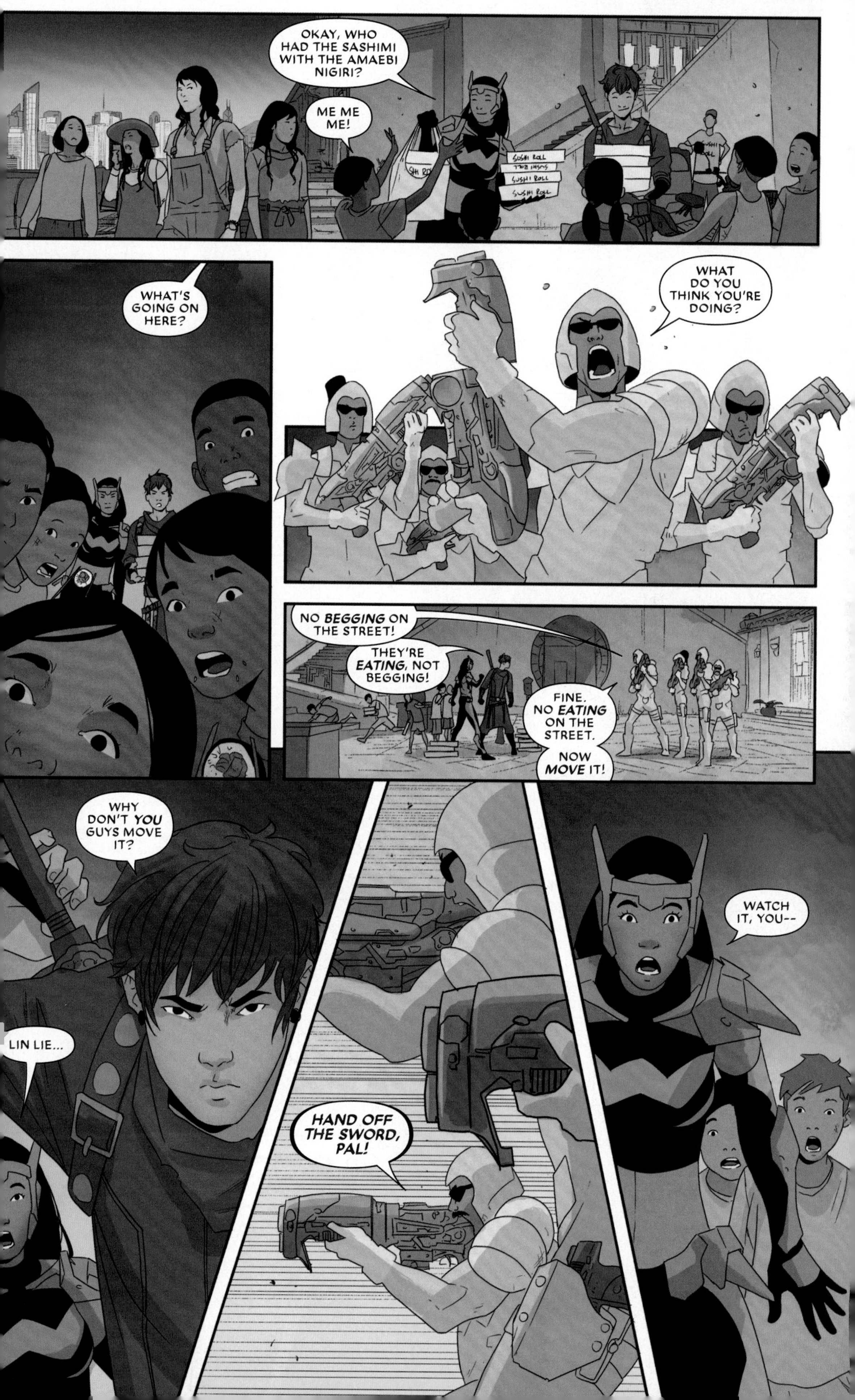
OKAY, WHO HAD THE SASHIMI WITH THE AMAEBI NIGIRI?
ME ME ME!
SUSHI ROLL
SUSHI ROLL
SUSHI ROLL
SUSHI ROLL
WHAT'S GOING ON HERE?
WHAT DO YOU THINK YOU'RE DOING?
NO BEGGING ON THE STREET!
THEY'RE EATING, NOT BEGGING!
FINE. NO EATING ON THE STREET.
NOW MOVE IT!
WHY DON'T YOU GUYS MOVE IT?
LIN LIE...
HAND OFF THE SWORD, PAL!
WATCH IT, YOU--

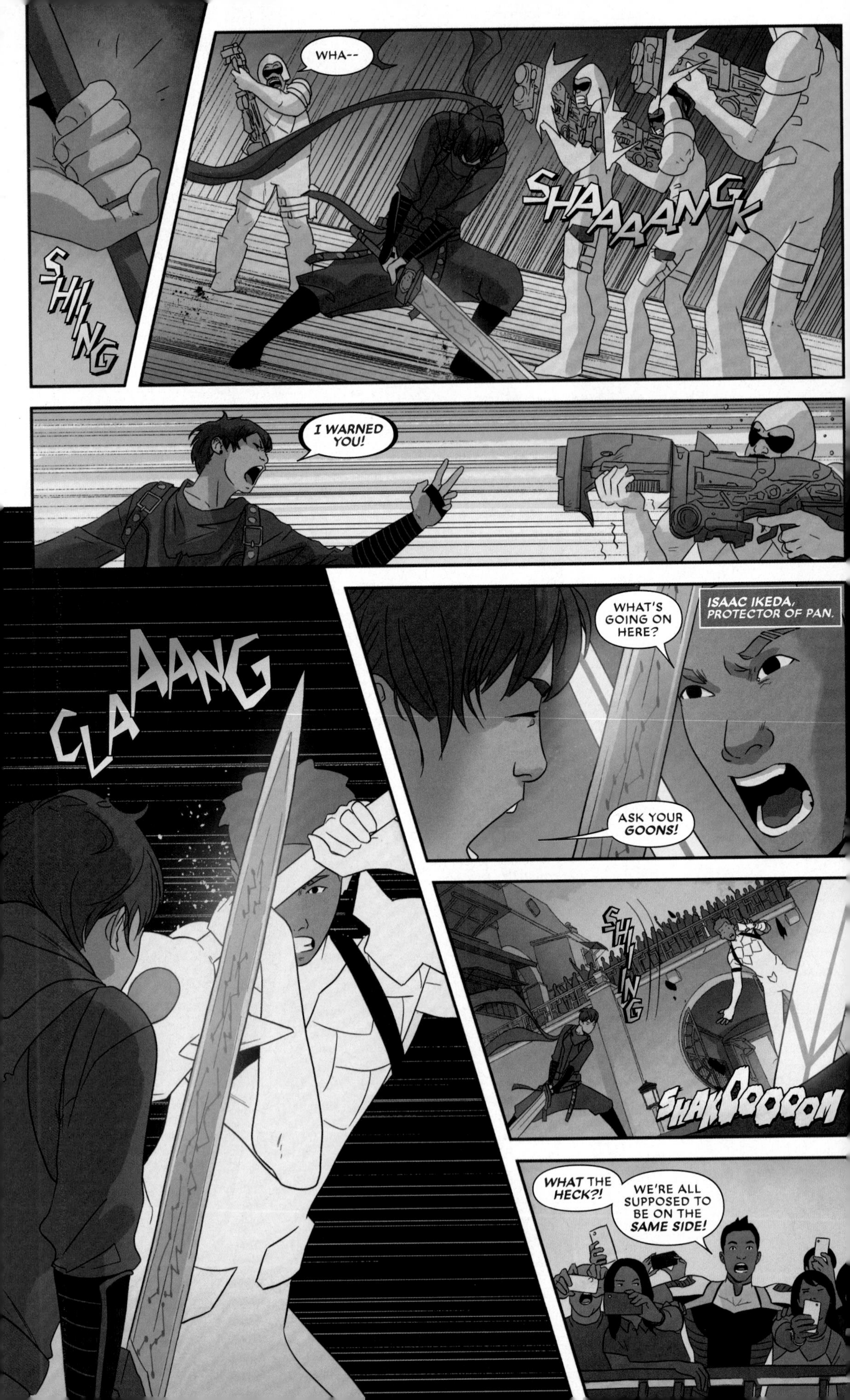

SHIING
WHA--
SHAAAANGK
I WARNED YOU!
CLAAANG
ISAAC IKEDA, PROTECTOR OF PAN.
WHAT'S GOING ON HERE?
ASK YOUR GOONS!
SHIING
SHAKDOOOOOM
WHAT THE HECK?!
WE'RE ALL SUPPOSED TO BE ON THE SAME SIDE!

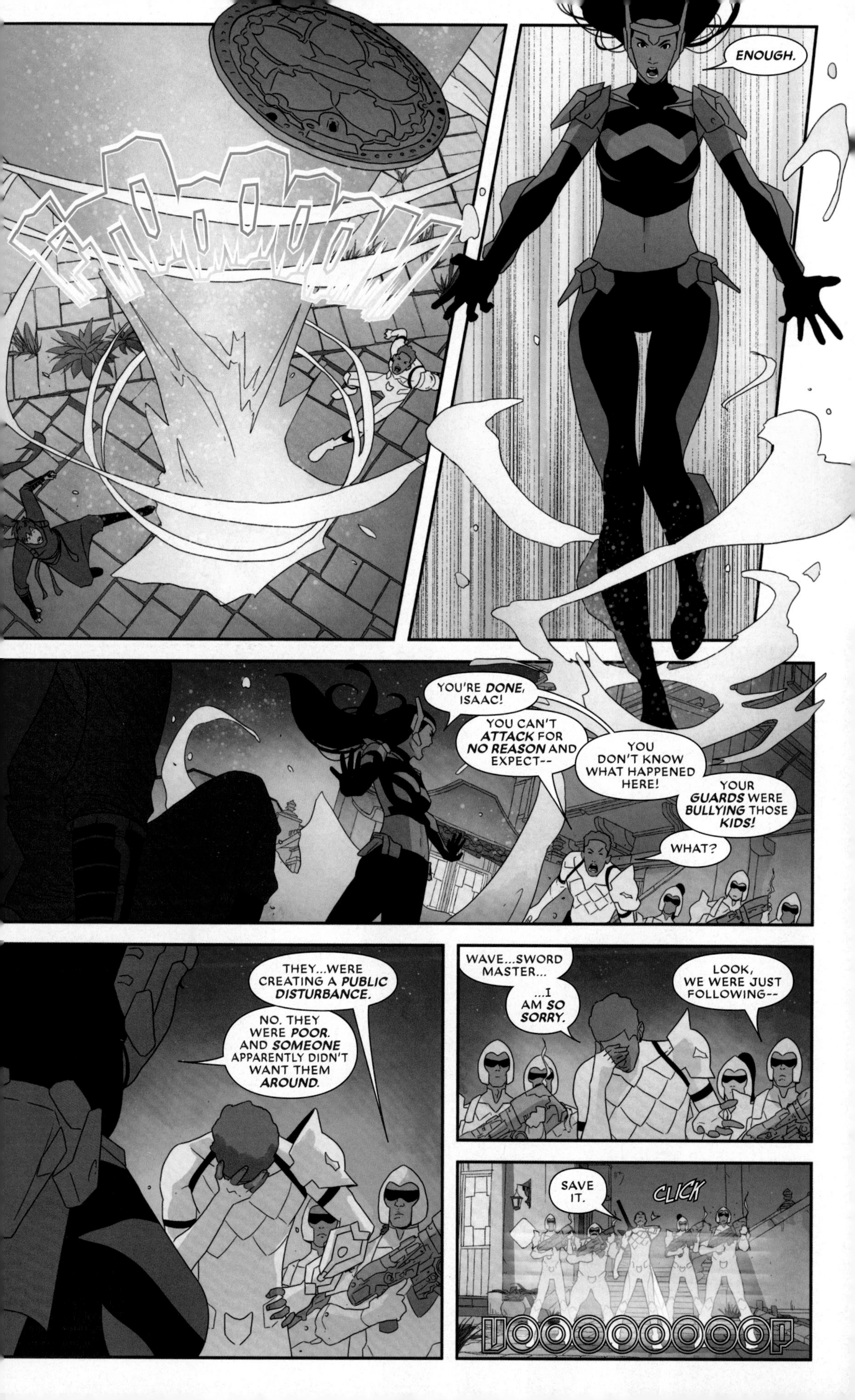

ENOUGH.
YOU'RE DONE, ISAAC!
YOU CAN'T ATTACK FOR NO REASON AND EXPECT--
YOU DON'T KNOW WHAT HAPPENED HERE!
YOUR GUARDS WERE BULLYING THOSE KIDS!
WHAT?
THEY...WERE CREATING A PUBLIC DISTURBANCE.
NO. THEY WERE POOR. AND SOMEONE APPARENTLY DIDN'T WANT THEM AROUND.
WAVE...SWORD MASTER...
...I AM SO SORRY.
LOOK, WE WERE JUST FOLLOWING--
SAVE IT.
CLICK
VOOOOOOOOOP

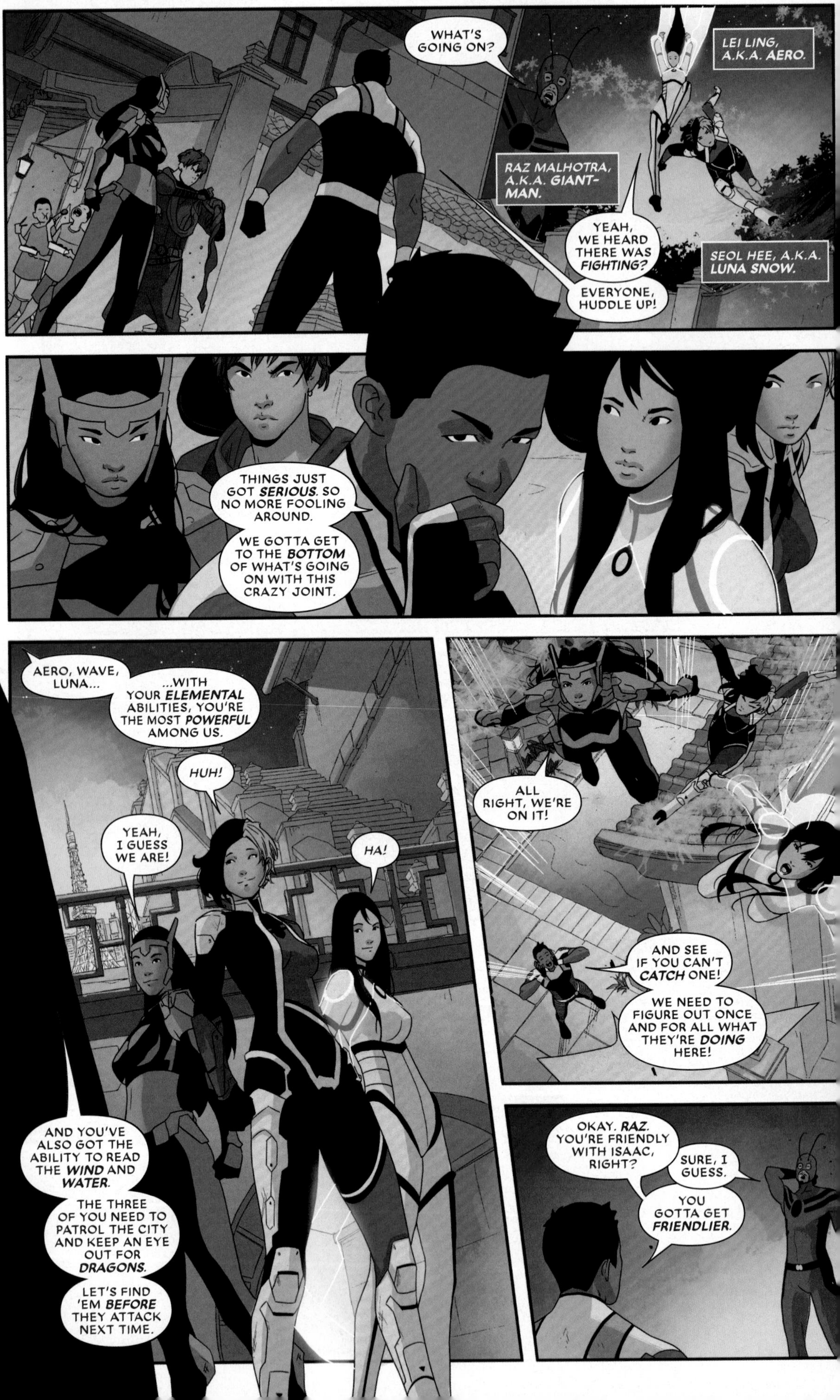
WHAT'S GOING ON?
LEI LING, A.K.A. AERO.
RAZ MALHOTRA, A.K.A. GIANT-MAN.
YEAH, WE HEARD THERE WAS FIGHTING?
SEOL HEE, A.K.A. LUNA SNOW.
EVERYONE, HUDDLE UP!
THINGS JUST GOT SERIOUS. SO NO MORE FOOLING AROUND.
WE GOTTA GET TO THE BOTTOM OF WHAT'S GOING ON WITH THIS CRAZY JOINT.
AERO, WAVE, LUNA...
...WITH YOUR ELEMENTAL ABILITIES, YOU'RE THE MOST POWERFUL AMONG US.
HUH!
YEAH, I GUESS WE ARE!
HA!
AND YOU'VE ALSO GOT THE ABILITY TO READ THE WIND AND WATER.
THE THREE OF YOU NEED TO PATROL THE CITY AND KEEP AN EYE OUT FOR DRAGONS.
LET'S FIND 'EM BEFORE THEY ATTACK NEXT TIME.
ALL RIGHT, WE'RE ON IT!
AND SEE IF YOU CAN'T CATCH ONE!
WE NEED TO FIGURE OUT ONCE AND FOR ALL WHAT THEY'RE DOING HERE!
OKAY. RAZ. YOU'RE FRIENDLY WITH ISAAC, RIGHT?
SURE, I GUESS.
YOU GOTTA GET FRIENDLIER.

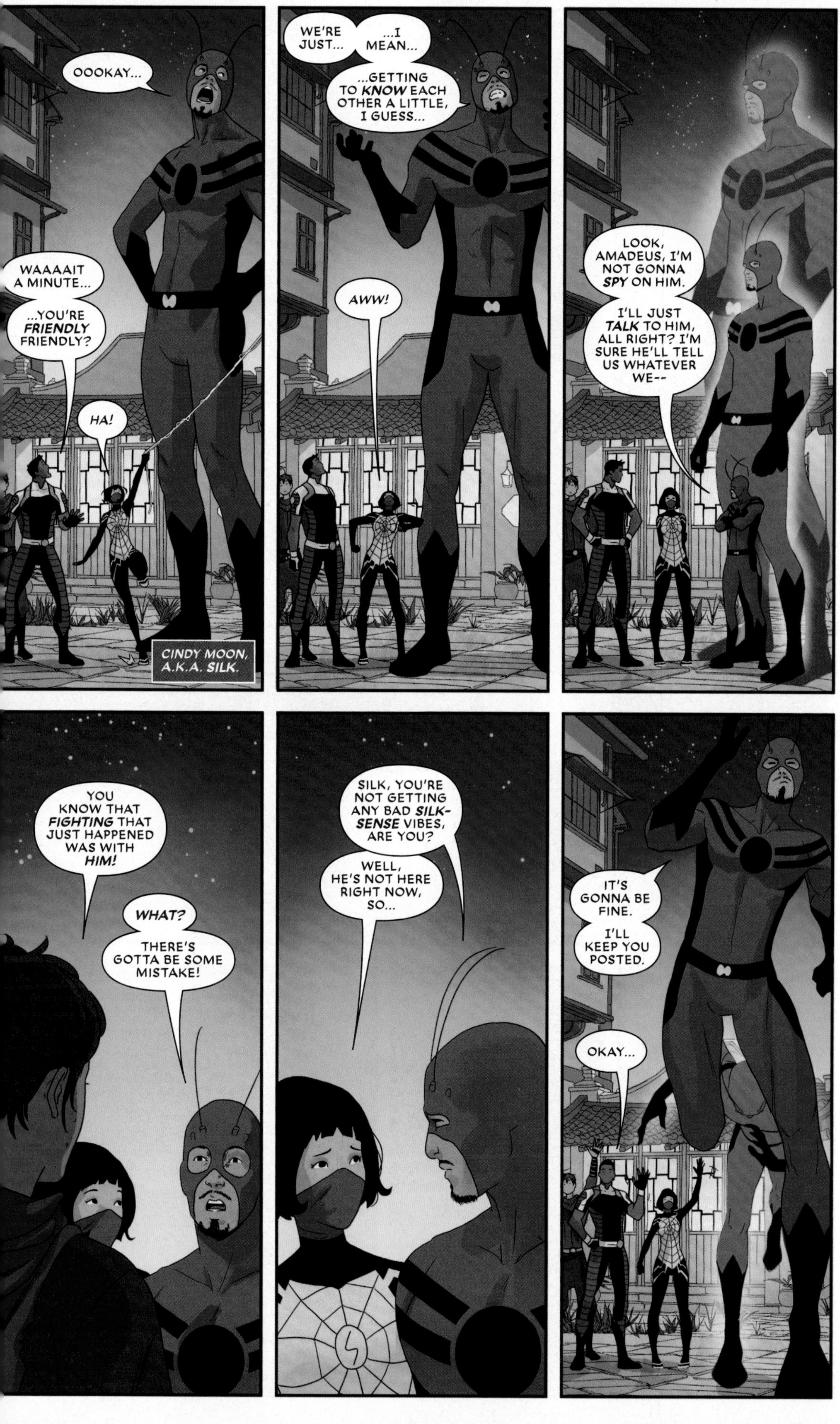
OOOKAY...
WAAAAIT A MINUTE...
...YOU'RE *FRIENDLY* FRIENDLY?
HA!
CINDY MOON, A.K.A. *SILK*.
WE'RE JUST...
...I MEAN...
...GETTING TO *KNOW* EACH OTHER A LITTLE, I GUESS...
AWW!
LOOK, AMADEUS, I'M NOT GONNA *SPY* ON HIM.
I'LL JUST *TALK* TO HIM, ALL RIGHT? I'M SURE HE'LL TELL US WHATEVER WE--
YOU KNOW THAT *FIGHTING* THAT JUST HAPPENED WAS WITH *HIM!*
WHAT?
THERE'S GOTTA BE SOME MISTAKE!
SILK, YOU'RE NOT GETTING ANY BAD *SILK-SENSE* VIBES, ARE YOU?
WELL, HE'S NOT HERE RIGHT NOW, SO...
IT'S GONNA BE FINE.
I'LL KEEP YOU POSTED.
OKAY...

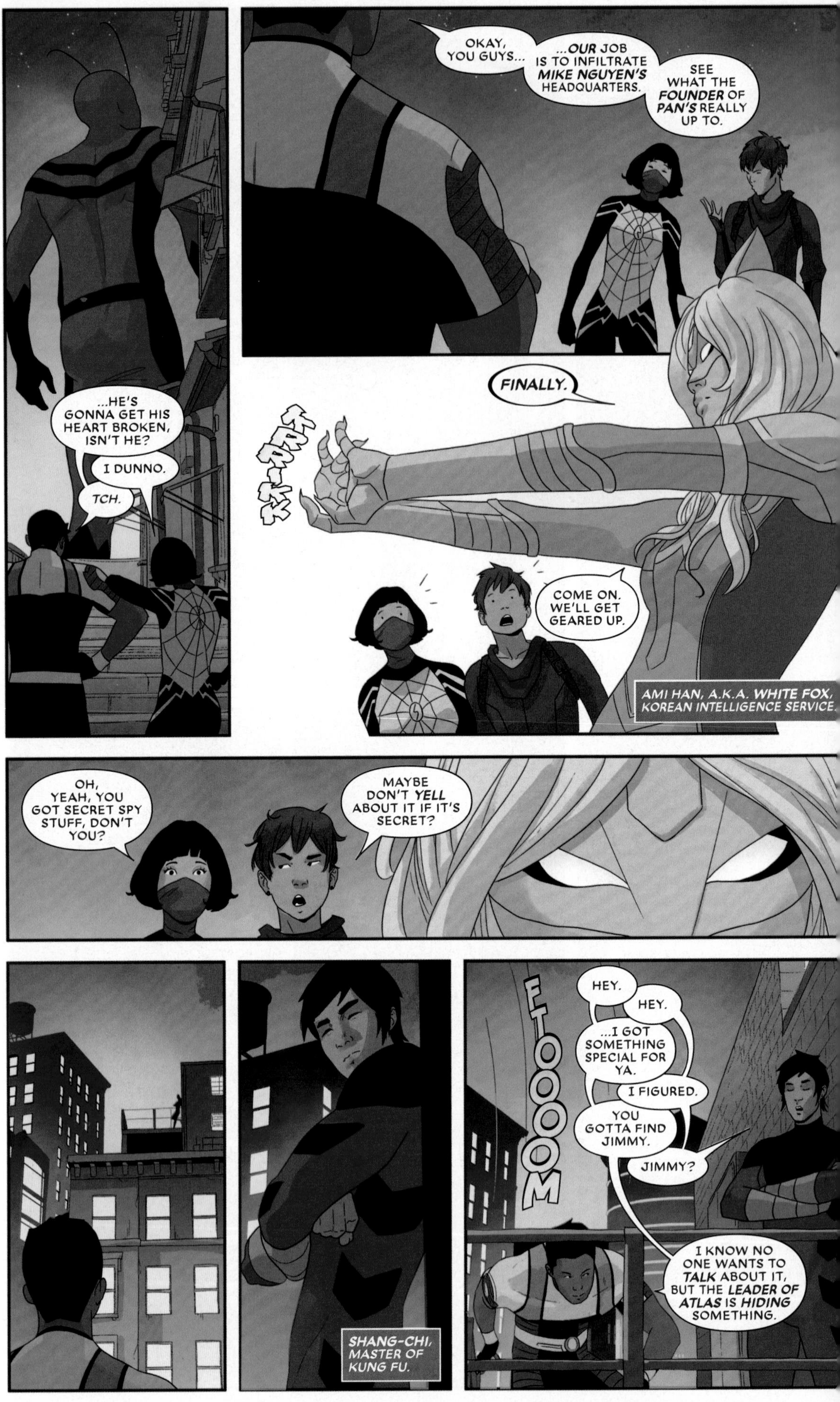
OKAY, YOU GUYS...
...OUR JOB IS TO INFILTRATE MIKE NGUYEN'S HEADQUARTERS.
SEE WHAT THE FOUNDER OF PAN'S REALLY UP TO.
FINALLY.
KRIKK
...HE'S GONNA GET HIS HEART BROKEN, ISN'T HE?
I DUNNO.
TCH.
COME ON. WE'LL GET GEARED UP.
AMI HAN, A.K.A. WHITE FOX, KOREAN INTELLIGENCE SERVICE.
OH, YEAH, YOU GOT SECRET SPY STUFF, DON'T YOU?
MAYBE DON'T YELL ABOUT IT IF IT'S SECRET?
SHANG-CHI, MASTER OF KUNG FU.
FTOOOOM
HEY.
HEY.
...I GOT SOMETHING SPECIAL FOR YA.
I FIGURED.
YOU GOTTA FIND JIMMY.
JIMMY?
I KNOW NO ONE WANTS TO TALK ABOUT IT, BUT THE LEADER OF ATLAS IS HIDING SOMETHING.

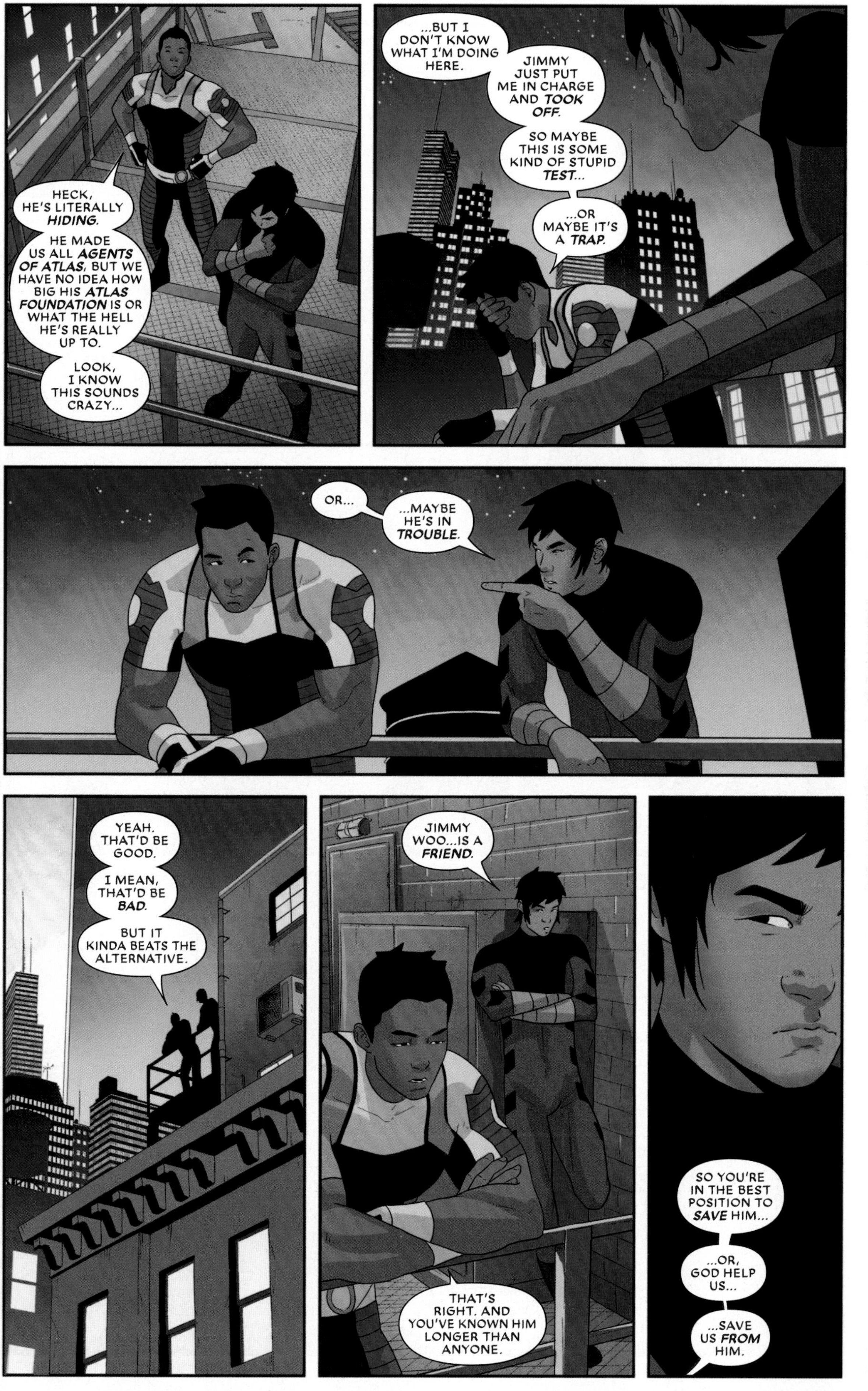
HECK, HE'S LITERALLY HIDING.
HE MADE US ALL AGENTS OF ATLAS, BUT WE HAVE NO IDEA HOW BIG HIS ATLAS FOUNDATION IS OR WHAT THE HELL HE'S REALLY UP TO.
LOOK, I KNOW THIS SOUNDS CRAZY...
...BUT I DON'T KNOW WHAT I'M DOING HERE.
JIMMY JUST PUT ME IN CHARGE AND TOOK OFF.
SO MAYBE THIS IS SOME KIND OF STUPID TEST...
...OR MAYBE IT'S A TRAP.
OR...
...MAYBE HE'S IN TROUBLE.
YEAH. THAT'D BE GOOD.
I MEAN, THAT'D BE BAD.
BUT IT KINDA BEATS THE ALTERNATIVE.
JIMMY WOO...IS A FRIEND.
THAT'S RIGHT. AND YOU'VE KNOWN HIM LONGER THAN ANYONE.
SO YOU'RE IN THE BEST POSITION TO SAVE HIM...
...OR, GOD HELP US...
...SAVE US FROM HIM.

PAN GUARDS, COME IN! WHAT THE HELL'S GOING ON HERE?!

SORRY, SIR! IT'S OUR NEW *ATTACK TANK*!

IT PROBABLY THOUGHT YOU *ABDUCTED* US!

SHUT IT DOWN!

WE--WE *CAN'T*!

BRRZZAAAM BRRAZZAM

VANCOUVER SECTOR OF PAN.

LET ME TRY.

HA HA! THANKS, RAZ!

STOMMMPP

HEY, YOU WANNA GO TO MADRIPOOR LATER? THERE'S A NEW NOODLE PLACE EVERYONE SAYS IS GREAT.

UH, YEAH, DEFINITELY!

BUT, UH...

SPPRRAAAK

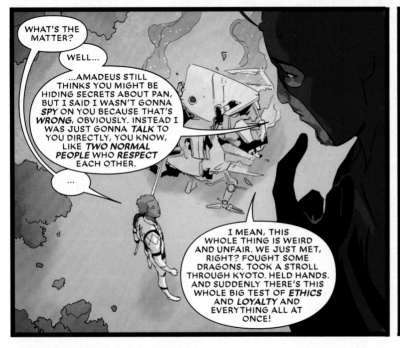

WHAT'S THE MATTER?

WELL...

...AMADEUS STILL THINKS YOU MIGHT BE HIDING SECRETS ABOUT PAN, BUT I SAID I WASN'T GONNA *SPY* ON YOU BECAUSE THAT'S *WRONG*, OBVIOUSLY. INSTEAD I WAS JUST GONNA *TALK* TO YOU DIRECTLY, YOU KNOW, LIKE *TWO NORMAL PEOPLE* WHO *RESPECT* EACH OTHER.

...

I MEAN, THIS WHOLE THING IS WEIRD AND UNFAIR. WE JUST MET, RIGHT? FOUGHT SOME *DRAGONS*. TOOK A STROLL THROUGH KYOTO. HELD HANDS. AND SUDDENLY THERE'S THIS WHOLE BIG TEST OF *ETHICS* AND *LOYALTY* AND EVERYTHING ALL AT ONCE!

... WHAT?

YOU'RE CUTE.

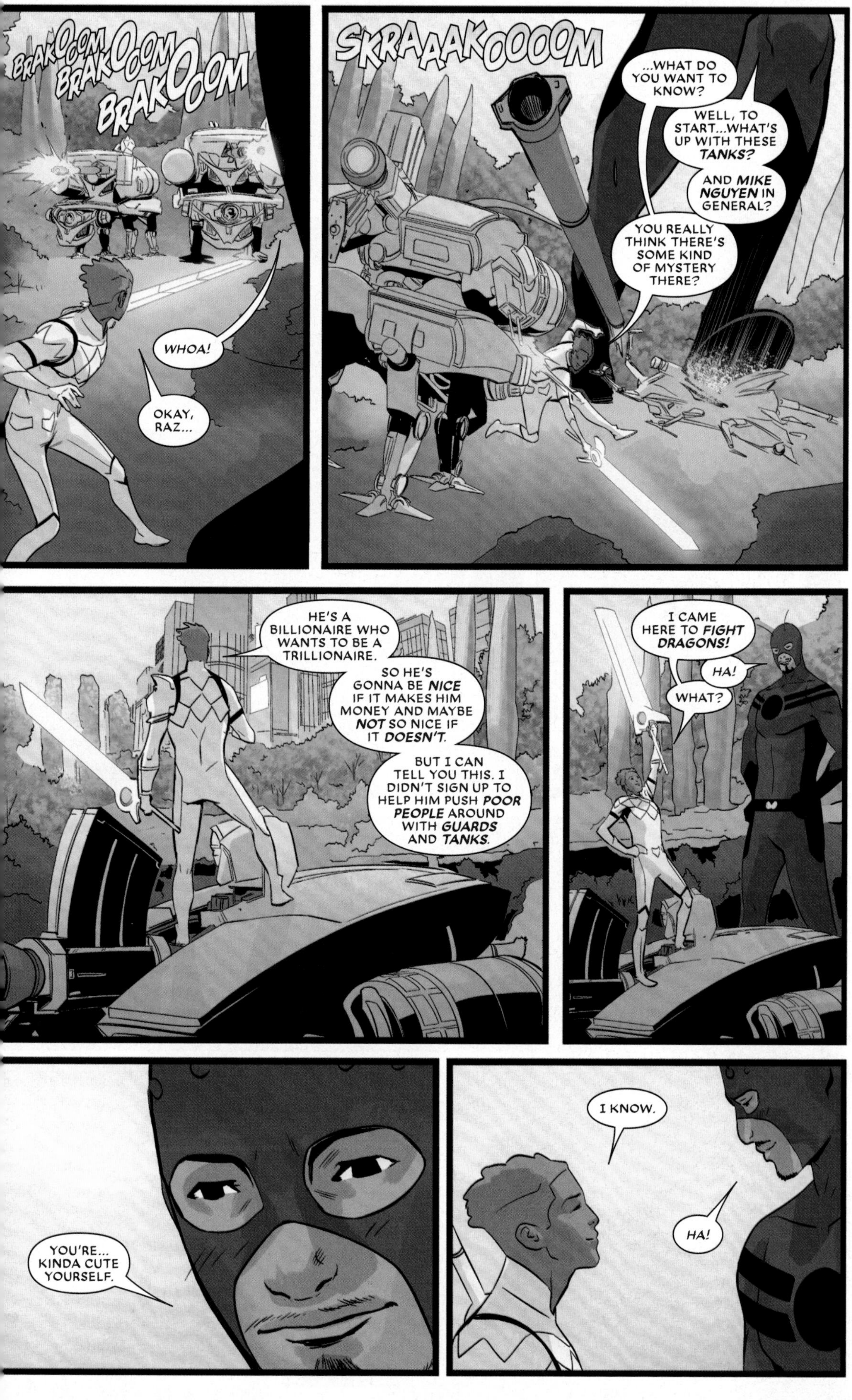
BRAKOOOM BRAKOOOM BRAKOOOM
WHOA!
OKAY, RAZ...
SKRAAAKOOOOM
...WHAT DO YOU WANT TO KNOW?
WELL, TO START...WHAT'S UP WITH THESE TANKS?
AND MIKE NGUYEN IN GENERAL?
YOU REALLY THINK THERE'S SOME KIND OF MYSTERY THERE?
HE'S A BILLIONAIRE WHO WANTS TO BE A TRILLIONAIRE.
SO HE'S GONNA BE NICE IF IT MAKES HIM MONEY AND MAYBE NOT SO NICE IF IT DOESN'T.
BUT I CAN TELL YOU THIS. I DIDN'T SIGN UP TO HELP HIM PUSH POOR PEOPLE AROUND WITH GUARDS AND TANKS.
I CAME HERE TO FIGHT DRAGONS!
HA!
WHAT?
YOU'RE... KINDA CUTE YOURSELF.
I KNOW.
HA!

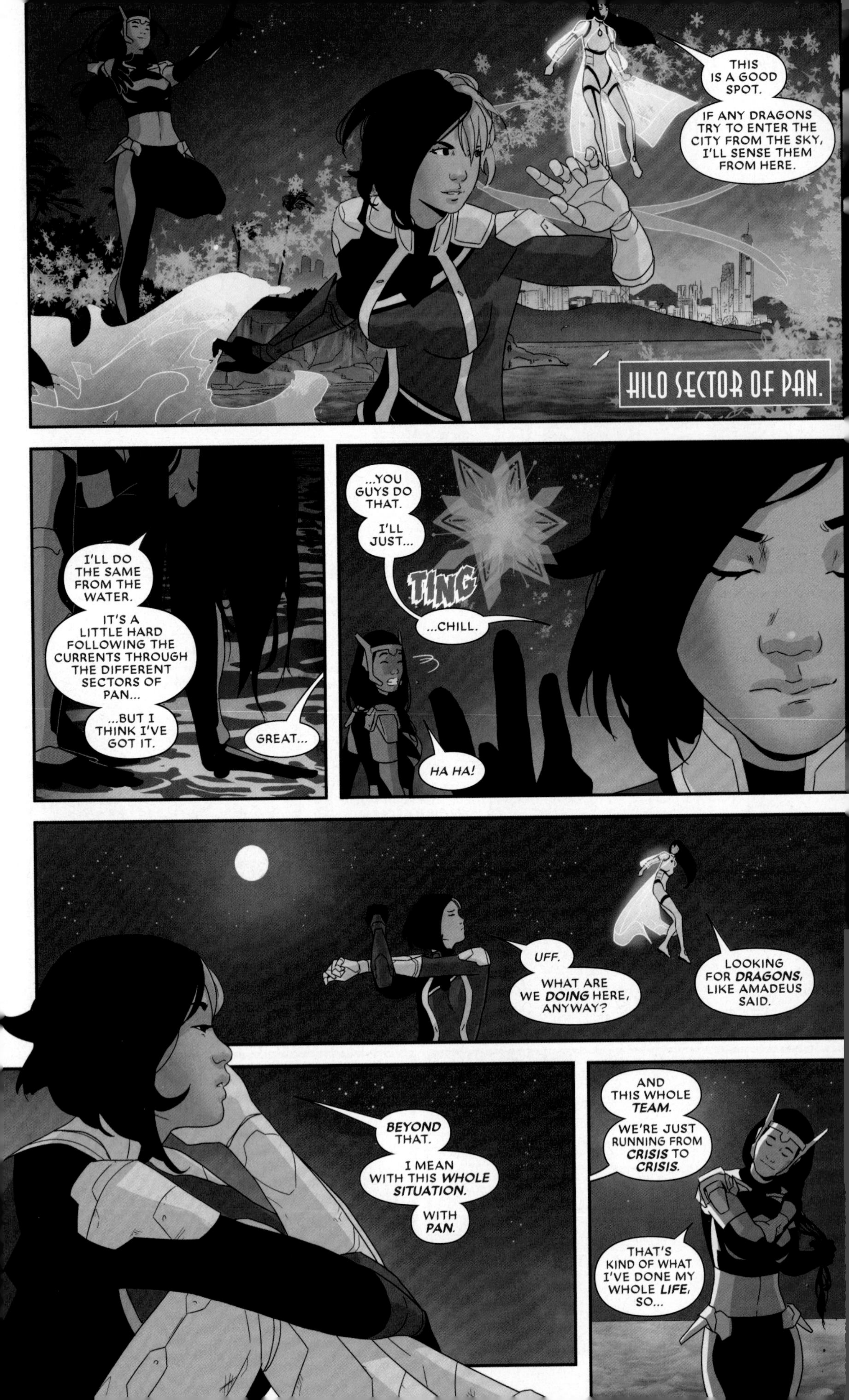

THIS IS A GOOD SPOT.
IF ANY DRAGONS TRY TO ENTER THE CITY FROM THE SKY, I'LL SENSE THEM FROM HERE.
HILO SECTOR OF PAN.
I'LL DO THE SAME FROM THE WATER.
IT'S A LITTLE HARD FOLLOWING THE CURRENTS THROUGH THE DIFFERENT SECTORS OF PAN...
...BUT I THINK I'VE GOT IT.
GREAT...
...YOU GUYS DO THAT.
I'LL JUST...
TING
...CHILL.
HA HA!
UFF.
WHAT ARE WE *DOING* HERE, ANYWAY?
LOOKING FOR *DRAGONS*, LIKE AMADEUS SAID.
BEYOND THAT.
I MEAN WITH THIS *WHOLE SITUATION.*
WITH *PAN*.
AND THIS WHOLE *TEAM*.
WE'RE JUST RUNNING FROM *CRISIS* TO *CRISIS*.
THAT'S KIND OF WHAT I'VE DONE MY WHOLE *LIFE*, SO...

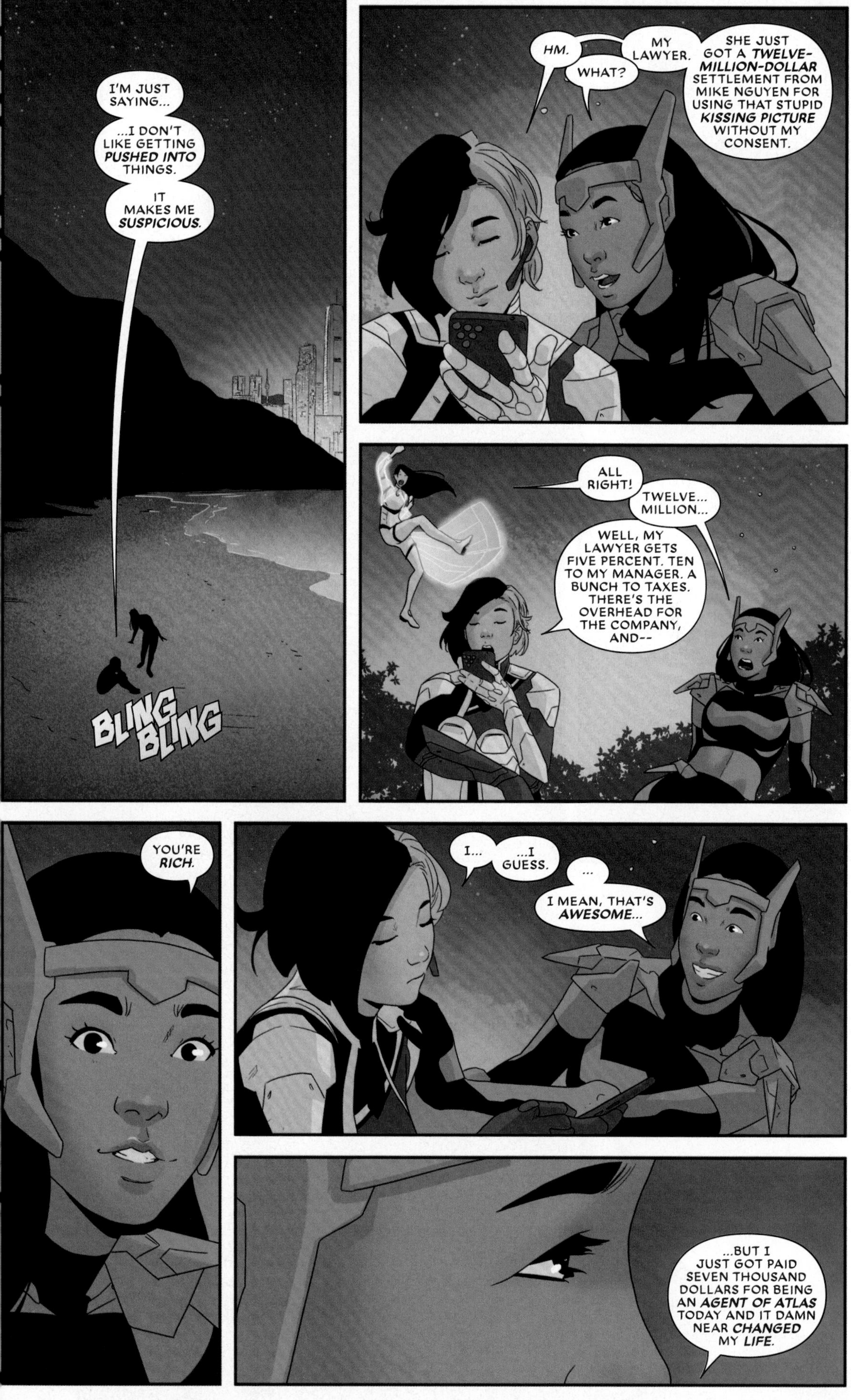
I'M JUST SAYING...
...I DON'T LIKE GETTING PUSHED INTO THINGS.
IT MAKES ME SUSPICIOUS.
BLING BLING
HM.
WHAT?
MY LAWYER.
SHE JUST GOT A TWELVE-MILLION-DOLLAR SETTLEMENT FROM MIKE NGUYEN FOR USING THAT STUPID KISSING PICTURE WITHOUT MY CONSENT.
ALL RIGHT!
TWELVE... MILLION...
WELL, MY LAWYER GETS FIVE PERCENT. TEN TO MY MANAGER. A BUNCH TO TAXES. THERE'S THE OVERHEAD FOR THE COMPANY, AND--
YOU'RE RICH.
I...
...I GUESS.
...
I MEAN, THAT'S AWESOME...
...BUT I JUST GOT PAID SEVEN THOUSAND DOLLARS FOR BEING AN AGENT OF ATLAS TODAY AND IT DAMN NEAR CHANGED MY LIFE.

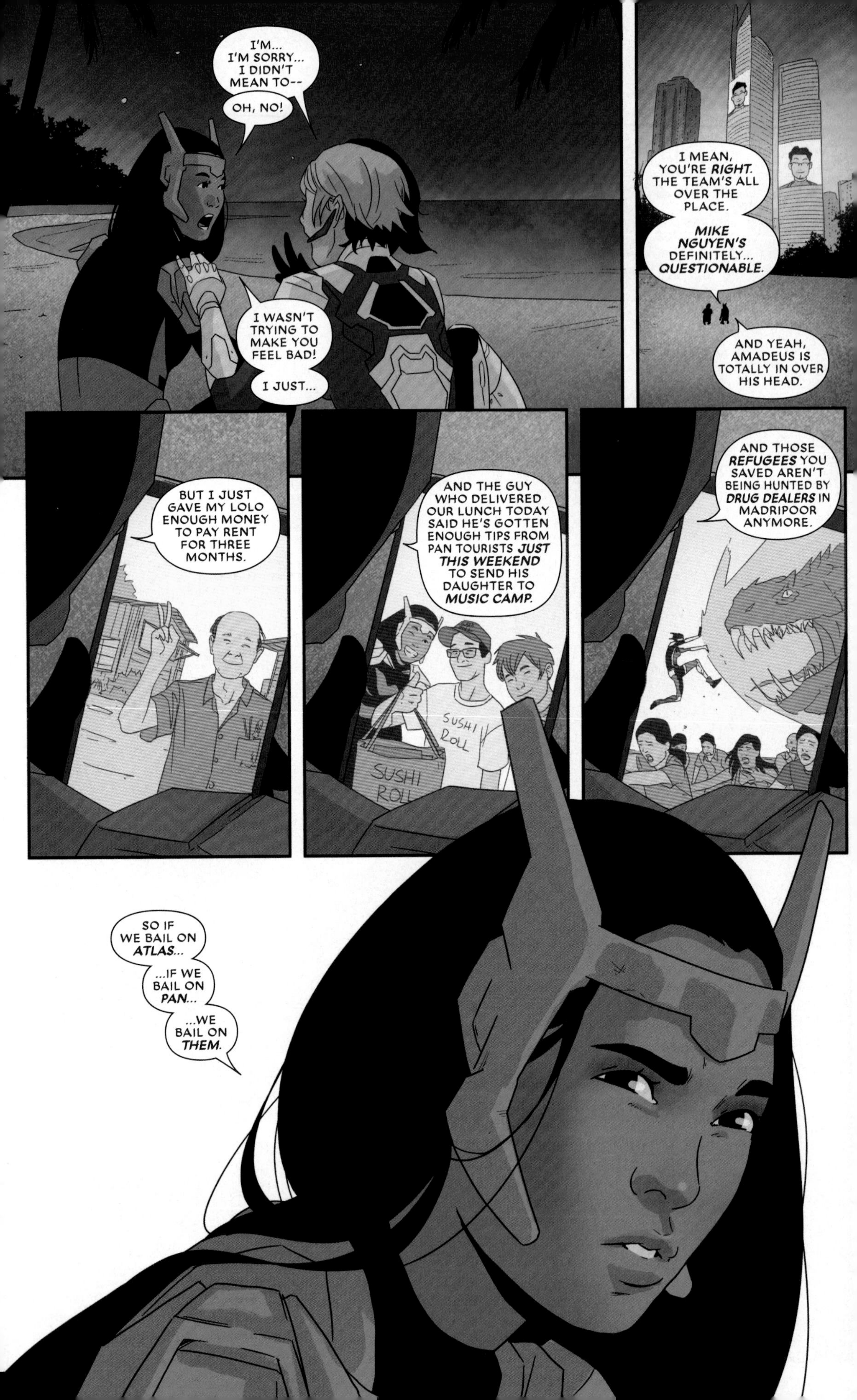
I'M... I'M SORRY... I DIDN'T MEAN TO--
OH, NO!
I WASN'T TRYING TO MAKE YOU FEEL BAD!
I JUST...
I MEAN, YOU'RE RIGHT. THE TEAM'S ALL OVER THE PLACE.
MIKE NGUYEN'S DEFINITELY... QUESTIONABLE.
AND YEAH, AMADEUS IS TOTALLY IN OVER HIS HEAD.
BUT I JUST GAVE MY LOLO ENOUGH MONEY TO PAY RENT FOR THREE MONTHS.
AND THE GUY WHO DELIVERED OUR LUNCH TODAY SAID HE'S GOTTEN ENOUGH TIPS FROM PAN TOURISTS JUST THIS WEEKEND TO SEND HIS DAUGHTER TO MUSIC CAMP.
SUSHI ROLL
SUSHI ROLL
AND THOSE REFUGEES YOU SAVED AREN'T BEING HUNTED BY DRUG DEALERS IN MADRIPOOR ANYMORE.
SO IF WE BAIL ON ATLAS...
...IF WE BAIL ON PAN...
...WE BAIL ON THEM.

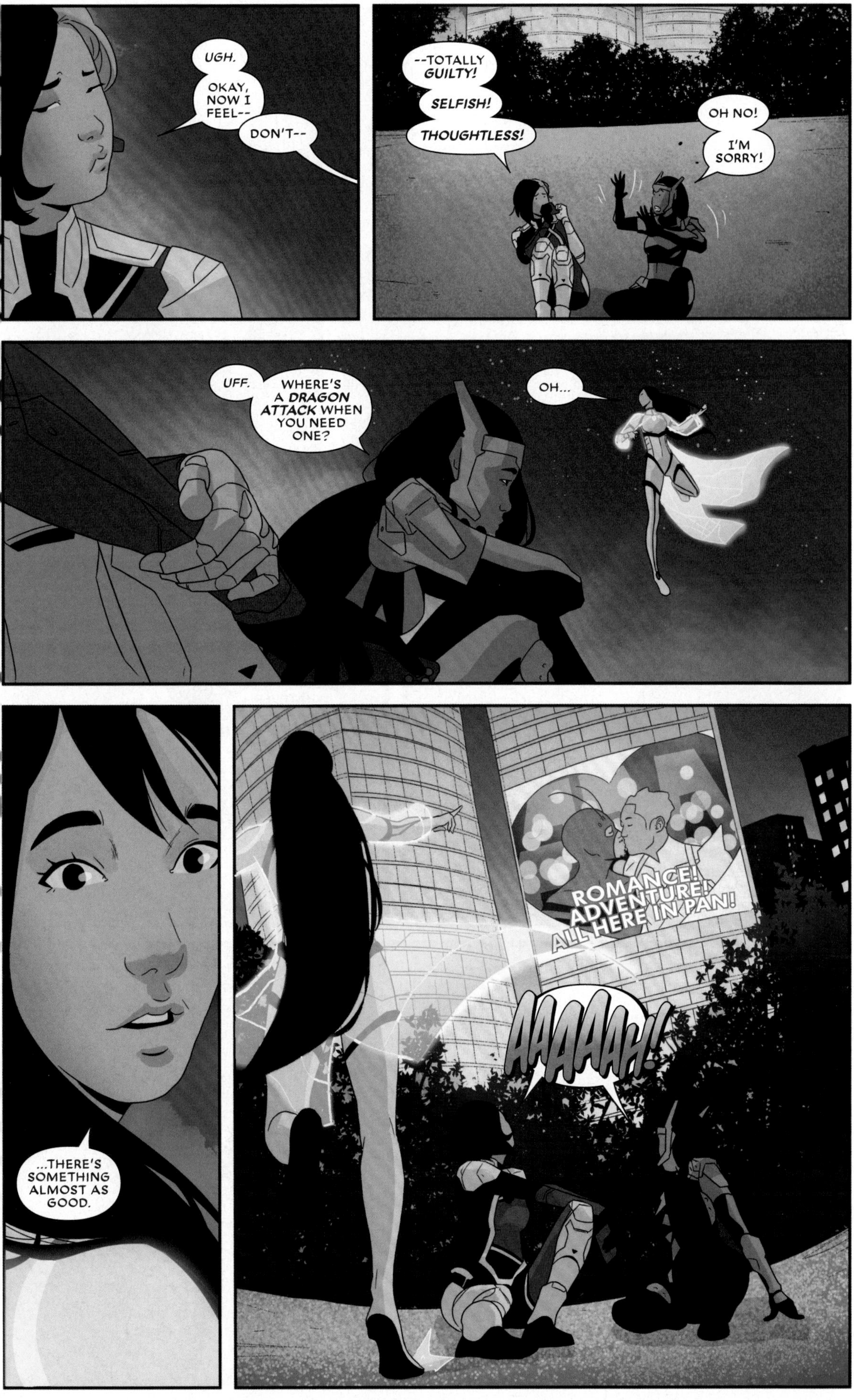
UGH.
OKAY, NOW I FEEL--
DON'T--
--TOTALLY GUILTY!
SELFISH!
THOUGHTLESS!
OH NO!
I'M SORRY!
UFF.
WHERE'S A DRAGON ATTACK WHEN YOU NEED ONE?
OH...
...THERE'S SOMETHING ALMOST AS GOOD.
ROMANCE! ADVENTURE! ALL HERE IN PAN!
AAAAAH!

OH BOY.

WELL. AT LEAST YOU AND *LUNA* ARE OFF THE HOOK.

YYYEAH...

ROMANCE! ADVENTURE! ALL HERE IN PAN!

WHAT WAS *THAT* ALL ABOUT, ANYWAY?

I DUNNO. I MEAN, *NOTHING.* WE JUST HAD A LITTLE MOMENT, I GUESS.

EH, IT NEVER WOULD HAVE WORKED.

WHAT?

LUNA WAS BORN AND RAISED IN *SEOUL.* YOU'RE TOO *AMERICAN.*

WHAT?

YOU SPEAK KOREAN LIKE A *LITTLE KID.*

HE SPEAKS *ENGLISH* THE SAME WAY.

WHATEVER!

LOOK, WE'RE HERE.

THE *HEART OF PAN.*

WHAT'S *KOREAN INTELLIGENCE* GOT FOR US, WHITE FOX?

ROMANCE! ADVENTURE! ALL HERE IN PAN!

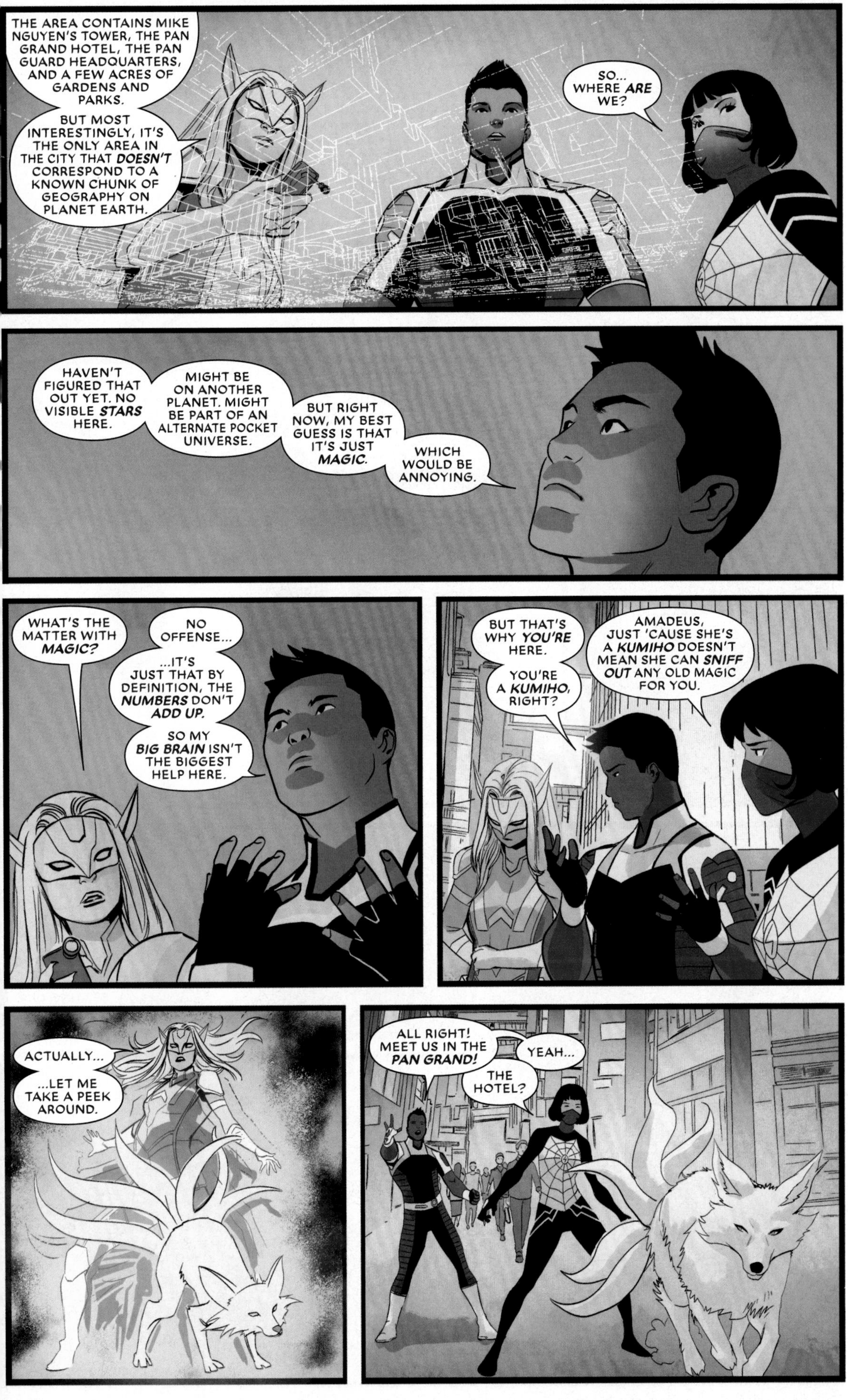
THE AREA CONTAINS MIKE NGUYEN'S TOWER, THE PAN GRAND HOTEL, THE PAN GUARD HEADQUARTERS, AND A FEW ACRES OF GARDENS AND PARKS.
BUT MOST INTERESTINGLY, IT'S THE ONLY AREA IN THE CITY THAT DOESN'T CORRESPOND TO A KNOWN CHUNK OF GEOGRAPHY ON PLANET EARTH.
SO... WHERE ARE WE?
HAVEN'T FIGURED THAT OUT YET. NO VISIBLE STARS HERE.
MIGHT BE ON ANOTHER PLANET. MIGHT BE PART OF AN ALTERNATE POCKET UNIVERSE.
BUT RIGHT NOW, MY BEST GUESS IS THAT IT'S JUST MAGIC.
WHICH WOULD BE ANNOYING.
WHAT'S THE MATTER WITH MAGIC?
NO OFFENSE...
...IT'S JUST THAT BY DEFINITION, THE NUMBERS DON'T ADD UP.
SO MY BIG BRAIN ISN'T THE BIGGEST HELP HERE.
BUT THAT'S WHY YOU'RE HERE.
YOU'RE A KUMIHO, RIGHT?
AMADEUS, JUST 'CAUSE SHE'S A KUMIHO DOESN'T MEAN SHE CAN SNIFF OUT ANY OLD MAGIC FOR YOU.
ACTUALLY...
...LET ME TAKE A PEEK AROUND.
ALL RIGHT! MEET US IN THE PAN GRAND!
YEAH...
THE HOTEL?

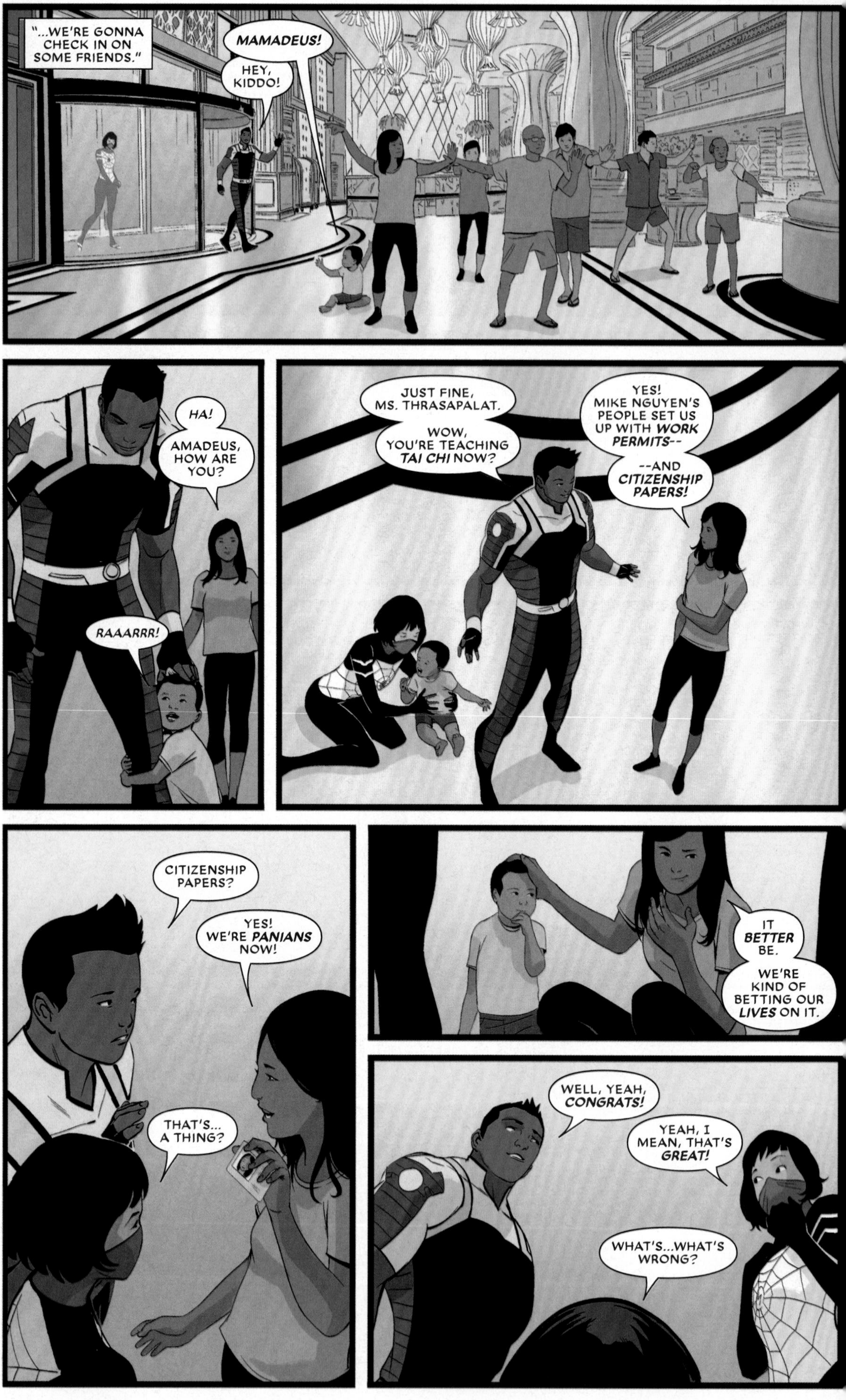
"...WE'RE GONNA CHECK IN ON SOME FRIENDS."
MAMADEUS!
HEY, KIDDO!
HA!
AMADEUS, HOW ARE YOU?
RAAARRR!
JUST FINE, MS. THRASAPALAT.
WOW, YOU'RE TEACHING TAI CHI NOW?
YES! MIKE NGUYEN'S PEOPLE SET US UP WITH WORK PERMITS--
--AND CITIZENSHIP PAPERS!
CITIZENSHIP PAPERS?
YES! WE'RE PANIANS NOW!
THAT'S... A THING?
IT BETTER BE.
WE'RE KIND OF BETTING OUR LIVES ON IT.
WELL, YEAH, CONGRATS!
YEAH, I MEAN, THAT'S GREAT!
WHAT'S...WHAT'S WRONG?

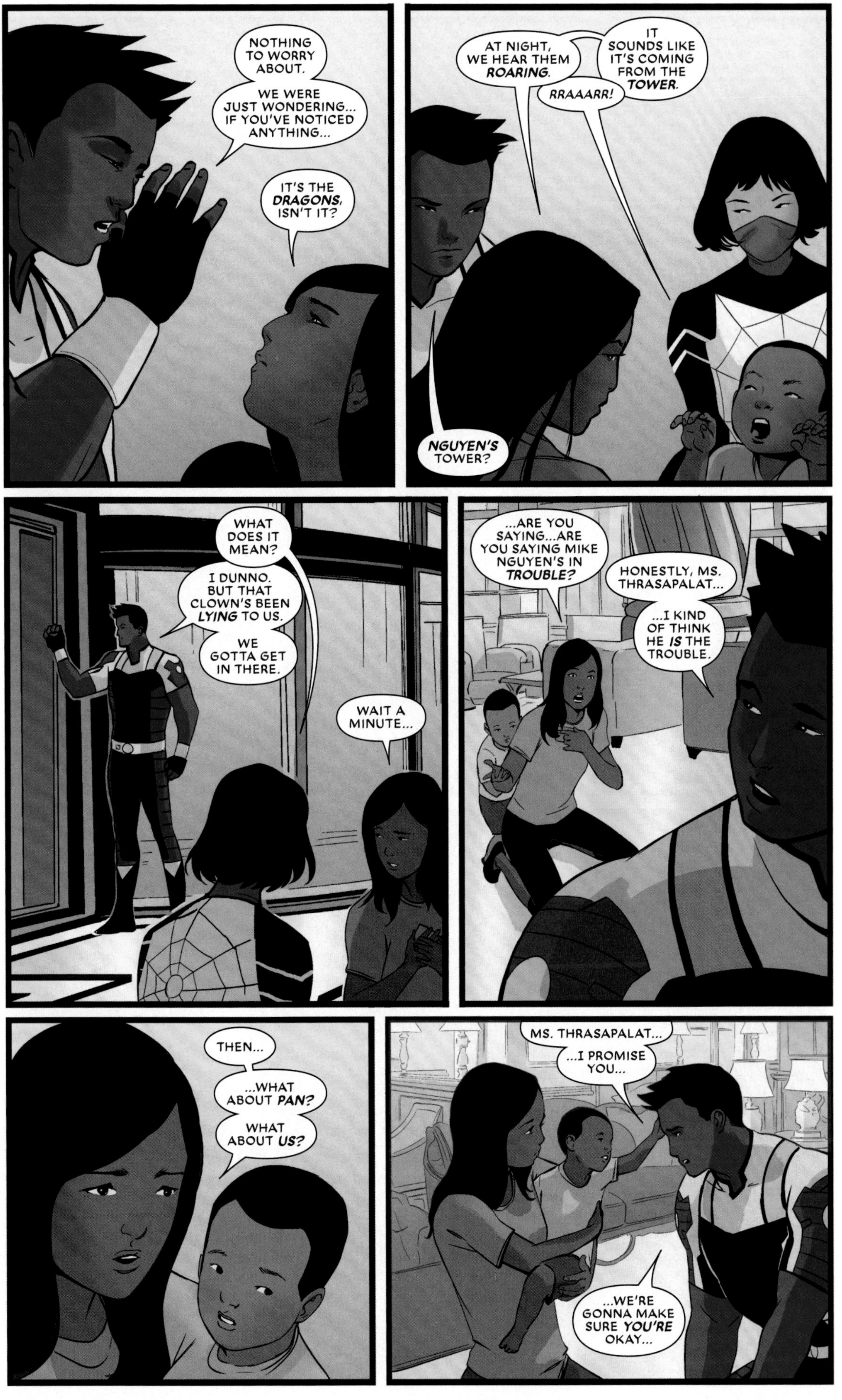
NOTHING TO WORRY ABOUT.
WE WERE JUST WONDERING... IF YOU'VE NOTICED ANYTHING...
IT'S THE *DRAGONS*, ISN'T IT?
AT NIGHT, WE HEAR THEM *ROARING*.
IT SOUNDS LIKE IT'S COMING FROM THE *TOWER*.
RRAAARR!
NGUYEN'S TOWER?
WHAT DOES IT MEAN?
I DUNNO. BUT THAT CLOWN'S BEEN *LYING* TO US.
WE GOTTA GET IN THERE.
WAIT A MINUTE...
...ARE YOU SAYING...ARE YOU SAYING MIKE NGUYEN'S IN *TROUBLE?*
HONESTLY, MS. THRASAPALAT...
...I KIND OF THINK HE *IS* THE TROUBLE.
THEN...
...WHAT ABOUT *PAN?*
WHAT ABOUT *US?*
MS. THRASAPALAT...
...I PROMISE YOU...
...WE'RE GONNA MAKE SURE *YOU'RE* OKAY...

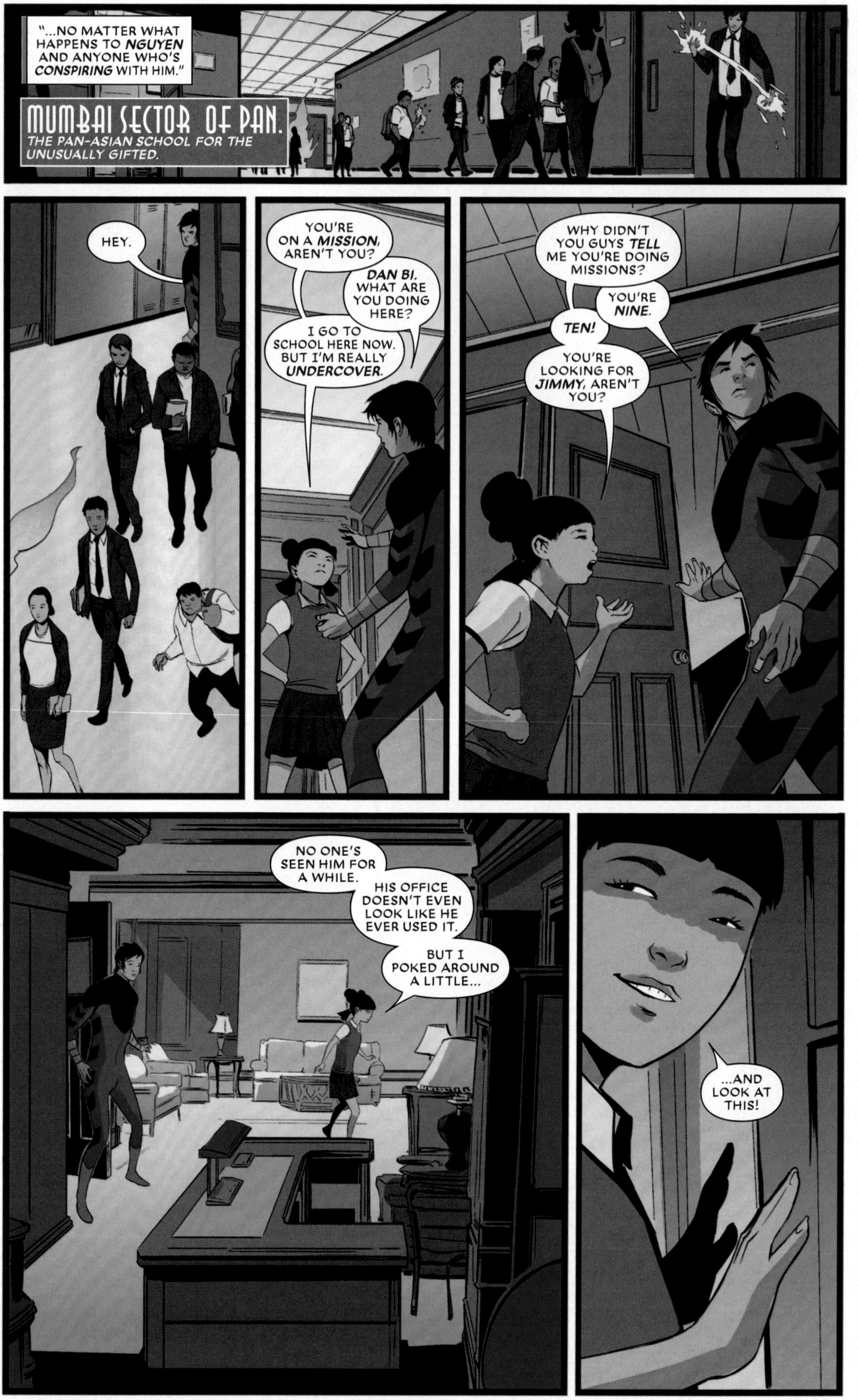

"...NO MATTER WHAT HAPPENS TO NGUYEN AND ANYONE WHO'S CONSPIRING WITH HIM."
MUMBAI SECTOR OF PAN.
THE PAN-ASIAN SCHOOL FOR THE UNUSUALLY GIFTED.
HEY.
YOU'RE ON A MISSION, AREN'T YOU?
DAN BI. WHAT ARE YOU DOING HERE?
I GO TO SCHOOL HERE NOW. BUT I'M REALLY UNDERCOVER.
WHY DIDN'T YOU GUYS TELL ME YOU'RE DOING MISSIONS?
YOU'RE NINE.
TEN!
YOU'RE LOOKING FOR JIMMY, AREN'T YOU?
NO ONE'S SEEN HIM FOR A WHILE.
HIS OFFICE DOESN'T EVEN LOOK LIKE HE EVER USED IT.
BUT I POKED AROUND A LITTLE...
...AND LOOK AT THIS!

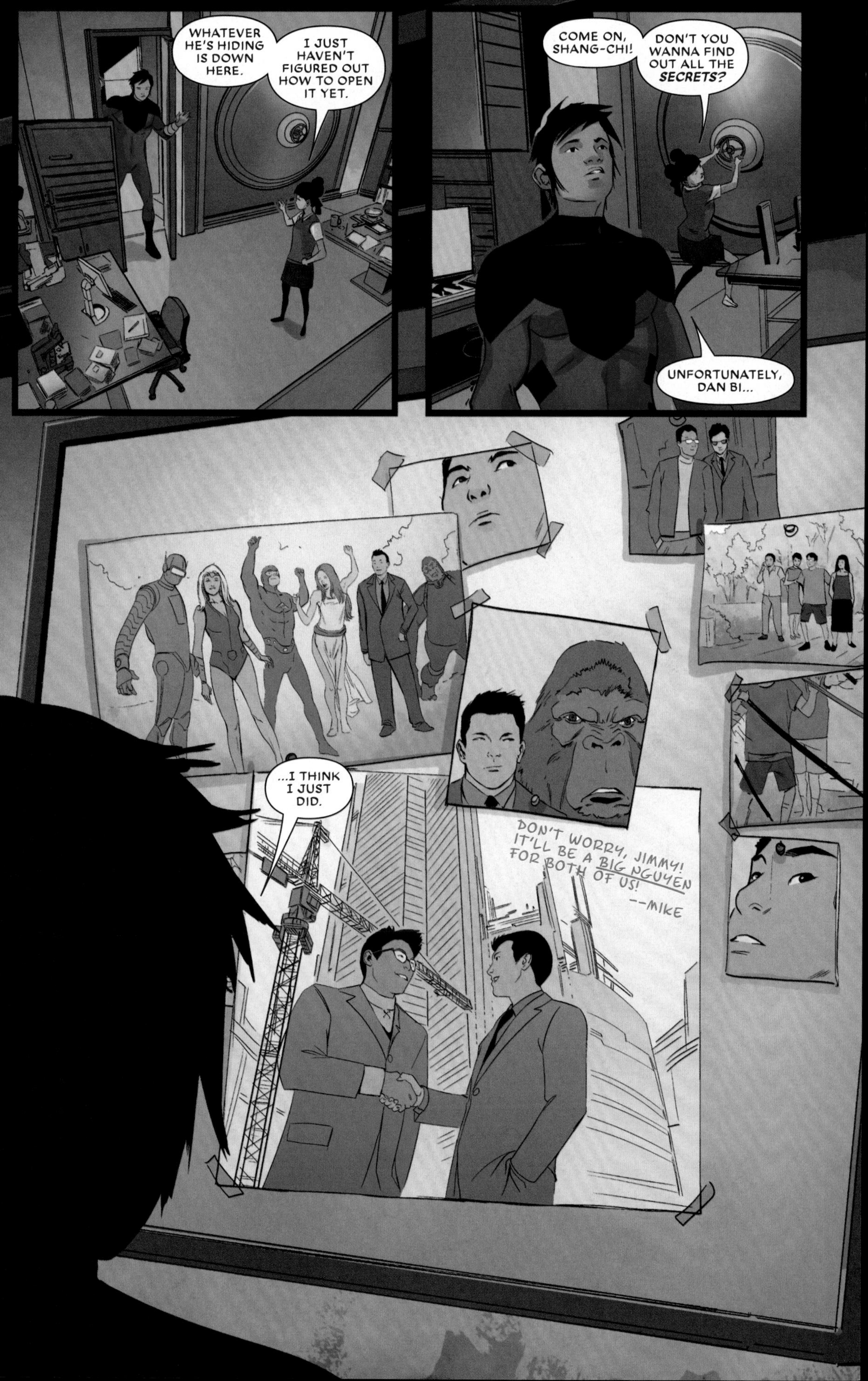
WHATEVER HE'S HIDING IS DOWN HERE.
I JUST HAVEN'T FIGURED OUT HOW TO OPEN IT YET.
COME ON, SHANG-CHI!
DON'T YOU WANNA FIND OUT ALL THE SECRETS?
UNFORTUNATELY, DAN BI...
...I THINK I JUST DID.
DON'T WORRY, JIMMY! IT'LL BE A BIG NGUYEN FOR BOTH OF US!
--MIKE

FIVE

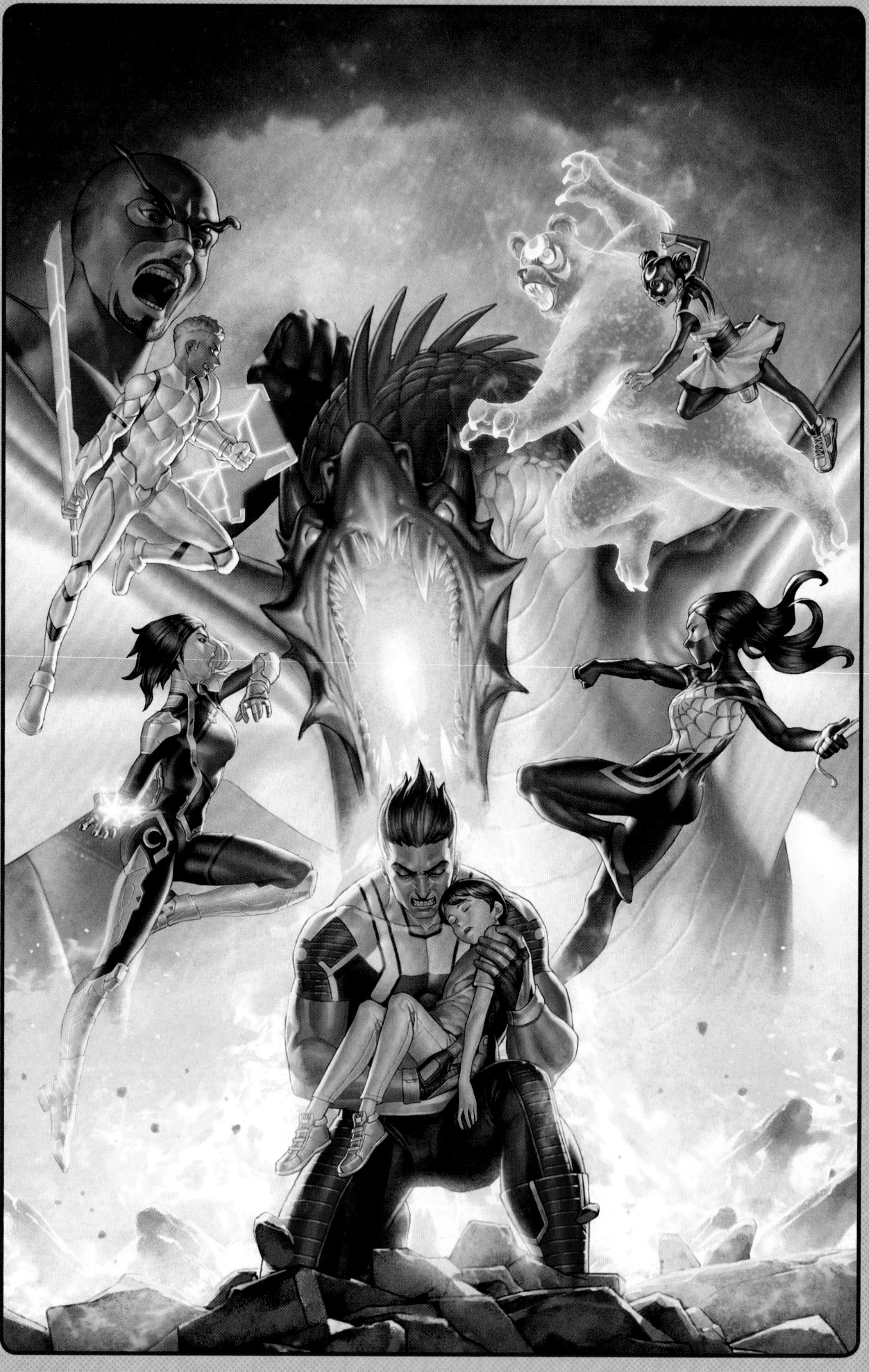

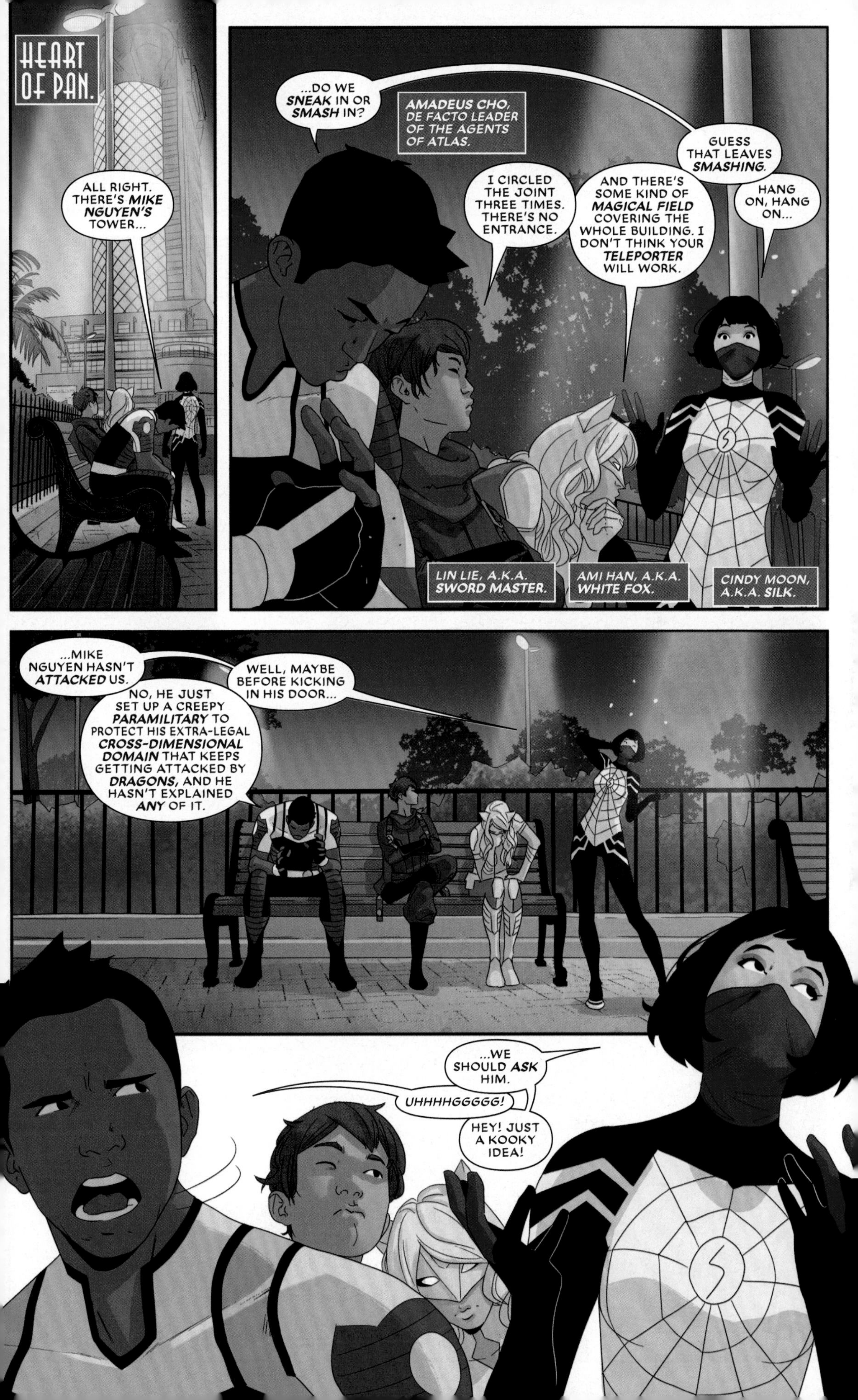
HEART OF PAN.
ALL RIGHT. THERE'S MIKE NGUYEN'S TOWER...
...DO WE SNEAK IN OR SMASH IN?
AMADEUS CHO, DE FACTO LEADER OF THE AGENTS OF ATLAS.
I CIRCLED THE JOINT THREE TIMES. THERE'S NO ENTRANCE.
AND THERE'S SOME KIND OF MAGICAL FIELD COVERING THE WHOLE BUILDING. I DON'T THINK YOUR TELEPORTER WILL WORK.
GUESS THAT LEAVES SMASHING.
HANG ON, HANG ON...
LIN LIE, A.K.A. SWORD MASTER.
AMI HAN, A.K.A. WHITE FOX.
CINDY MOON, A.K.A. SILK.
...MIKE NGUYEN HASN'T ATTACKED US.
WELL, MAYBE BEFORE KICKING IN HIS DOOR...
NO, HE JUST SET UP A CREEPY PARAMILITARY TO PROTECT HIS EXTRA-LEGAL CROSS-DIMENSIONAL DOMAIN THAT KEEPS GETTING ATTACKED BY DRAGONS, AND HE HASN'T EXPLAINED ANY OF IT.
...WE SHOULD ASK HIM.
UHHHHGGGGG!
HEY! JUST A KOOKY IDEA!

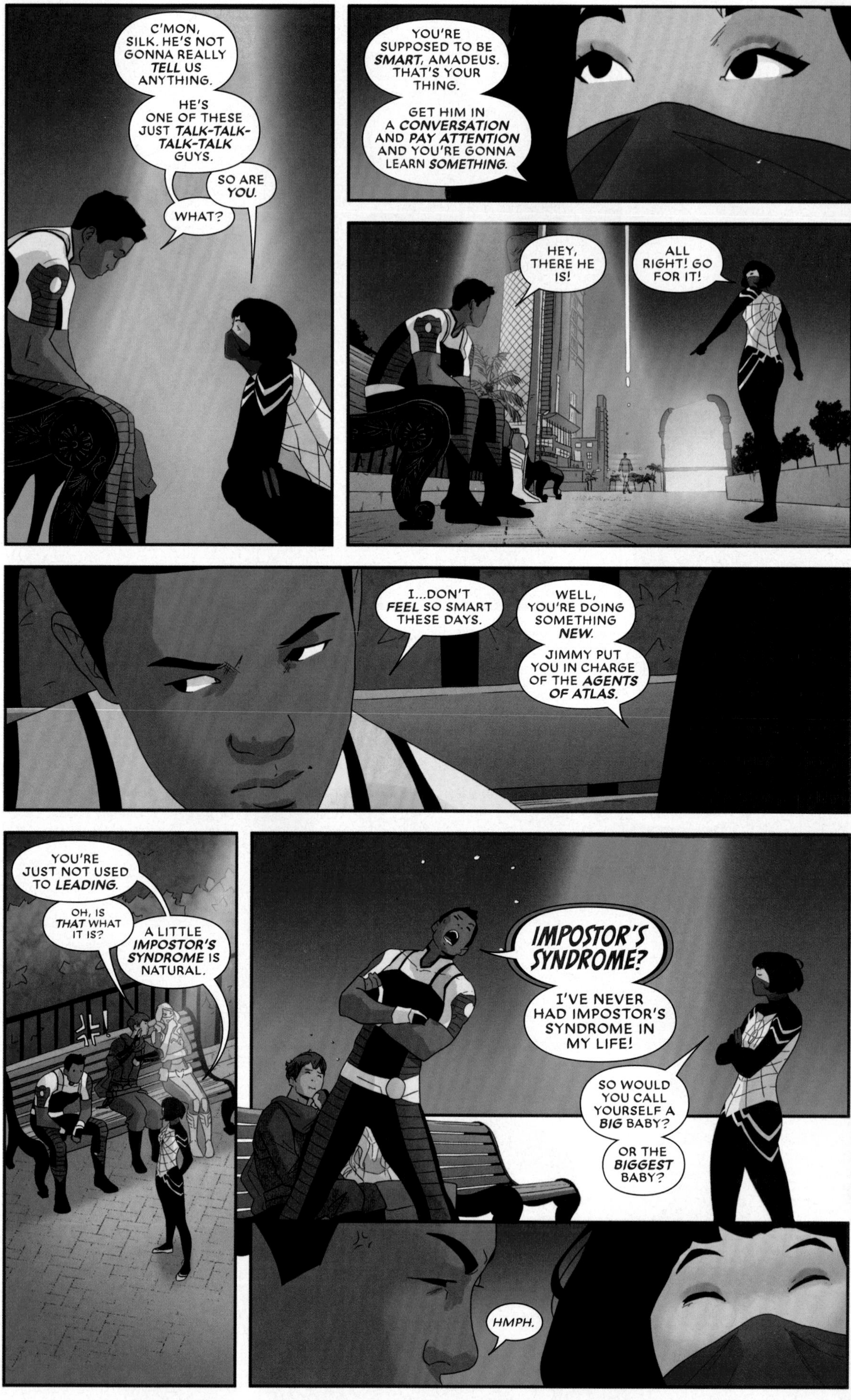
C'MON, SILK. HE'S NOT GONNA REALLY TELL US ANYTHING.
HE'S ONE OF THESE JUST TALK-TALK-TALK-TALK GUYS.
SO ARE YOU.
WHAT?
YOU'RE SUPPOSED TO BE SMART, AMADEUS. THAT'S YOUR THING.
GET HIM IN A CONVERSATION AND PAY ATTENTION AND YOU'RE GONNA LEARN SOMETHING.
HEY, THERE HE IS!
ALL RIGHT! GO FOR IT!
I...DON'T FEEL SO SMART THESE DAYS.
WELL, YOU'RE DOING SOMETHING NEW.
JIMMY PUT YOU IN CHARGE OF THE AGENTS OF ATLAS.
YOU'RE JUST NOT USED TO LEADING.
OH, IS THAT WHAT IT IS?
A LITTLE IMPOSTOR'S SYNDROME IS NATURAL.
IMPOSTOR'S SYNDROME?
I'VE NEVER HAD IMPOSTOR'S SYNDROME IN MY LIFE!
SO WOULD YOU CALL YOURSELF A BIG BABY?
OR THE BIGGEST BABY?
HMPH.

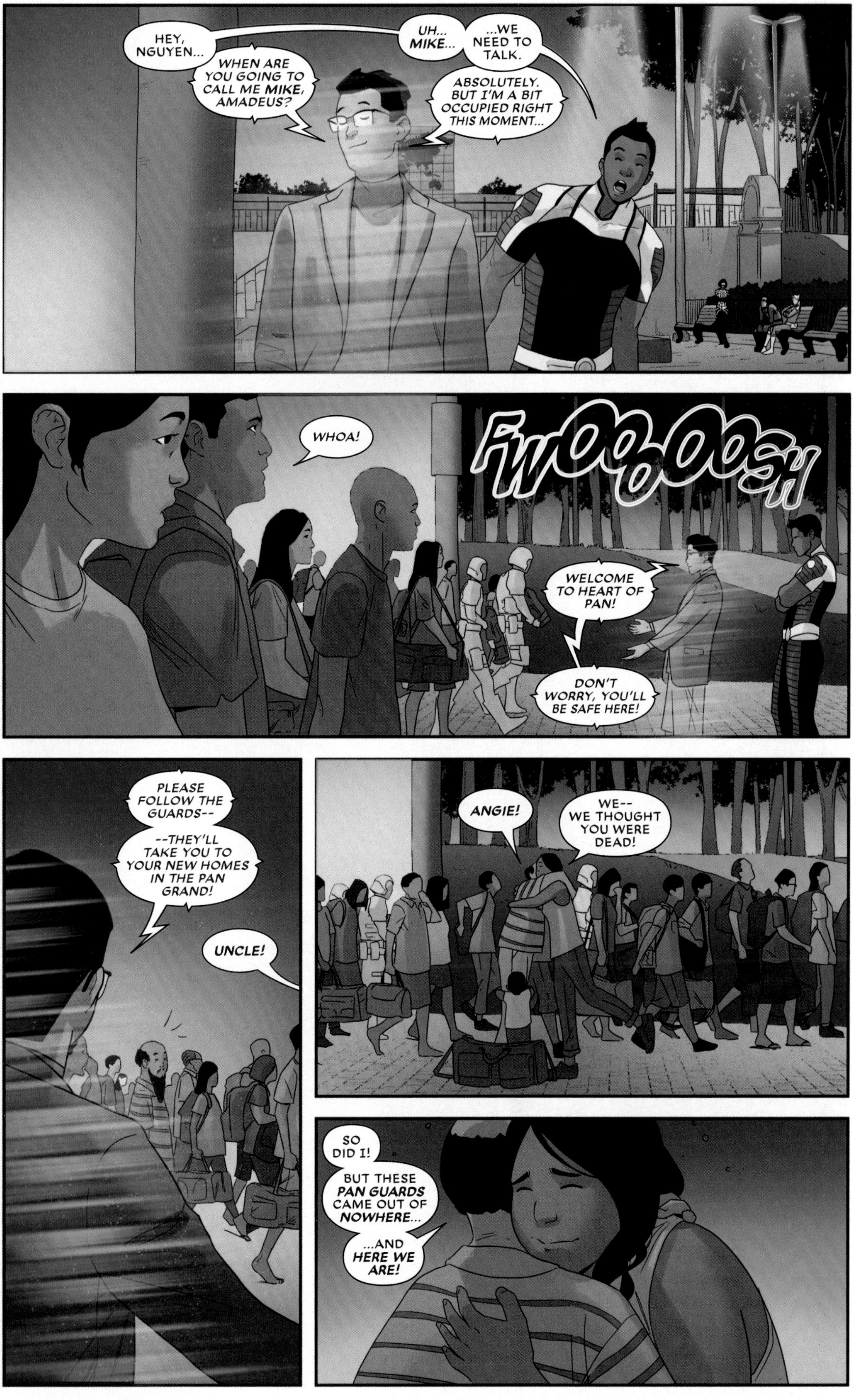
HEY, NGUYEN...
WHEN ARE YOU GOING TO CALL ME MIKE, AMADEUS?
UH... MIKE...
...WE NEED TO TALK.
ABSOLUTELY. BUT I'M A BIT OCCUPIED RIGHT THIS MOMENT...
WHOA!
FWOOOOOOSH
WELCOME TO HEART OF PAN!
DON'T WORRY, YOU'LL BE SAFE HERE!
PLEASE FOLLOW THE GUARDS--
--THEY'LL TAKE YOU TO YOUR NEW HOMES IN THE PAN GRAND!
UNCLE!
ANGIE!
WE-- WE THOUGHT YOU WERE DEAD!
SO DID I!
BUT THESE PAN GUARDS CAME OUT OF NOWHERE...
...AND HERE WE ARE!

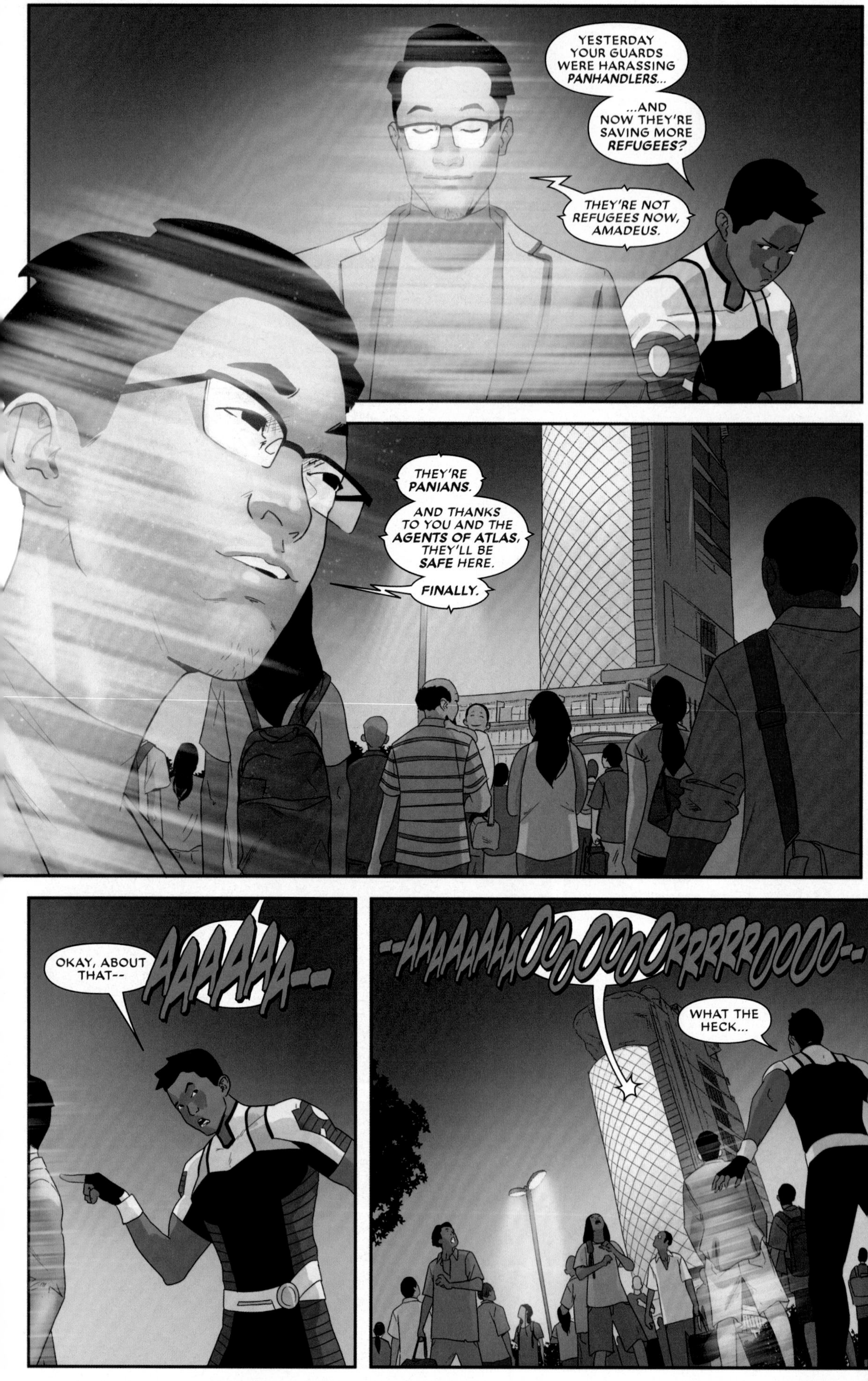
YESTERDAY YOUR GUARDS WERE HARASSING PANHANDLERS...
...AND NOW THEY'RE SAVING MORE REFUGEES?
THEY'RE NOT REFUGEES NOW, AMADEUS.
THEY'RE PANIANS.
AND THANKS TO YOU AND THE AGENTS OF ATLAS, THEY'LL BE SAFE HERE.
FINALLY.
OKAY, ABOUT THAT--
AAAAAA--
--AAAAAAAAOOOOOOOORRRRROOOOO--
WHAT THE HECK...

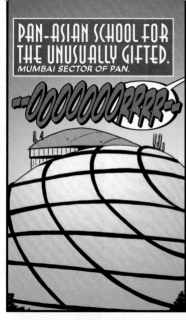

PAN-ASIAN SCHOOL FOR
THE UNUSUALLY GIFTED.
MUMBAI SECTOR OF PAN.

-OOOOOOOORRRR-

-RRRR-
-OOOOOOOOI!

WHOA.

HM.

DAN BI, A.K.A.
CRESCENT.

SHANG-CHI,
MASTER OF
KUNG FU.

CHO, THIS
IS SHANG-CHI.
WHAT'S GOING
ON?

GREAT
QUESTION.

NGUYEN!
WHAT'S GOING
ON?

THAT'S
SOME WIND,
HUH?

DON'T
WORRY, I
DON'T.

LISTEN,
I FOUND
SOMETHING
OVER HERE.

JIMMY
WOO AND
NGUYEN HAVE
BEEN WORKING
TOGETHER.

WHAT?

JIMMY...
MIGHT HAVE
HELPED BUILD
PAN.

DANG IT.
ALL RIGHT, YOU
TRACK DOWN
JIMMY...

YOU'RE
WITH NGUYEN?
DON'T TRUST
HIM!

I'M ON
NGUYEN--

WE'LL
CATCH UP SOON,
AMADEUS!

HEY,
WAIT!

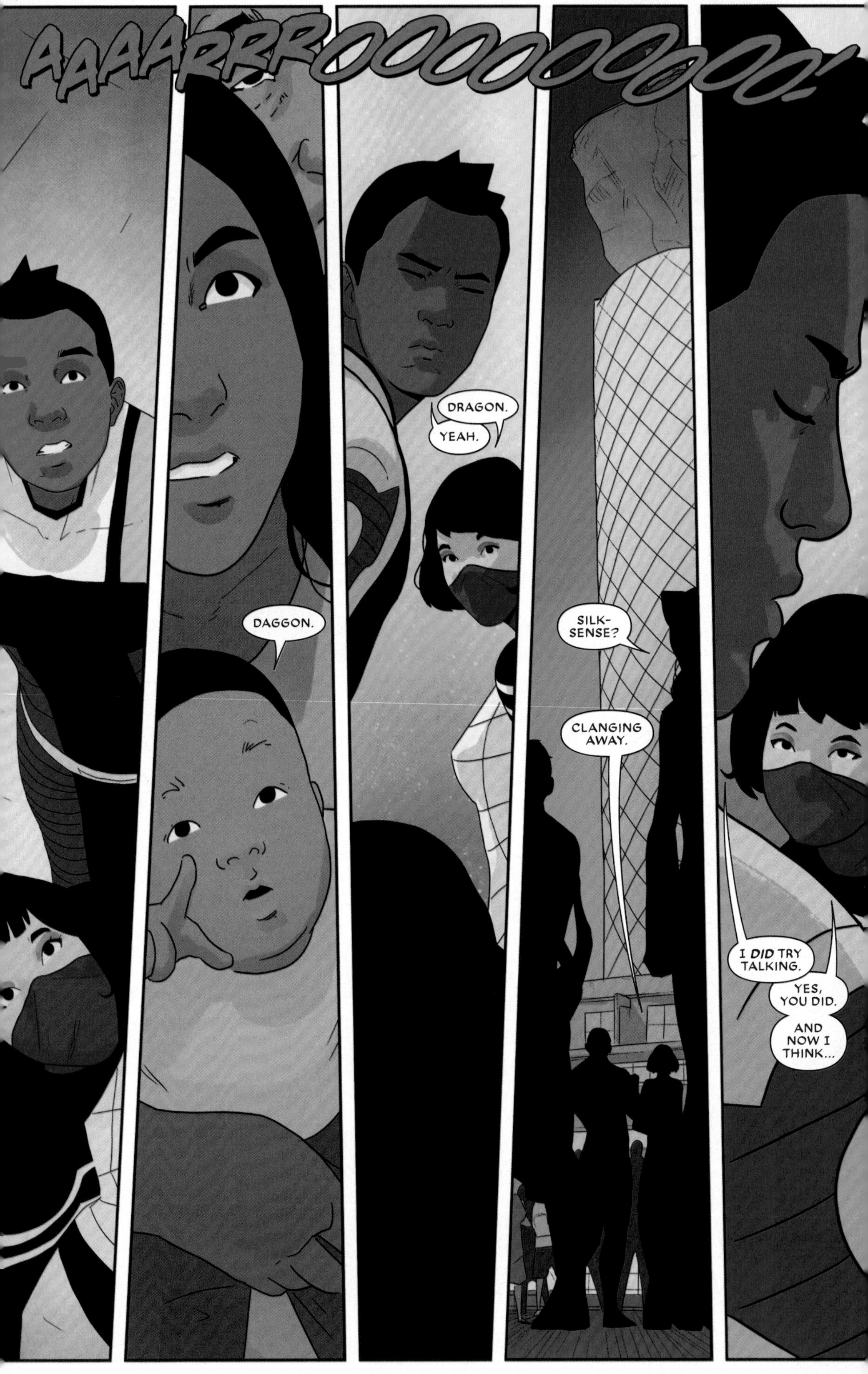

AAAARRROOOOOOOOOO!
DAGGON.
DRAGON.
YEAH.
SILK-SENSE?
CLANGING AWAY.
I *DID* TRY TALKING.
YES, YOU DID.
AND NOW I THINK...

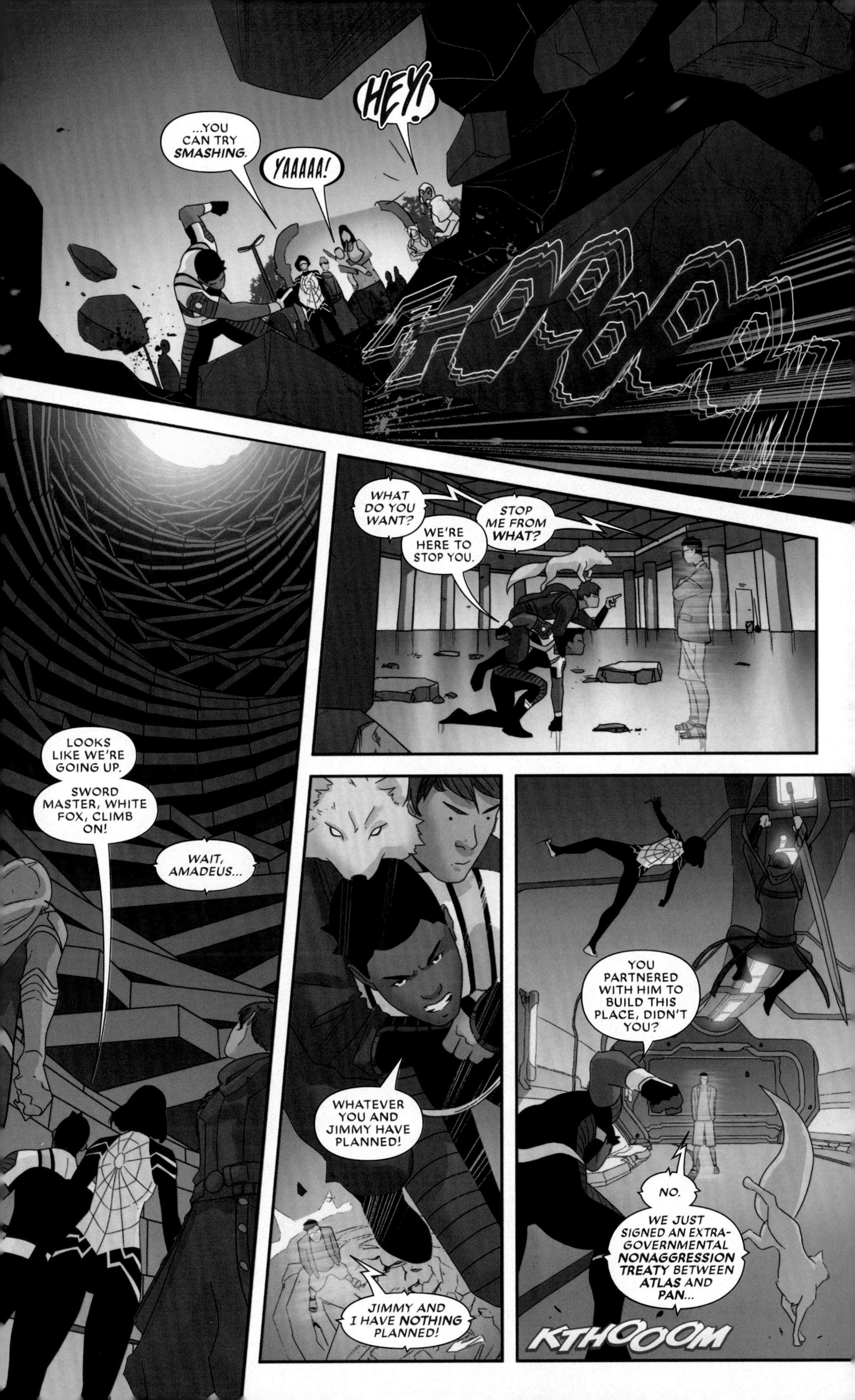
...YOU CAN TRY SMASHING.
YAAAAA!
HEY!
LOOKS LIKE WE'RE GOING UP.
SWORD MASTER, WHITE FOX, CLIMB ON!
WAIT, AMADEUS...
WHAT DO YOU WANT?
WE'RE HERE TO STOP YOU.
STOP ME FROM WHAT?
WHATEVER YOU AND JIMMY HAVE PLANNED!
JIMMY AND I HAVE NOTHING PLANNED!
YOU PARTNERED WITH HIM TO BUILD THIS PLACE, DIDN'T YOU?
NO.
WE JUST SIGNED AN EXTRA-GOVERNMENTAL NONAGGRESSION TREATY BETWEEN ATLAS AND PAN...
KTHOOOOM

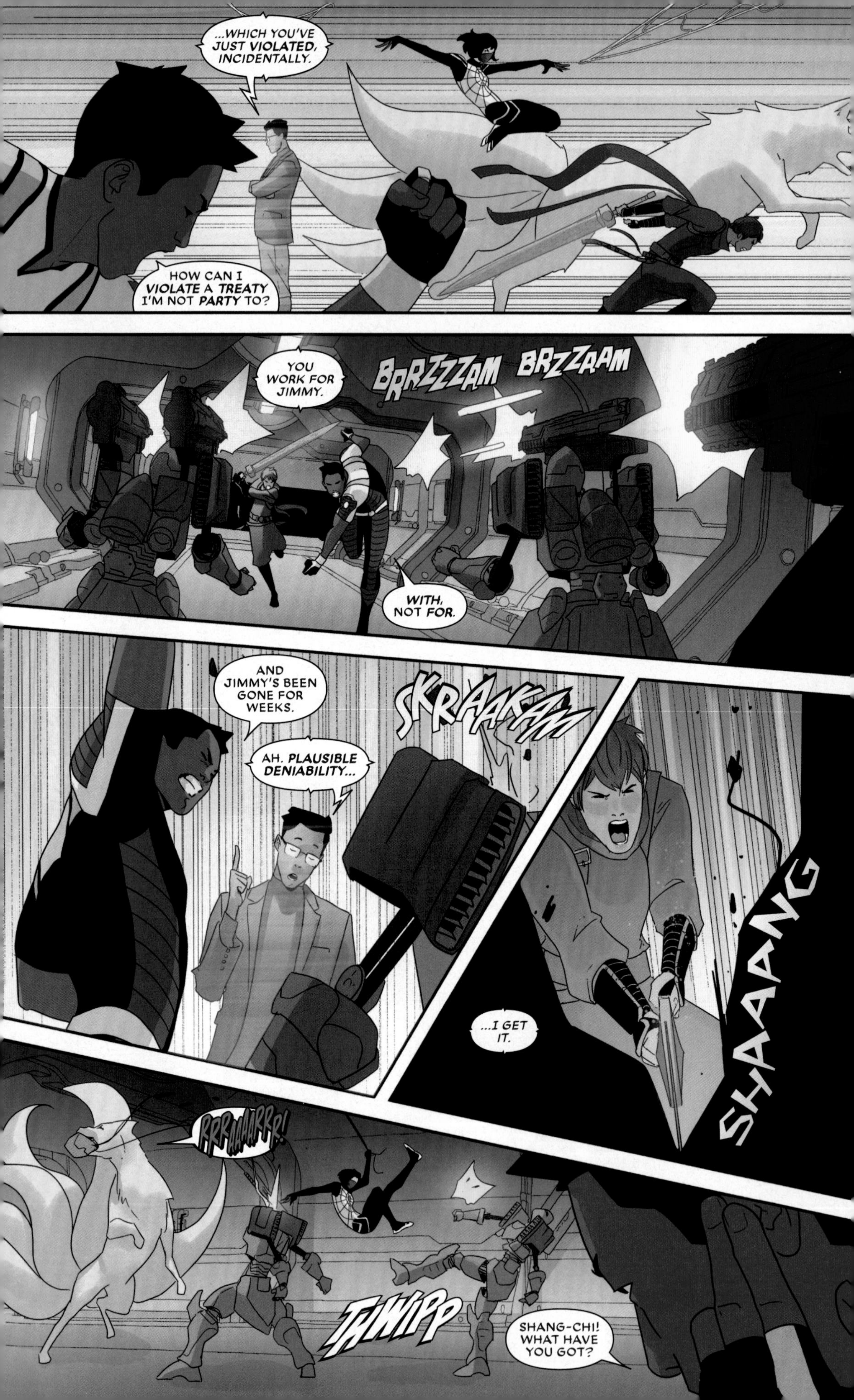
...WHICH YOU'VE JUST VIOLATED, INCIDENTALLY.
HOW CAN I VIOLATE A TREATY I'M NOT PARTY TO?
YOU WORK FOR JIMMY.
BRRZZZAM BRZZAAM
WITH, NOT FOR.
AND JIMMY'S BEEN GONE FOR WEEKS.
SKRAAKAM
AH. PLAUSIBLE DENIABILITY...
...I GET IT.
SHAAANG
RRRAAAARRR!
THWIPP
SHANG-CHI! WHAT HAVE YOU GOT?

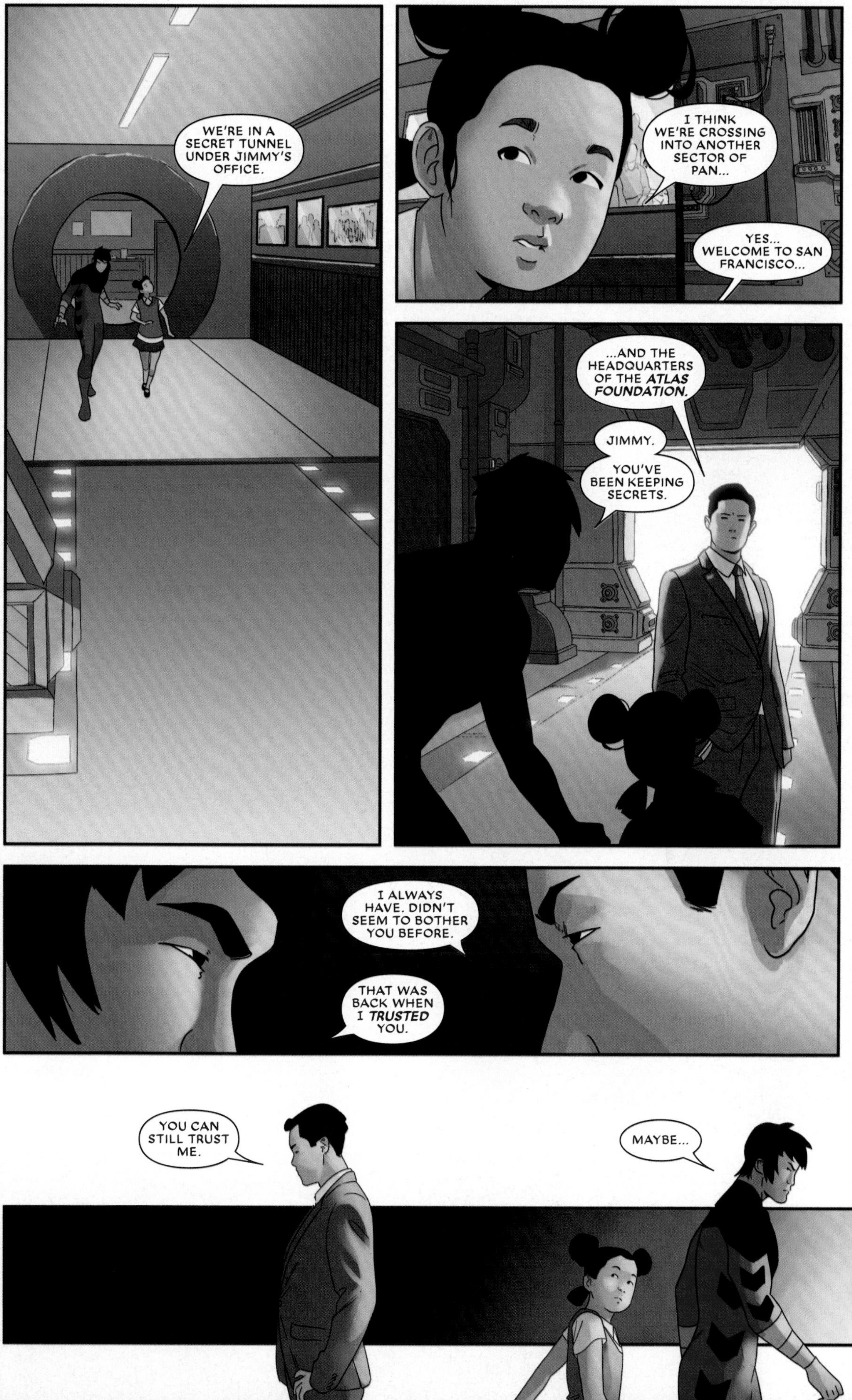
WE'RE IN A SECRET TUNNEL UNDER JIMMY'S OFFICE.
I THINK WE'RE CROSSING INTO ANOTHER SECTOR OF PAN...
YES... WELCOME TO SAN FRANCISCO...
...AND THE HEADQUARTERS OF THE ATLAS FOUNDATION.
JIMMY.
YOU'VE BEEN KEEPING SECRETS.
I ALWAYS HAVE. DIDN'T SEEM TO BOTHER YOU BEFORE.
THAT WAS BACK WHEN I TRUSTED YOU.
YOU CAN STILL TRUST ME.
MAYBE...

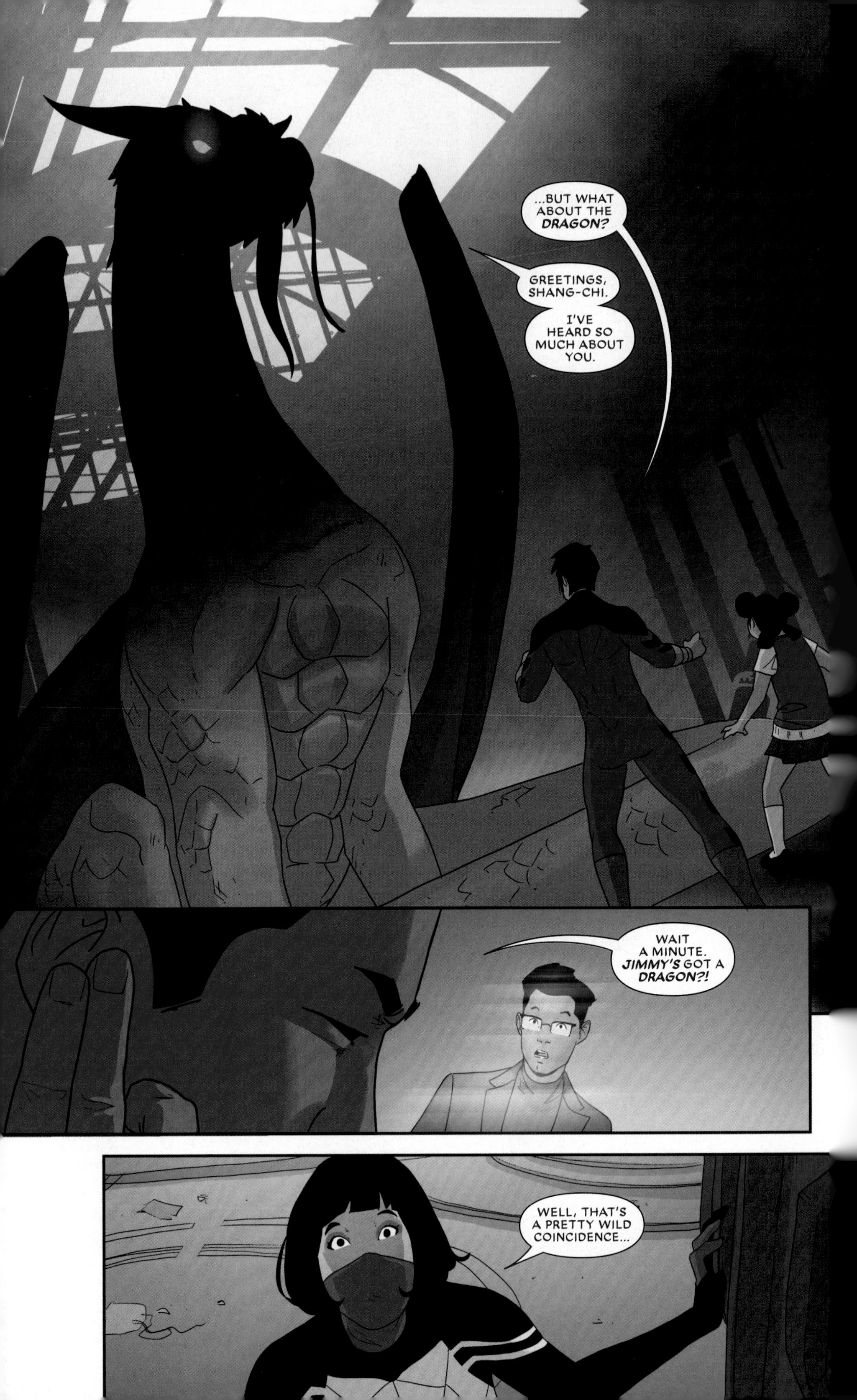
...BUT WHAT ABOUT THE **DRAGON?**
GREETINGS, SHANG-CHI.
I'VE HEARD SO MUCH ABOUT YOU.
WAIT A MINUTE. **JIMMY'S** GOT A **DRAGON?!**
WELL, THAT'S A PRETTY WILD COINCIDENCE...

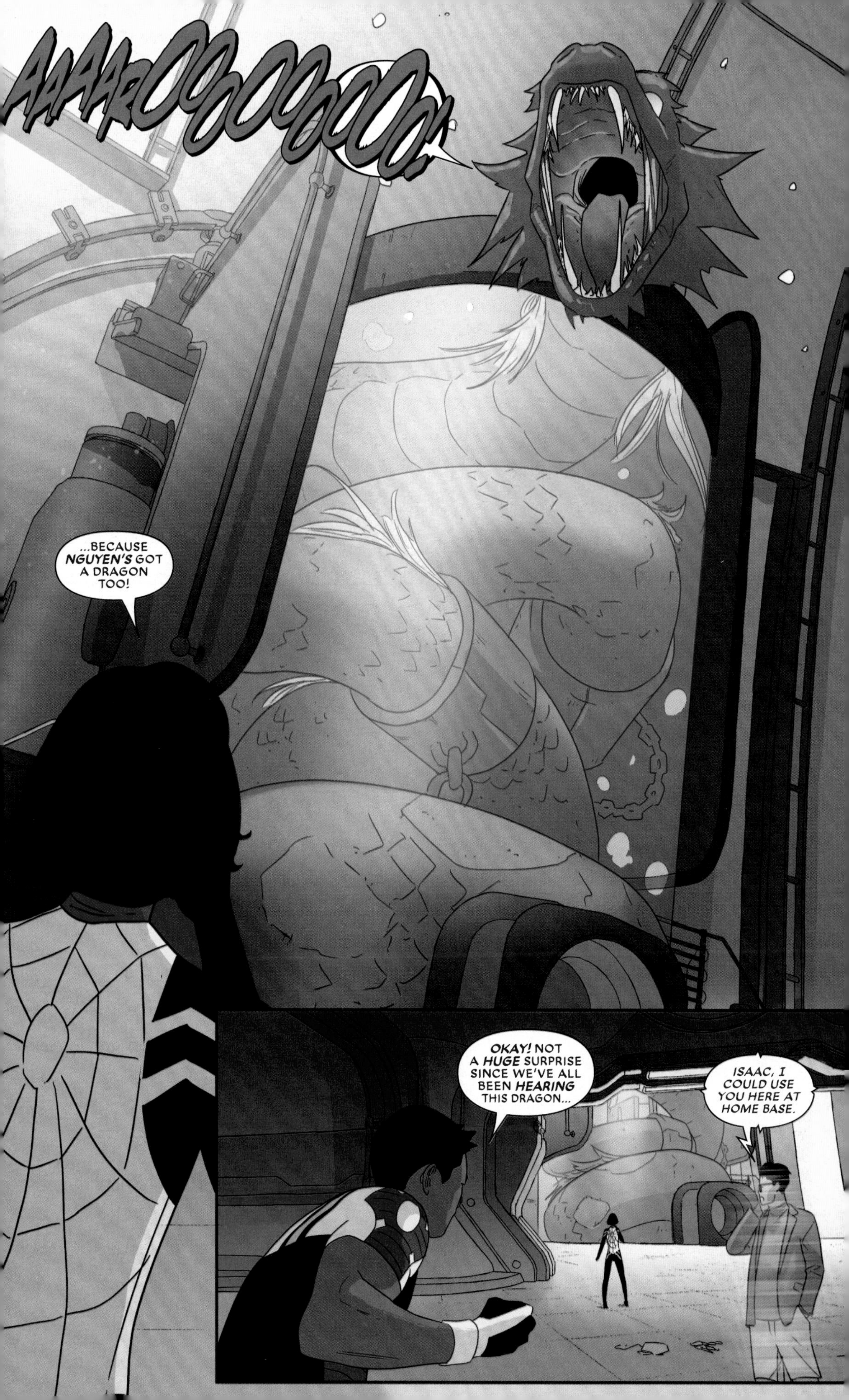
AAAAROOOOOOOOOO!
...BECAUSE NGUYEN'S GOT A DRAGON TOO!
OKAY! NOT A HUGE SURPRISE SINCE WE'VE ALL BEEN HEARING THIS DRAGON...
ISAAC, I COULD USE YOU HERE AT HOME BASE.

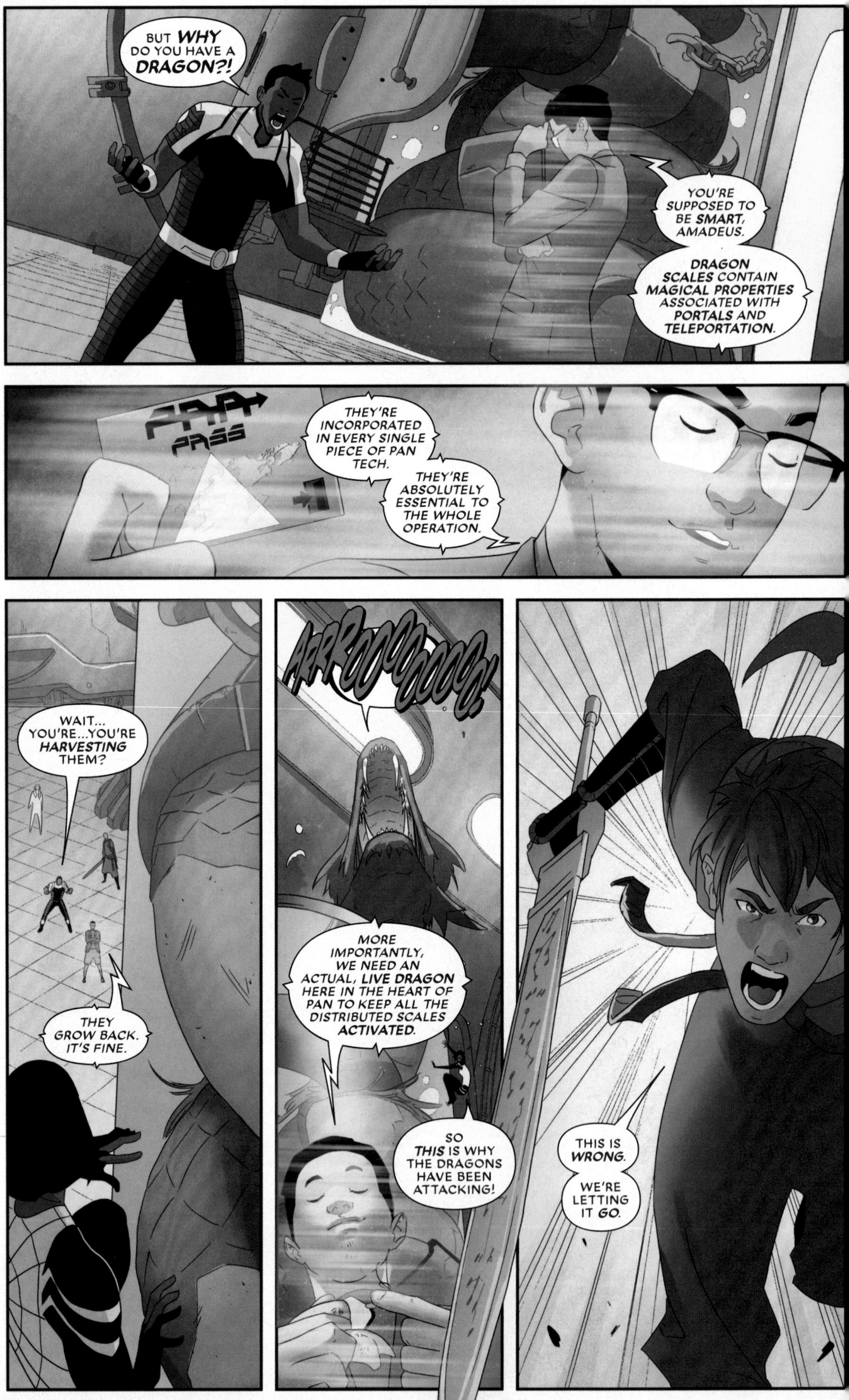
BUT WHY DO YOU HAVE A DRAGON?!
YOU'RE SUPPOSED TO BE SMART, AMADEUS.
DRAGON SCALES CONTAIN MAGICAL PROPERTIES ASSOCIATED WITH PORTALS AND TELEPORTATION.
PASS
THEY'RE INCORPORATED IN EVERY SINGLE PIECE OF PAN TECH.
THEY'RE ABSOLUTELY ESSENTIAL TO THE WHOLE OPERATION.
WAIT... YOU'RE...YOU'RE HARVESTING THEM?
THEY GROW BACK. IT'S FINE.
ARRROOOOOOOOO!
MORE IMPORTANTLY, WE NEED AN ACTUAL, LIVE DRAGON HERE IN THE HEART OF PAN TO KEEP ALL THE DISTRIBUTED SCALES ACTIVATED.
SO THIS IS WHY THE DRAGONS HAVE BEEN ATTACKING!
THIS IS WRONG.
WE'RE LETTING IT GO.

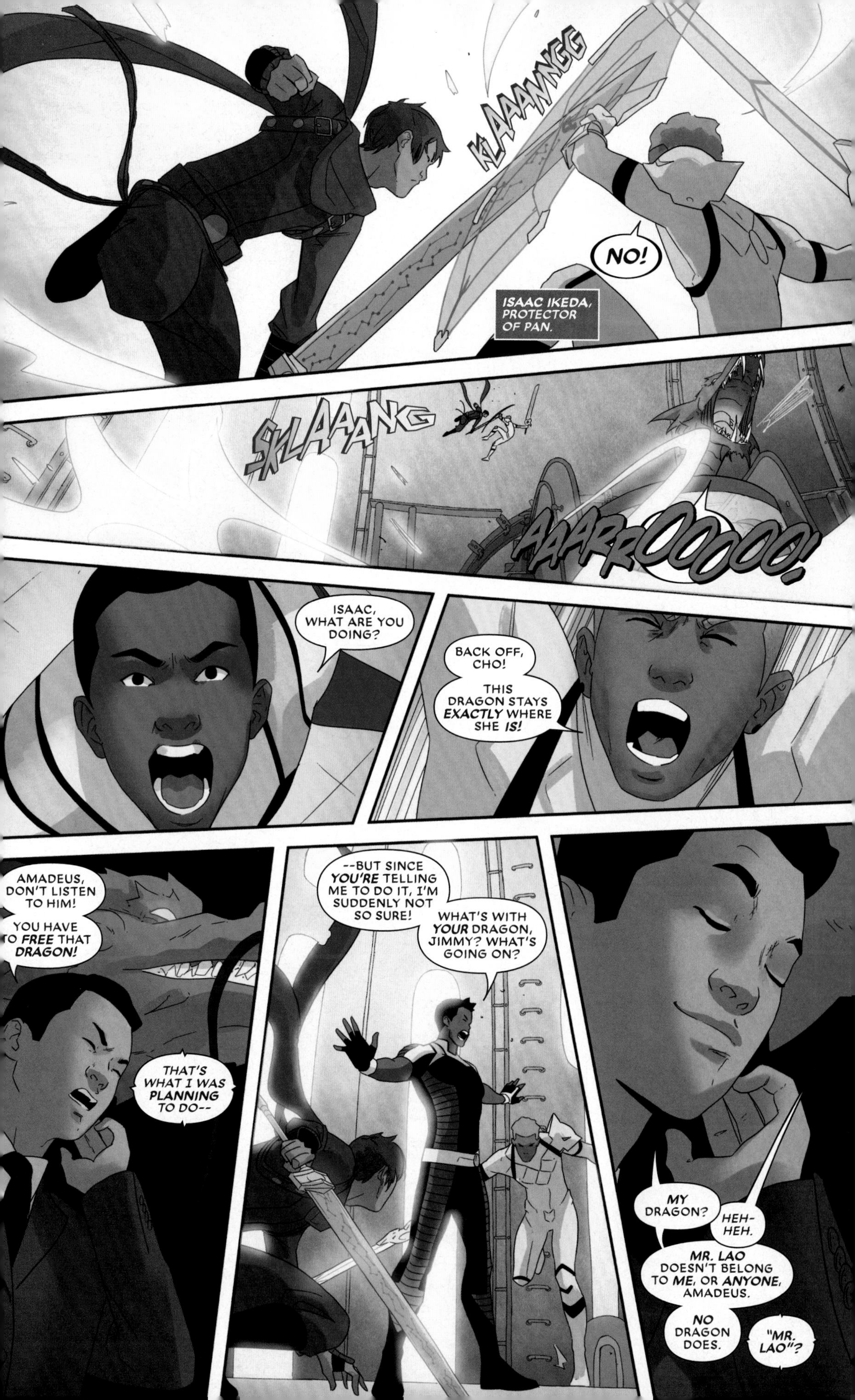
KLAAANNGG
NO!
ISAAC IKEDA, PROTECTOR OF PAN.
SKLAAANG
AAARROOOOOO!
ISAAC, WHAT ARE YOU DOING?
BACK OFF, CHO!
THIS DRAGON STAYS EXACTLY WHERE SHE IS!
AMADEUS, DON'T LISTEN TO HIM!
YOU HAVE TO FREE THAT DRAGON!
THAT'S WHAT I WAS PLANNING TO DO--
--BUT SINCE YOU'RE TELLING ME TO DO IT, I'M SUDDENLY NOT SO SURE!
WHAT'S WITH YOUR DRAGON, JIMMY? WHAT'S GOING ON?
MY DRAGON?
HEH-HEH.
MR. LAO DOESN'T BELONG TO ME, OR ANYONE, AMADEUS.
NO DRAGON DOES.
"MR. LAO"?

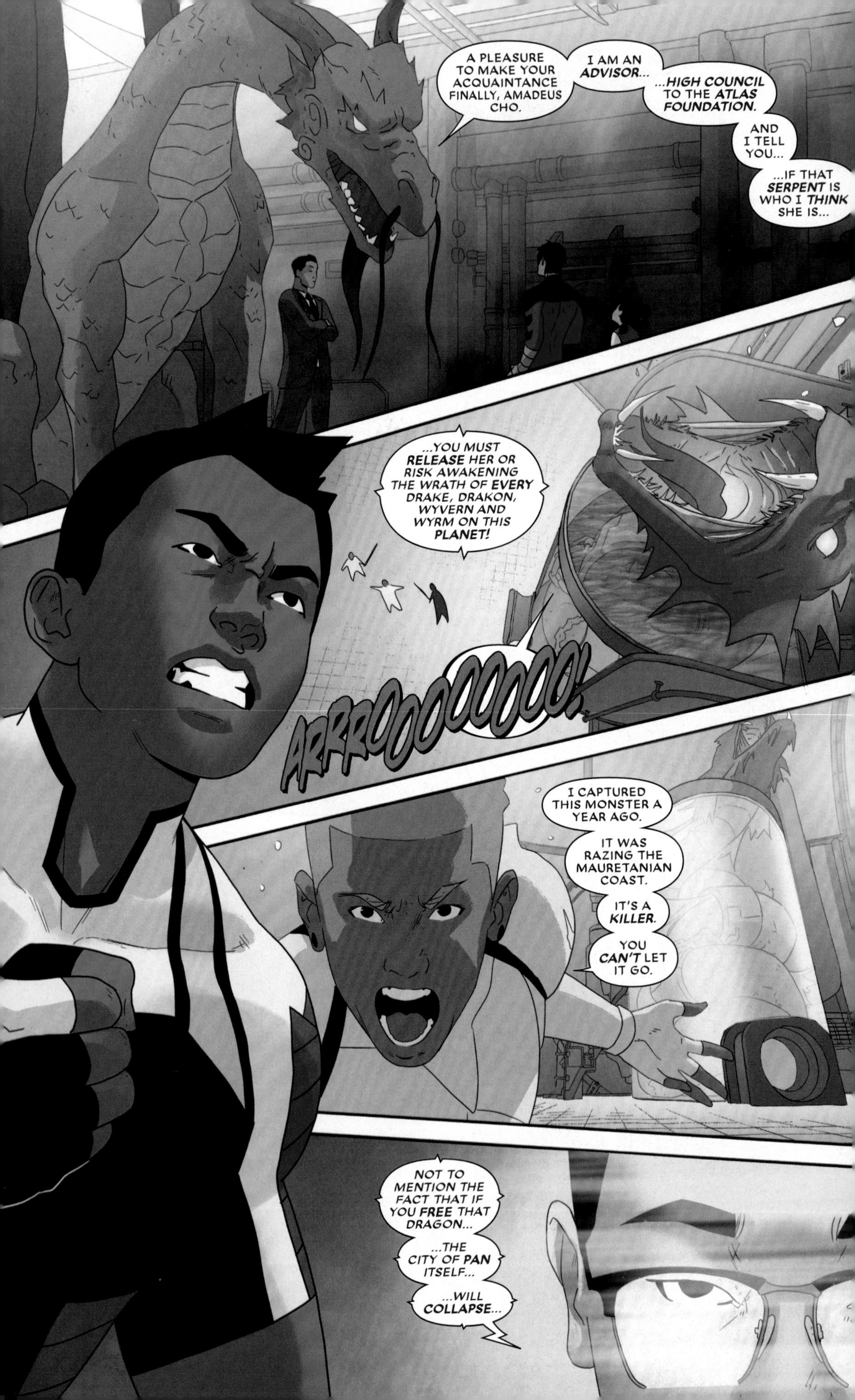

A PLEASURE TO MAKE YOUR ACQUAINTANCE FINALLY, AMADEUS CHO.
I AM AN ADVISOR...
...HIGH COUNCIL TO THE ATLAS FOUNDATION.
AND I TELL YOU...
...IF THAT SERPENT IS WHO I THINK SHE IS...
...YOU MUST RELEASE HER OR RISK AWAKENING THE WRATH OF EVERY DRAKE, DRAKON, WYVERN AND WYRM ON THIS PLANET!
ARRROOOOOOOOO!
I CAPTURED THIS MONSTER A YEAR AGO.
IT WAS RAZING THE MAURETANIAN COAST.
IT'S A KILLER.
YOU CAN'T LET IT GO.
NOT TO MENTION THE FACT THAT IF YOU FREE THAT DRAGON...
...THE CITY OF PAN ITSELF...
...WILL COLLAPSE...

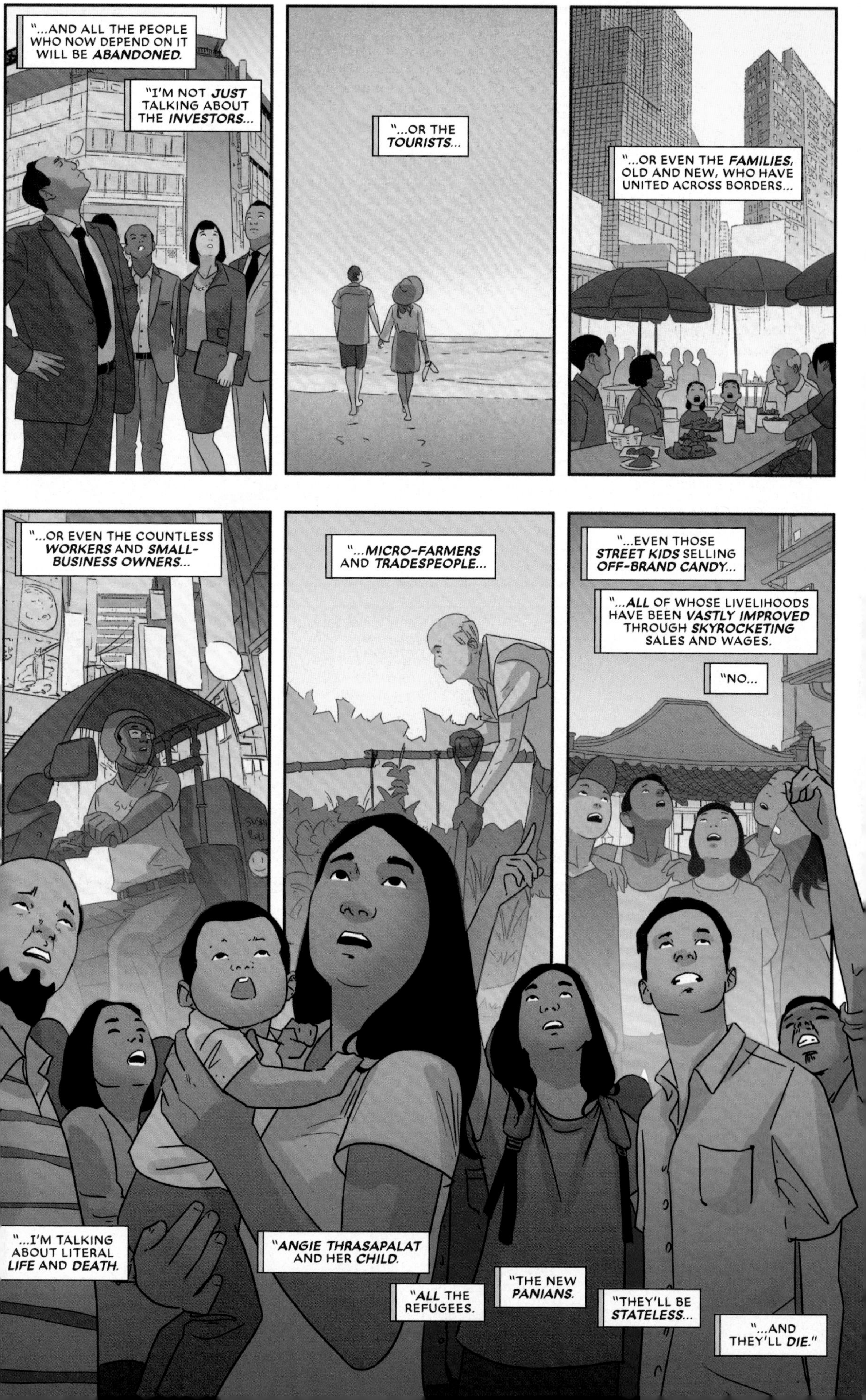
"...AND ALL THE PEOPLE WHO NOW DEPEND ON IT WILL BE ABANDONED.
"I'M NOT JUST TALKING ABOUT THE INVESTORS...
"...OR THE TOURISTS...
"...OR EVEN THE FAMILIES, OLD AND NEW, WHO HAVE UNITED ACROSS BORDERS...
"...OR EVEN THE COUNTLESS WORKERS AND SMALL-BUSINESS OWNERS...
"...MICRO-FARMERS AND TRADESPEOPLE...
"...EVEN THOSE STREET KIDS SELLING OFF-BRAND CANDY...
"...ALL OF WHOSE LIVELIHOODS HAVE BEEN VASTLY IMPROVED THROUGH SKYROCKETING SALES AND WAGES.
"NO...
"...I'M TALKING ABOUT LITERAL LIFE AND DEATH.
"ANGIE THRASAPALAT AND HER CHILD.
"ALL THE REFUGEES.
"THE NEW PANIANS.
"THEY'LL BE STATELESS...
"...AND THEY'LL DIE."

YOU... YOU SET THIS ALL UP.

ROPED IN ALL KINDS OF GOOD PEOPLE.

LET IN *JUST* AS MANY REFUGEES AS YOU NEEDED FOR THIS *VERY SCENARIO.*

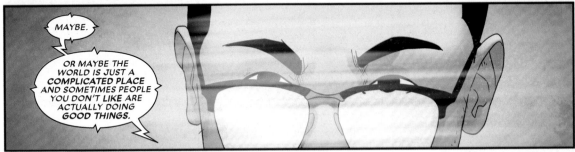

MAYBE.

OR MAYBE THE WORLD IS JUST A *COMPLICATED PLACE* AND SOMETIMES PEOPLE YOU DON'T *LIKE* ARE ACTUALLY DOING *GOOD THINGS.*

SOMETIMES THERE'S NO PURE COURSE OF ACTION.

SOMETIMES YOU HAVE TO MAKE *CHOICES.*

YOU DIRTY LITTLE--

AMADEUS. JIMMY HERE. YOU HAVE ABOUT 30 SECONDS TO MAKE A DECISION.

AND I KNOW THAT'S *UNFAIR,* BECAUSE I SHOULD HAVE TOLD YOU SO MUCH *MORE* SO MUCH *EARLIER.*

BUT THE WORLD AS YOU KNOW IT ONLY *ENDURES* BECAUSE OF A FRAGILE *BALANCE OF POWER* BETWEEN THESE DRAGONS.

OUR SECRET JOB AS AGENTS OF ATLAS IS TO *SAVE* THE *WORLD* BY *PRESERVING* THAT *BALANCE.*

SO NO MATTER WHAT NGUYEN SAYS, YOU *HAVE* TO *FREE* THAT SERPENT.

TRUST ME.

YOU KNOW, JIMMY...

...YOU'RE *RIGHT...*

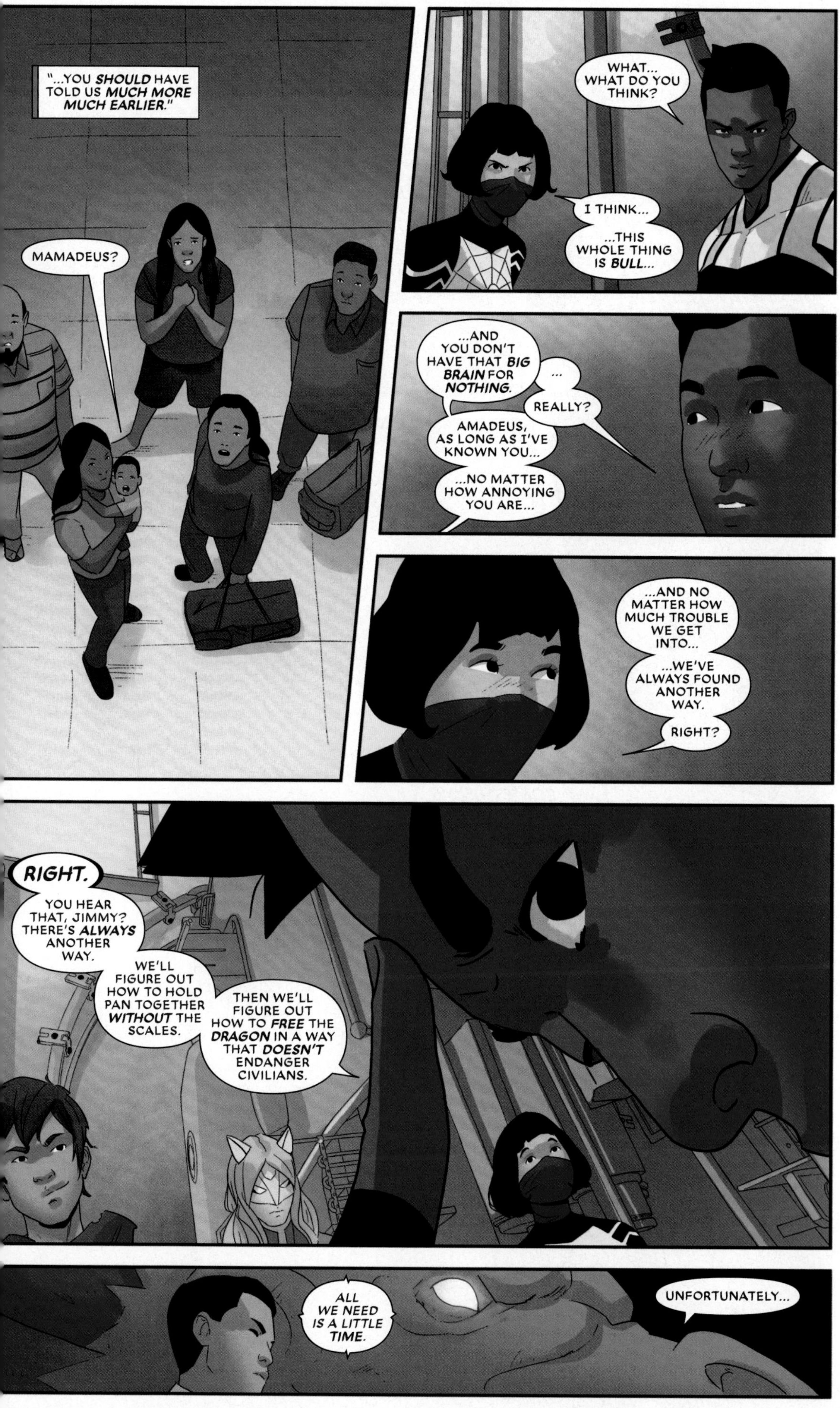
"...YOU SHOULD HAVE TOLD US MUCH MORE MUCH EARLIER."
MAMADEUS?
WHAT... WHAT DO YOU THINK?
I THINK...
...THIS WHOLE THING IS BULL...
...AND YOU DON'T HAVE THAT BIG BRAIN FOR NOTHING.
...
REALLY?
AMADEUS, AS LONG AS I'VE KNOWN YOU...
...NO MATTER HOW ANNOYING YOU ARE...
...AND NO MATTER HOW MUCH TROUBLE WE GET INTO...
...WE'VE ALWAYS FOUND ANOTHER WAY.
RIGHT?
RIGHT.
YOU HEAR THAT, JIMMY? THERE'S ALWAYS ANOTHER WAY.
WE'LL FIGURE OUT HOW TO HOLD PAN TOGETHER WITHOUT THE SCALES.
THEN WE'LL FIGURE OUT HOW TO FREE THE DRAGON IN A WAY THAT DOESN'T ENDANGER CIVILIANS.
ALL WE NEED IS A LITTLE TIME.
UNFORTUNATELY...

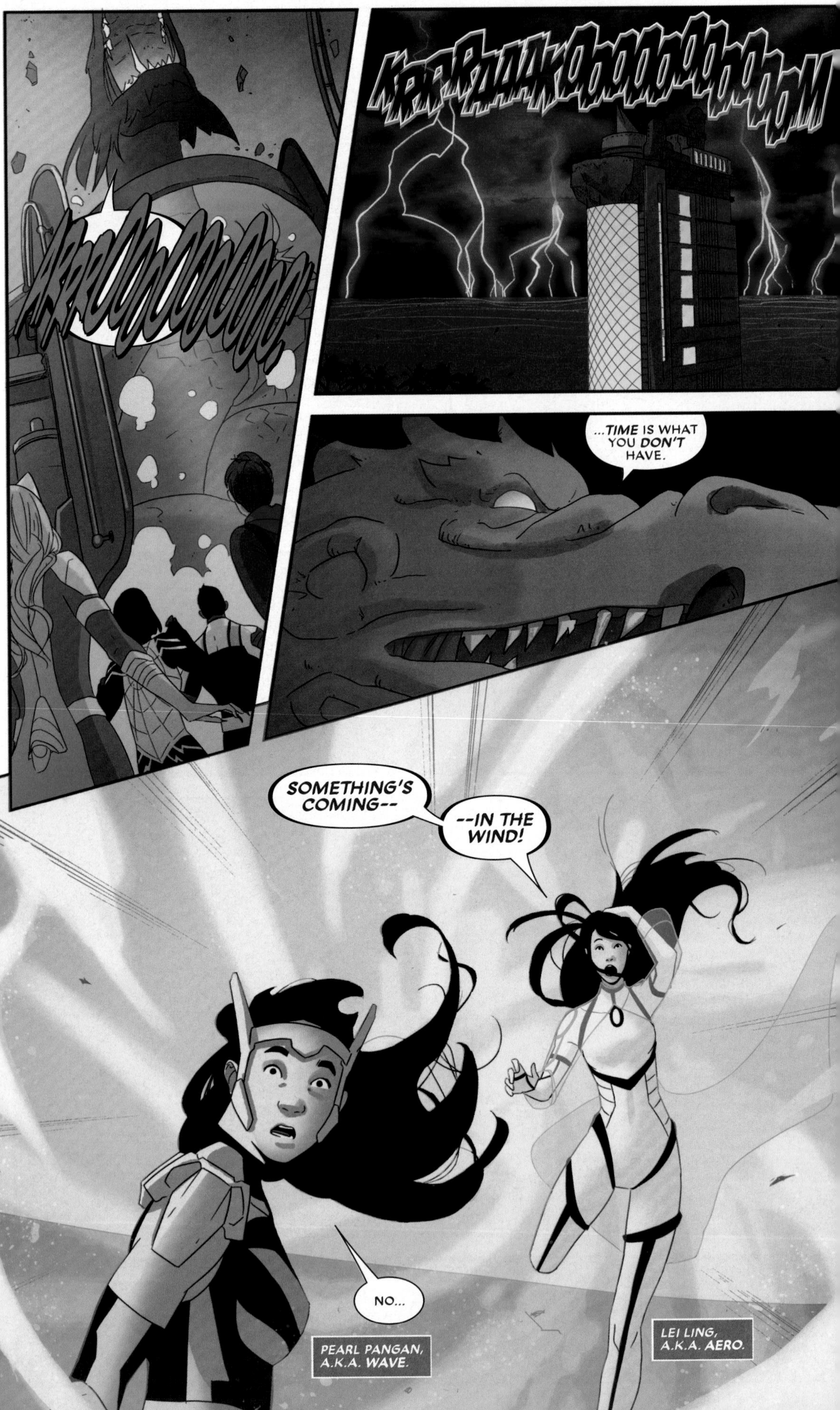
...TIME IS WHAT YOU DON'T HAVE.
SOMETHING'S COMING--
--IN THE WIND!
NO...
PEARL PANGAN, A.K.A. WAVE.
LEI LING, A.K.A. AERO.

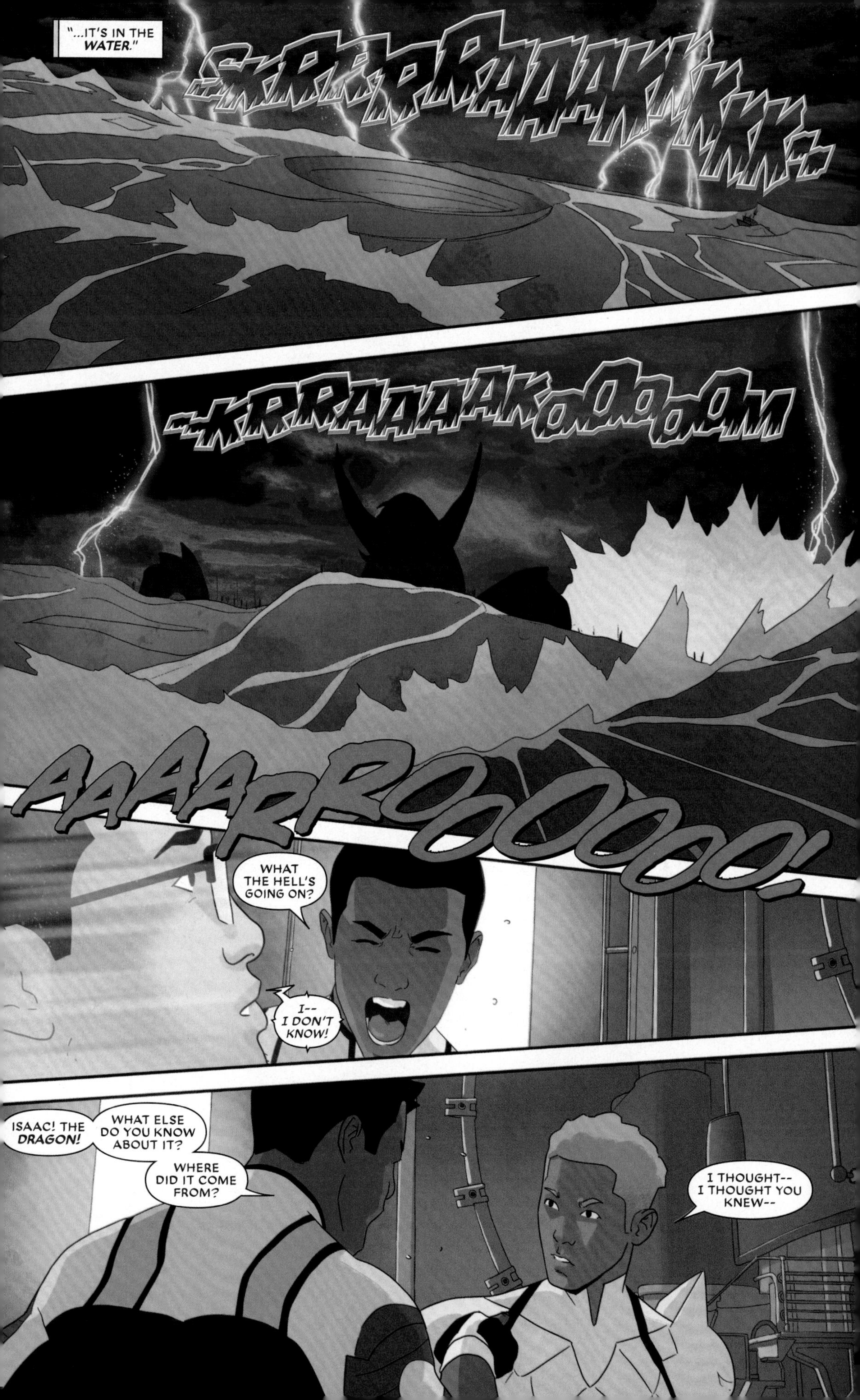
"...IT'S IN THE WATER."
SKRRRRAAAKKKKK--
--KRRAAAAKOOOOOM
AAAARROOOOOOO!
WHAT THE HELL'S GOING ON?
I-- I DON'T KNOW!
ISAAC! THE DRAGON!
WHAT ELSE DO YOU KNOW ABOUT IT?
WHERE DID IT COME FROM?
I THOUGHT-- I THOUGHT YOU KNEW--

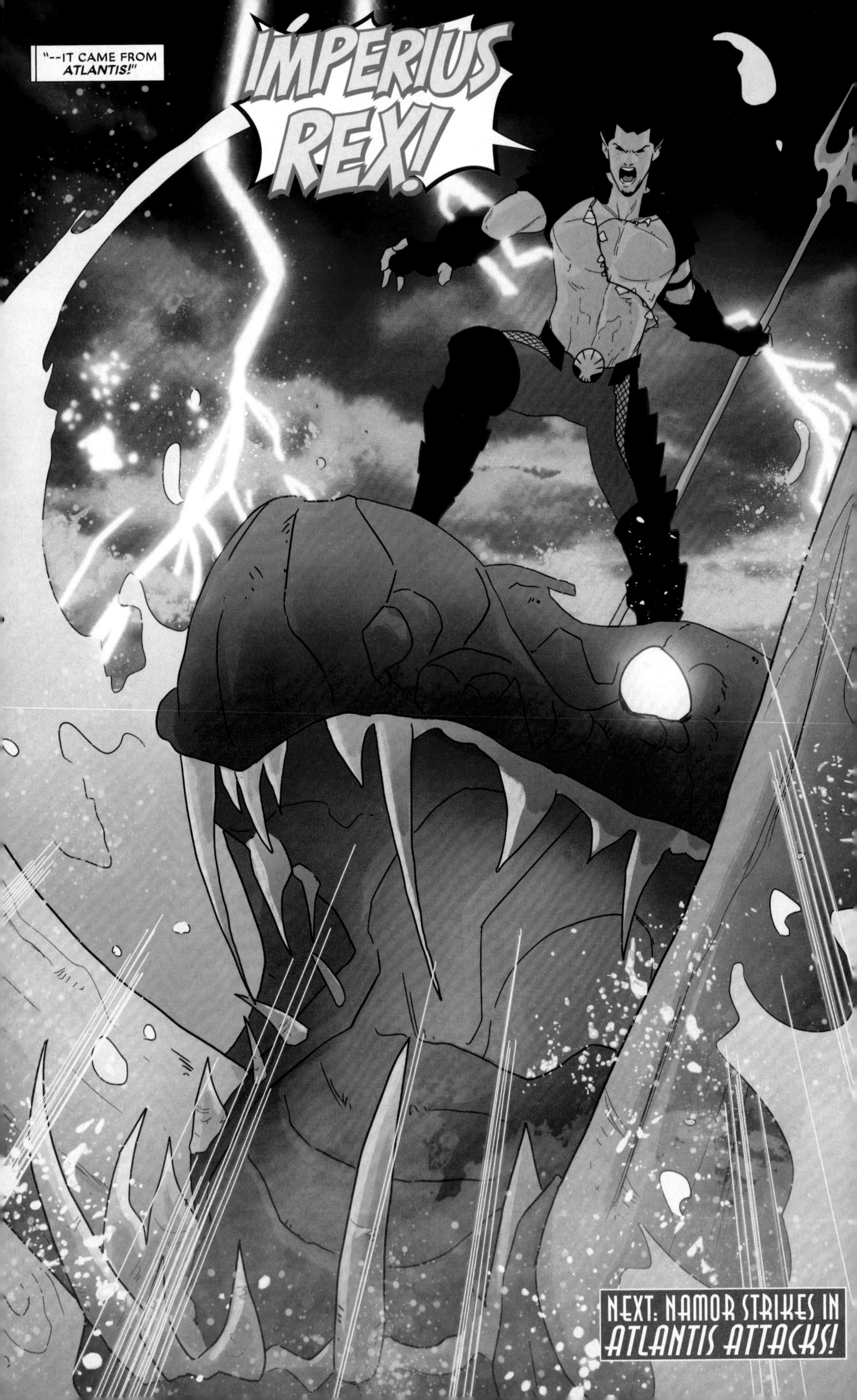

"--IT CAME FROM ATLANTIS!"
IMPERIUS REX!
NEXT: NAMOR STRIKES IN ATLANTIS ATTACKS!

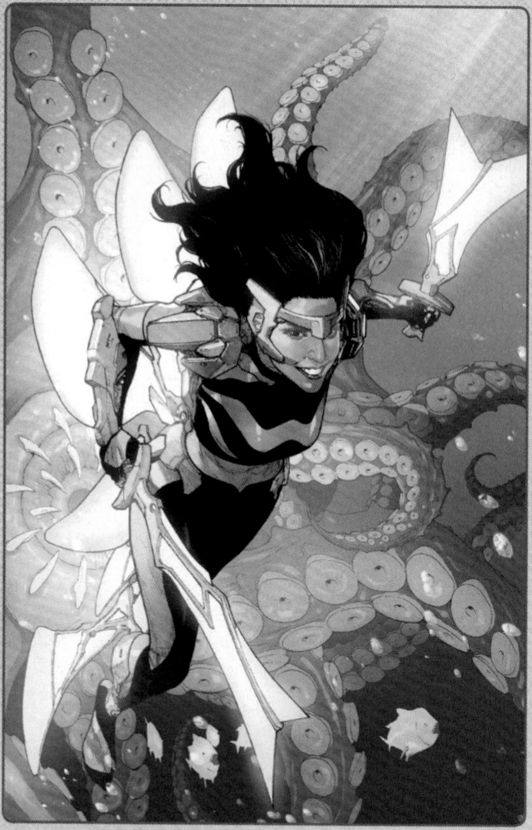

Leinil Francis Yu & **Sunny Gho**
1 VARIANT

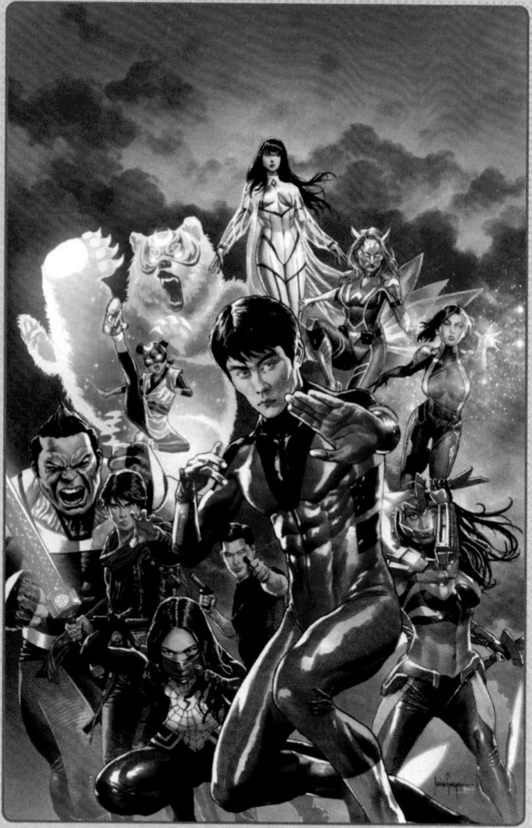

Mico Suayan & **Rain Beredo**
1 VARIANT

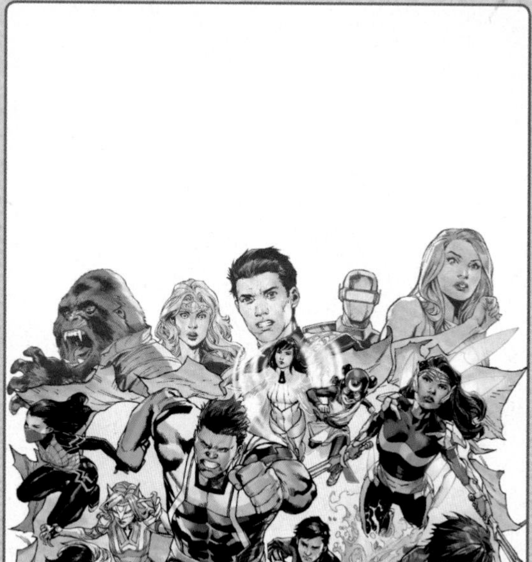

Carlo Pagulayan, **Jason Paz** & **Federico Blee**
1 VARIANT

Skottie Young
1 VARIANT

Sabine Rich
2 VARIANT

Stonehouse
3 VARIANT